MW01097742

Dyn

This book provides new insights into the opportunities, risks, and unintended consequences for the American economy, legacy industries, global multinational corporations, and financial institutions having pledged to transition to a net-zero-carbon economy. It places specific emphasis on "systems analysis," as well as the unprecedented pace needed for our sustainability transition. It examines the implications of organizations purchasing voluntary carbon credits that are not regulated, not insured, and potentially not scientifically validated. It scrutinizes how financial markets are driving corporate sustainability while at the same time conservative policymakers seek to ban environmental and social governance investments. The author discusses national security as well as the growing rural–urban divide, seemingly widened by transitions toward zero-emission electric vehicles and renewable energy. Using empirical evidence to chart the effect of our sustainability transition on the government, the military, and corporations, this book is an invaluable resource for researchers, graduate students, policymakers, and industry professionals.

JAY S. GOLDEN is Pontarelli Professor of Environmental Sustainability and Finance in the Maxwell School at Syracuse University, where he also directs the Dynamic Sustainability Lab. Dr. Golden is regularly called on by global corporations and governments to advise and consult on sustainability strategies and policies. He is the author of more than 150 articles and recipient of the Faculty Pioneer Award from the Aspen Institute.

"Professor Golden's book should be read by every early-career believer who wants to become a sustainability leader, as well as every mid- or late-career professional who is expected to be one. All of society is or will be on this journey; don't set off without reading this book."

Francis Bouchard, Managing Director, Climate, Marsh McLennan

"Organizational pledges to net-zero-carbon emissions without taking action are empty promises. Golden provides a compelling and insightful analysis of the many policy implications, digital requirements, and new technology roadmaps that will be required for the American economy to truly move towards a net-zero-carbon ecosystem. He provides some important implications for long-term and short-term actions that senior executives, government policy makers, and academics should consider as we move into the next decade."

Rob Handfield, Executive Director of Supply Chain Resource Cooperative and Bank of America University Distinguished Professor of Operations and Supply Chain Management, North Carolina State University

"The world is transitioning out of necessity to electricity and clean, renewable energy and storage across all energy sectors. What are the implications of such a technology transition on society, policies, markets, and national security? This well-crafted book answers these questions with a plethora of facts woven into an engaging narrative. I strongly recommend it."

Mark Z. Jacobson, Stanford University; author of No Miracles Needed: How Today's Technology Can Save Our Climate and Clean Our Air

Dynamic Sustainability
Implications for Policy, Markets, and National Security

JAY S. GOLDEN
Syracuse University

CAMBRIDGE
UNIVERSITY PRESS

Shaftesbury Road, Cambridge CB2 8EA, United Kingdom

One Liberty Plaza, 20th Floor, New York, NY 10006, USA

477 Williamstown Road, Port Melbourne, VIC 3207, Australia

314–321, 3rd Floor, Plot 3, Splendor Forum, Jasola District Centre,
New Delhi – 110025, India

103 Penang Road, #05–06/07, Visioncrest Commercial, Singapore 238467

Cambridge University Press is part of Cambridge University Press & Assessment,
a department of the University of Cambridge.

We share the University's mission to contribute to society through the pursuit of
education, learning and research at the highest international levels of excellence.

www.cambridge.org
Information on this title: www.cambridge.org/9781009298674

DOI: 10.1017/9781009298711

First published 2024

A catalogue record for this publication is available from the British Library.

A Cataloging-in-Publication data record for this book is available from the Library of Congress.

ISBN 978-1-009-29867-4 Hardback
ISBN 978-1-009-29868-1 Paperback

Cambridge University Press & Assessment has no responsibility for the persistence
or accuracy of URLs for external or third-party internet websites referred to in this
publication and does not guarantee that any content on such websites is, or will remain,
accurate or appropriate.

For
Dina, for her love and support
Samantha, who keeps me humble and laughing
Shea, who inspires me to be my best
and
Evelyn and Mort, for pointing me in the right direction

Contents

About the Author

Dr. Jay Golden is an internationally recognized sustainable systems researcher, academic, and adviser to government and industry leaders around the globe. Golden serves as Pontarelli Professor of Environmental Sustainability and Finance in the Maxwell School at Syracuse University, where he also founded and directs the pan-university Dynamic Sustainability Lab.[1]

---

[1] www.dynamicslab.org.

Prior to Syracuse, Dr. Golden was a faculty member and faculty chair of the Business and Environment program at Duke University, where he also directed the Duke Center for Sustainability and Commerce and was the executive-in-charge of the Duke Corporate Relations Office working with global companies, chief executive officers, and boards. Dr. Golden served as Vice Chancellor at East Carolina University and President of Wichita State University.

Dr. Golden was one of the first faculty members in the newly created School of Sustainability located at Arizona State University (ASU), where he held secondary appointments in the Ira A. Fulton Schools of Engineering and in the Supply Chain Department at the W. P. Carey School of Business. At ASU, Dr. Golden directed the National Center of Excellence on SMART Innovations.

Later, Dr. Golden founded and codirected the Sustainability Consortium, a leading academic–industry research partnership and at the time the largest consortium of industry focused on sustainability, which included many of the world's largest manufacturers, brands, and retailers from around the world.

Author of more than 150 articles, Dr. Golden has participated in 100 invited presentations and more than 150 media interviews around the world. He has testified before Congress and participated in more than $150 million in research funding. Dr. Golden has served as a guest editor on urban sustainability for the *Proceedings of the National Academies* and cochaired National Academy of Engineering conferences/workshops on sustainability, with a focus on innovation in manufacturing.

Dr. Golden was presented with the Faculty Pioneer Award by the Aspen Institute for his leadership in the field of sustainable business education and research. He was also inducted in the Phi Kappa Phi Honors Society and the Scientific Research Honor Society Sigma Xi, and was named one of the 100 most influential people in business ethics by the Ethisphere Institute.

In 2017, Dr. Golden was appointed to the Board of Scientific Counselors for the US Environmental Protection Agency and was reappointed in 2022 to the executive committee. He has also served on a number of boards and committees, including for the United Nations Environment Programme on Environmental Life Cycle Modeling.

Dr. Golden received his Ph.D. in engineering from the University of Cambridge (Wolfson College) and his master's degree in environmental engineering from a joint program of the Massachusetts Institute of Technology and the University of Cambridge. He also holds an Organizational Mastery of Project Management from Stanford University and an M.L.E. from Harvard University. Dr. Golden attended the University of Phoenix and Arizona State University as an undergraduate and earned a B.A. in management.

Dr. Golden brings both an entrepreneurial and business background to sustainability, having founded a small environmental engineering services company that grew to have operations throughout the west and southwest of the United States. He has also held leadership positions in the private sector, including a Fortune 150 international service and technology company. He currently serves as an adviser to a number of manufacturing and service companies.

Preface

My career at the nexus of sustainability, policy, and business has spanned time in government, the private sector, and academia. My journey has taken me into the corporate boardroom of the world's largest company, Walmart, to help their executives develop arguably one of the more impactful sustainable strategies that would affect over 60,000 of their direct suppliers, many of whom are the best-known brands and manufacturers in the world.

I have spent considerable time both advising and tracking governmental and industry policies and actions. I have been invited to testify before the Congress of the United States, dine at the House of Lords in Parliament, and give presentations to public and business officials around the globe.

During all this time my primary focus was to support these key decision- and policymakers with both the aspirational and pragmatic benefits of choosing a sustainability transition through the adoption of a new generation of sustainable technologies, strategies, policies, and finance. Yet recently I have become increasingly concerned that all the progress made to date, and especially the advancements set in motion, are potentially at risk, in part because of the projected pace and breadth of the sustainability and net-zero-carbon economy transitions.

I use the term *dynamic sustainability* to define this unique juncture in the history of our epic sustainability transition. At one end of the spectrum, government policies and technology advancements are inching us closer to achieving the long-sought-after goal of transitioning from a fossil-fuel-based economy to a low-carbon, green economy. This transition is dependent on a new generation of sustainable technologies that are accelerating at an unprecedented pace. In part this has been bolstered by both national and regional government policies since the 2015 Paris Climate Agreement. In many cases these policies are not meant to simply ensure a healthier environment but are also intended to achieve near-term and longer-term economic gains. Similarly, there now exist growing corporate governance pressures from consumers, shareholders, and financial regulators, as evidenced by the shareholder-driven environmental and social governance (ESG) paradigm, which is further accelerating the sustainability transition but also causing political tensions.

However, at the other end of the spectrum, society is challenged by unprecedented competition and pressures for critical natural resources necessary to power the transition that in part are further driving increased nationalistic policies impacting global trade and raising national security concerns. In the United States, domestic pressures are rising from both the rural–urban divide and blue–red divide in national and local politics. Concerns over environmental justice and social equity further complicate the sustainability transition and, as presented in this book, raise the real possibility of unintended consequences and risks to our environment, our society, and the global economy.

In many ways, the sustainability transition of today is analogous to the first (1760–1820) and second (1871–1914) industrial revolutions in regard to advances in research and development and the creation of disruptive technologies. Yet our current industrial revolution is far more complicated and globally interconnected, and it comes at a time of unprecedented global population increases, rapid urbanization, and expansion of the global middle class. In the United States the most recent presidential election is emblematic of a rising rural–urban divide and blue–red divide, which the sustainable transition may further exacerbate.

For many, the abstraction of sustainability is being supplanted by the realities of impactful policies and the deployment of disruptive technologies. Around the world, national and regional governments as well as multinational corporations are developing plans and commitments to achieve short-term (2030) and longer-term (2050) greenhouse gas emission reductions. This includes committing to "net-zero" targets as a follow-up to the 2015 Paris Climate Agreement. A recent report by the University of Oxford [1] indicates that 61 percent of countries have committed to net zero and over a fifth of the major companies on the Forbes list, with annual sales of nearly $14 trillion, have also made net-zero commitments. Far more governments and industries have also published interim targets as they seek to adopt a new generation of sustainable technologies and organizational strategies to achieve net zero.

One of the clearer examples of the dynamics of sustainability is found in the pace and growth of the transition to electric vehicles (EVs). Consider that in less than three months, between September and November 2020, both California as the world's fifth largest economy and the United Kingdom as the world's sixth largest economy announced policy changes that have triggered what is likely to be the demise of the internal combustion vehicle. By

2035 every new car sold in California will be required to be emission free and the United Kingdom has brought forward its similar plans to ban new petrol cars by 2030.

Even before these policy announcements were formalized, the financial markets had already rewarded the vision of sustainable mobility. Tesla, which sold approximately 500,000 vehicles (all electric) in 2020 as compared to Ford's 4.2 million cars sold, achieved a market cap of $480 billion, which is higher than the next twelve global auto manufacturers combined, excluding Toyota.

Legacy automakers around the globe facing the pressures of new government policies and shareholder expectations lined up to make public announcements about their transition to the EV market. This is exemplified by General Motors, who in January 2021 announced their plans to exclusively offer zero emission vehicles by 2035.

While the transition to a more sustainable form of transportation provides the promise of reduced environmental impacts, especially greenhouse gas emissions, the dynamics of this transition present many risks and the potential for unintended consequences that, if not planned for, can ultimately impair the sustainability transition.

Notably, the transition will drive a significant demand for additional electricity generation. The average EV requires 30 kilowatt-hours to travel 100 miles – the same amount of electricity a typical American home uses each day. A US Department of Energy study [2] found that electric capacity needs to double to power 186 million light-duty EVs in 2050.

For the transition to EVs to meet the goals of advancing sustainability, the increased demand for electricity must be met by renewable sources, such as wind, solar, and potentially green hydrogen. In the United States the transportation sector accounted for 29 percent of greenhouse gas emissions in 2019, which was the largest percentage of emissions by sector. It was closely followed by electricity generation at 25 percent [3].

To meet the demand for renewable electricity in the United States, there will likely be a significant expansion of offshore wind. The Biden Administration has in fact proposed installing 30 gigawatts of offshore wind energy by 2030 [4], which is a substantial increase for a country with only one offshore wind farm in place as of 2021.

This rapid expansion is likely to raise social and political tensions driven in part by the $9.7 billion fishing industry, tourism industry, and real-estate developers, who fear the possible visual impacts of offshore wind turbines. Environmentalists including non-governmental organizations are already voicing concern over the environmental risks, such as those caused by ocean-based seismic surveys, which are known to have adverse impacts on whales, other cetaceans, pinnipeds, and turtles, as well as fish and possibly other marine creatures. The effects of such operations on species can occur over very large areas in the ocean and include disruption of communication, stress, and behavioral changes such as avoidance of key habitat.

The dynamics are further complicated by the fact that there is a growing dependence on the critical earth resources necessary to produce key components in EVs, charging stations, and renewable energy sources such as onshore and offshore wind turbines. The EV transition and resultant dependence on the growth of the renewable energy sector hinge on the availability of specific critical earth elements including certain rare-earth elements, such as neodymium, praseodymium, and dysprosium, for the production of permanent magnet electric generators. The United States is highly dependent on limited numbers of foreign sources of critical earth elements. In fact, between 2014 and 2017 China supplied 80 percent of the rare earths to the United States. China is home to at least 85 percent of the world's capacity to process rare-earth elements and processes 220,000 tons per year, which is five times the combined capacity of the rest of the world.

Increased nationalism and growing trade tensions have resulted in China limiting exports of critical earth elements to ensure the growth of their own sustainable technology sectors. The United States is aggressively seeking to open or reopen domestic mining operations to reduce reliance on foreign supplies. These new mining operations come with additional environmental implications. Because of national security concerns, in 2020 the US Department of Defense issued a number of contracts as part of the Defense Production Act to increase the supply and production of rare earths and rare-earth salts.

In part, these national security concerns are playing into complex diplomatic movements, which are witnessing countries making plays in regions with conflict and high risk, as China is doing in Africa. Further, Russia, the United States, and other countries are also racing to take advantage of how climate change is altering conditions in the Arctic. The opening of waterways due to ice melt provides new potential to control and acquire newly available resources, where estimates [5] place 13 percent of the world's undiscovered oil (90 bb of oil), 30 percent of its undiscovered gas (669 Tcf), and an abundance of critical earth resources such as uranium and rare-earth minerals. The strategic importance is witnessed as Russia develops new bases and refurbishes former Cold War bases in the Kola Peninsula near the city of Murmansk and NATO develops counter-strategies.

Finally, the dynamics of the sustainability transition into EVs will also have strong implications for legacy industries. The oil and gas industry in the United

States supports over 10.3 million jobs and represents nearly 8 percent of gross domestic product. In 2020, consumption of finished motor gasoline averaged about 8.03 million b/d (337 million gallons per day), which was equal to about 44 percent of total US petroleum consumption. This is in large part supported by 76,000 miles of pipeline and 141 operable petroleum refineries.

The current sustainability transition comes at a time of stress for the American farmer and rural America due to trade policies that have seen American agricultural exports to China fall from \$15.8 billion in 2017 to \$5.9 billion in 2018 and continue to remain depressed. Both corn, which is used in ethanol production, and soy, an additive for biodiesel, are important economic drivers for rural America. Corn, primarily grown in the Midwest, is the United States' largest crop, covering over 91.7 million acres in 2019 – about 69 million football fields. One-third of US corn is used to produce the renewable fuel additive ethanol. In 2019 this amounted to over 15.8 billion gallons of fuel ethanol with an economic impact of more than 68,600 direct jobs and \$43 billion added to gross domestic product – a significant economic driver for rural America [6, 7].

Each of these exogenous factors coupled with the unprecedented rapid pace of the sustainable technology transition is creating unique challenges and pressures that have the potential to result in unintended consequences for the environment, economy, and society, as well as risking the desired outcomes of the sustainability transition. Some of these challenges are near term, easier to quantify, and likely reversible. Other challenges from the transition have unknown implications and outcomes.

Yet, each of these dynamics also provides opportunities, such as repurposing American agriculture used for renewable ethanol to support the growth of renewable fuels in aviation and shipping, which cannot implement electrification in scale for the mid-term. Additionally, agriculture and portions of the fossil fuel-processing capacity can be used to develop a much more expansive transition to a green chemistry industrial sector. Further, legacy fossil fuel companies have recently shown interest in and are funding research and development to repurpose the large domestic fossil fuels infrastructure to advance the development of a domestic green hydrogen sector. This can also support coproduced solid carbon byproducts that have the potential to transition industries, including metal processing and cement manufacturing sectors, by the substitution of metals and cement with carbon byproducts from hydrogen production. And all of this is occurring at a time of enhanced pressures and governance through the emergence of ESG standards by institutional investors and shareholders who are exerting their strength to drive corporations to carbon neutrality and sustainable transitions.

To take us through this journey, we will explore together our race to green by 2035 by better understanding the trends, policies, and industry actions being taken. This will include introducing a dynamic sustainability trade-off framework to help us better understand the risks, unintended consequences, and opportunities presented by the dynamics of the sustainability transition. This book will not be able to provide the solutions or even all the questions, but what I do hope to offer is a platform through which there can be a convergence of ideas and science brought together to more effectively manage the sustainability transition in a way that protects not just society and the environment but also our economy and national security.

References

1. University of Oxford (2021). Taking Stock: A Global Assessment of Net Zero Targets. https://ca1-eci.edcdn.com/reports/ECIU-Oxford_Taking_Stock.pdf?mtime=20210323005817&focal=none.
2. Department of Energy (2021, January). The National Renewable Energy Laboratory's Electrification Futures Study. www.nrel.gov/analysis/electrification-futures.html.
3. US Environmental Protection Agency (2022). Inventory of U.S. Greenhouse Gas Emissions and Sinks. www.epa.gov/ghgemissions/inventory-us-greenhouse-gas-emissions-and-sinks.
4. *New York Times* (2021). Biden Administration Announces a Major Offshore Wind Plan. www.nytimes.com/2021/03/29/climate/biden-offshore-wind.html.
5. US Geological Survey (2008). Circum-Arctic Resource Appraisal: Estimates of Undiscovered Oil and Gas North of the Arctic Circle. Fact Sheet 2008–3049. https://pubs.usgs.gov/fs/2008/3049.
6. J. Daystar, R. B. Handfield, J. Pascual-Gonzalez, E. McConnell, and J. S. Golden (2020). An Economic Impact Analysis of the U.S. Biobased Products Industry: 2019 Update. Volume IV. A Joint Publication of the Supply Chain Resource Cooperative at North Carolina State University and the College of Engineering and Technology at East Carolina University. www.rd.usda.gov/sites/default/files/usda_rd_economic_impact_analysis_us_biobased_products_industry.pdf.
7. J. S. Golden, R. Handfield, J. Pascual-Gonzalez, and B. C. Morrison (2020). 2017 Indicators of the U.S. Biobased Economy, U.S. Department of Agriculture, Office of the Chief Economist. www.usda.gov/sites/default/files/documents/BIOINDICATORS.pdf.

Acknowledgments

My thanks go out to so many who have influenced, encouraged, and supported me to finally take the deep plunge and spend considerable time and energy putting into words what I present in lectures, invited talks, and informal settings.

I am grateful for the energy and level of inquiry of my student researchers in the Dynamic Sustainability Lab, who are in fact the reason I wake up in the morning excited to make the daily commute to campus.

I have been very fortunate to have a career filled with incredible colleagues and mentors who have inspired me through their generosity, ethics, and intellectual curiosity. Each is an incredible researcher and mentor in their own right:

- Bob Sutton at Stanford University
- Jonathon Fink at Arizona State University
- Richard Fenner at the University of Cambridge
- Peter Guthrie OBE at the Royal Academy of Engineering and the University of Cambridge.

I also want to thank my colleagues at Duke University, especially Lincoln Pratson and Tim Profetta, who brought me to the gorgeous Duke campus from Arizona State University, and to former engineering dean Thomas Katsouleas – a visionary leader.

Without question, one of my most fulfilling times as an academic and administrator to date happened at East Carolina University. The eastern half of North Carolina houses one of the most productive agriculture regions in the country, some of our largest military installations spanning the branches, and the beautiful outer banks, including Kitty Hawk. A huge thank you to the faculty, staff, and students at East Carolina University but especially to the team at the research, economic development, and engagement division that I led. I gained more than I could have imagined from having the privilege to serve the people and communities of eastern North Carolina, home to some of the hardest-working, kindest, and most community-minded individuals I have ever met. Go Pirates!

To the thought leaders who over the years have had to put up with my incessant calls and emails to discuss sustainability ideas – I am in your debt for your kindness. The list is long, and I cannot add all, but I would be remiss not to mention Kevin Dooley, Billie Turner, Karen Seto, Kira Matus, Kamil Kaloush, Christopher Boone, Andy Hoffman, Maggie Dalmas, Reide Corbett, Robert Handfield, Doug Nowacek, Janire Pascual, and Antoni Aguilar Mogas.

I would also like to thank Dean David Van Slyke, another visionary leader, and all of Orange Nation at Syracuse University, especially the Maxwell School. I feel honored to be among an incredible roster of faculty in what is continually ranked as the top college in the country for public policy.

Finally, thank you to all my students, especially those I have had the privilege to supervise. Watching your progress and the impacts you are making makes me a very proud and fulfilled person.

Abbreviations

°C	degrees Celsius
BEV	battery electric vehicle
BOEM	Bureau of Ocean Energy Management within the US Department of the Interior
carbon credit	1 ton of carbon dioxide or the equivalent in other greenhouse gases (also known as carbon offsets)
CO_2	carbon dioxide
DoD	US Department of Defense
EPA	US Environmental Protection Agency
ESG	environmental and social governance
EU	European Union
EV	electric vehicle
EVSE	electric vehicle supply equipment
FCEV	fuel cell electric
g CO_2	grams of carbon dioxide
g CO_2/km	grams of carbon dioxide per kilometer
GWh	gigawatt-hour
HEV	full hybrid electric
HVIP	Hybrid and Zero-Emission Truck and Bus Voucher Incentive Project (California)
ICE	internal combustion engine
IEA	International Energy Agency
km	kilometer
km/lge	kilometer per liter of gasoline equivalent
kW	kilowatt
KWh	kilowatt-hours
L/100 km	liters per 100 kilometers

lbs	pounds
LDV	light-duty vehicle
LFP	lithium-iron-phosphate
Li-ion	lithium-ion
mb/d	million barrels per day
MHEV	mild hybrid electric
MJ	megajoule (equal to 1,000,000 joules)
Mt CO_2-eq	million tons of carbon-dioxide equivalent
MW	megawatt
OEM	original equipment manufacturer
PHEV	plug-in hybrid electric
PLDV	passenger light-duty vehicle
SDS	sustainable development scenario
t CO_2	ton of carbon dioxide
t CO_2-eq	ton of carbon-dioxide equivalent
Tbtu	1 trillion British thermal units (Btus) (a Btu is defined as the amount of heat required to raise the temperature of 1 pound of water by 1 degree Fahrenheit)
Tg	teragrams (a unit of mass equal to 10^{12} [1 trillion grams])
TW	terawatt
TWh	terawatt-hour
ZETI	Zero-Emission Technology Inventory
ZEV	zero-emission vehicle

PART I

Introduction and Global Trends

In this part we will explore the physical, economic, and social changes that are taking place on our planet that taken in totality are creating dynamics of sustainability.

1

Introducing Dynamic Sustainability

> Dynamic sustainability is a systems approach to support decision-makers in identifying and managing the risk, unintended consequences, and opportunities of the net-zero-carbon economy transition.
>
> *Jay Golden, 2022*

Humans have repeatedly faced the challenge of resource scarcity resulting from population pressure and spatial or temporal variation in environmental conditions. In many instances, societies have successfully met these challenges through a variety of innovations – sociocultural, technological, governance, and economic. At other times, conflicts were the result in part of market shocks and demands for natural resources. All we need to do is consider what has occurred during the last few years as Russia invaded the Ukraine and as COVID-19 impacted access to resources because of supply-chain interruptions. Throughout the history of industrialization, nations have sought both access to and control of global oil supplies.

Further, after continued growth of industrialization and realization of the implications for our planet of human-induced climate change, the sustainability challenges that our society faces today are fundamentally different from the past as they are more global and interconnected [1].

The world has become *bigger* through rapid urbanization, global population increase, an exploding middle-class, and dependence on low-labor multinational trade, resulting in the expanded production–consumption systems of our earth's natural resources. The world has also become *smaller* because of increasingly advanced mobility, e–commerce, global financing, virtual meetings, and other technologies such as social media platforms.

In the context of global climate change, nations and multinational companies are increasingly seeking pathways to address and ultimately reverse human-caused climate impacts. These actions are resulting in both private companies and countries competing for renewable resources and critical earth elements essential for the next generation of sustainable technologies, as well as economic and national security. The rise of nationalistic policies, territorial disputes, and conflicts around the globe is threatening the availability of these resources, which threatens our industrial complex, jobs, the economy, defense, and national security.

In this book, I introduce you to the term "dynamic sustainability,"[1] which I use to define this unique juncture in the history of our epic sustainability transition. At one end of the spectrum government policies and technology advancements are inching us closer to achieving the long-sought-after goal of transitioning from a fossil-fuel-based economy to a renewable green economy – what we call the net-zero-carbon economy or zero-carbon economy. This transition is dependent on a new generation of sustainable technologies that are accelerating at an unprecedented pace. In part this has been bolstered by both national and regional government policies since the 2015 Paris Climate Agreement. In many cases these policies are not meant simply to ensure a healthier environment but also have the added benefit of achieving near-term and longer-term economic gains.

Similarly, there now exist growing corporate governance pressures exuded by consumers, shareholders, and financial institutions, as evidenced by the shareholder-driven environmental and social governance (ESG) paradigm, which is further accelerating the sustainability transition by placing pressure on corporate executives to commit to a roster of sustainability commitments, including both significant greenhouse gas (GHG) emission reductions and enhanced governance of supply chains to protect environmental and social imperatives.

Yet, at the same time, society is being challenged by unprecedented competition and pressures for critical natural resources necessary to power the transition, which in part are further driving increased nationalistic policies impacting global trade and raising national security concerns. In the United States, domestic pressures are rising from both the rural–urban divide and the blue–red divide in national and local politics. Concerns over environmental justice and social equity further complicate the sustainability transition. As presented in this book, they raise the real possibilities for unintended consequences and risks to our environment, our society, national security, and the global economy.

---

[1] Dynamic sustainability was previously used by Chambers, Glasgow, and Stange (2013) in "The Dynamic Sustainability Framework: Addressing the Paradox of Sustainment amid Ongoing Change," *Implementation Science*, 8: 117 for health services research.

In many ways, the sustainability transition of today is analogous to the first (1760–1820) and second (1871–1914) industrial revolutions in regard to advances in research and development and the creation of disruptive technologies. Yet our current industrial revolution is far more complicated and globally interconnected and comes at a time of unprecedented global pressures and civil unrest. In the United States the 2020 presidential election was emblematic of a rising rural–urban divide and red–blue divide, which the dynamics of the sustainable transition will further exasperate if not properly considered.

For many, the abstraction of sustainability is being supplanted by the realities of impactful policies and deployment of disruptive technologies. Around the world, national and regional governments as well as multinational corporations are developing plans and commitments to achieve short-term (2030) and longer-term (2050) GHG reductions. This includes committing to "net-zero" targets as a follow-up to the 2015 Paris Agreement. A recent report by the University of Oxford [2] indicates that 61 percent of countries have committed to net zero and over a fifth of the major companies on the Forbes list, with annual sales of nearly $14 trillion, have also made net-zero commitments. Many more governments and industries have also published interim targets as they seek to adopt a new generation of sustainable technologies and adopt organizational strategies to achieve net zero.

One of the clearer examples of dynamic sustainability is found in the pace and growth of the transition to electric vehicles (EVs), as presented in Figure 1.1.

Consider that in a matter of less than three months between September and November 2020, both California (the world's fifth largest economy) and the United Kingdom (the world's sixth largest economy) announced policy changes that have triggered what is likely to be the longer-term demise of the internal combustion vehicle. By 2035 every new car sold in California will be required to be emission free [3] and the United Kingdom moved up its similar plans to ban new petrol cars by 2030 [4].

Even before these policy announcements were formalized, the financial markets had already rewarded the vision of sustainable mobility. Tesla, which sold approximately 500,000 EVs in 2020 as compared to Ford's 4.2 million cars (primarily internal combustion), achieved a market cap of $480 billion, which is higher than the next nine global auto manufacturers combined, excluding Toyota [5].

Legacy automakers around the world facing the pressures of new government policies and shareholder expectations lined up to make public announcements about their transition to the EV market. This is best exemplified by

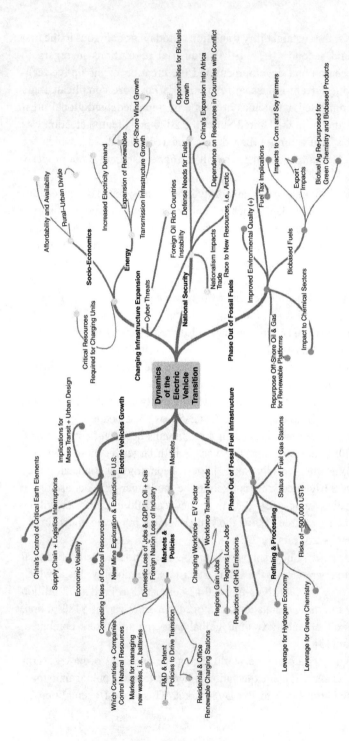

Figure 1.1 Dynamics of the electric vehicle transition.

General Motors who in January 2021 announced their plans to exclusively offer Zero Emission Vehicles by 2035 [6].

While the transition to a more sustainable form of transportation provides the promise of reduced environmental impacts, especially GHG emissions, the dynamics of this transition present many risks and the potential for unintended consequences that, if not planned for, can ultimately impair the sustainability transition.

Notably, the transition will drive a significant demand for additional electricity generation. The average EV requires 30 kilowatt-hours to travel 100 miles – the same amount of electricity a typical American home uses each day [7]. A US Department of Energy study found that US electricity capacity needs to double to power 186 million light-duty EVs in 2050 [8].

If the transition to EVs to meet the goals of advancing sustainability is to be successful, then the increased demand for electricity must be met by renewable sources, such as wind, solar, and potentially green hydrogen. In the United States the transportation sector accounted for 29 percent of GHG emissions in 2019, which was the largest amount of emissions by sector. It was closely followed by electricity generation at 25 percent [9].

To meet the demand for renewable electricity in the United States, there will likely be a significant expansion of offshore wind. The recently elected Biden Administration has proposed installing 30 gigawatts of new offshore wind energy by 2030,[2] which is a substantial increase for a country with only one offshore wind farm in place as of 2021 [10].

While key to meeting the needs of a net-zero economy, this rapid expansion of offshore wind is likely to expose growing tensions with the $5.5 billion fishing industry [11], tourism industry, and real-estate developers who fear the impacts of offshore wind turbines on fishing production, as well as the visual impacts from shorelines. Even environmentalists including non-governmental organizations are voicing concern over the potential environmental risks of wind blades to birds and of ocean-based seismic surveys used for locating wind turbines, which are known to have adverse impacts on whales, other cetaceans, pinnipeds, turtles, fish, and possibly other marine creatures [12]. The effects of such operations on species can occur over very large areas in the ocean and include disruption of communication, increase stress, and cause behavioral changes such as avoidance of key habitat. The dynamics are further complicated by the fact that there is a growing dependence on the critical earth resources necessary to produce key components in

---

[2] www.nytimes.com/2021/03/29/climate/biden-offshore-wind.html.

EVs, charging stations and renewable energy sources such as onshore and offshore wind turbines.

The EV transition and resultant dependence on the growth of the renewable energy sector hinges on the availability of specific critical earth elements including certain rare-earth elements (REs) including neodymium (Nd), praseodymium (Pr), and dysprosium (Dy) for the production of permanent magnet electric generators [13]. The United States as well as the rest of the world are highly dependent on limited numbers of foreign sources of raw and processed critical earth elements. In fact, between 2014 and 2017 China supplied 80 percent of the rare earths (a subset of critical earth elements) to the United States. China is home to at least 85 percent of the world's capacity to process RE elements [14]. China's dominance in this sphere is a result of a very strategic global engagement strategy, including access to these resources throughout the world via their Belt and Road strategy, while the United States in recent years has taken an isolationist policy pathway with limited engagement with countries with rich critical earth resources. Additionally, in part due to environmental concerns and burdensome permitting processes, the United States has lagged in the development of mining and processing of critical earth minerals.

With near-monopolistic control coupled with increased nationalism and growing trade tensions with the United States, China has threatened limiting exports of critical earth elements, which will impact the US military who require these resources for advanced avionics and munitions. Limiting access to critical minerals can also ensure the growth of China's sustainable technology sectors, including the race for dominance in the EV sector [15].

So how are the United States and other countries responding to both the unprecedented demand for critical earth elements and other resources and the domination of China? One example that highlights national security concerns is exemplified by the US Department of Defense in 2020 issuing a number of contracts as part of the Defense Production Act to increase the supply and production of REs and RE salts [16].

Another route to resource independence is the race to locate new and untapped reserves. Currently, Russia, the United States, China and other countries are racing to take advantage of how global climate change is altering conditions and access to the Arctic. The opening of waterways due to ice melt provides new opportunities to acquire resources where estimates place 13 percent of the world's undiscovered oil (90 bb of oil), 30 percent of its undiscovered gas (669 T cu ft), and an abundance of critical earth resources such as uranium and rare-earth minerals [17, 18]. The strategic importance is witnessed as Russia developed new bases[3] and refurbished former Cold War bases in the Kola Peninsula near the city of Murmansk and NATO developed counterstrategies [19].

Closer to home, the dynamics of the sustainability transition will have strong implications for legacy industries of the US economy. Consider the implications as we transition to non-internal combustion engine vehicles powered by renewable electricity. In 2020, America continued to be the world's leading producer of oil and natural gas [20] and, according to an industry-sponsored report, supported over 11.3 million jobs and accounted for up to 7.9 percent of the US GDP in 2019 [21]. In 2020, US petroleum consumption averaged about 17 million barrels per day (b/d), not including biofuels, which was about 13 percent lower than the pre-COVID-19 years [22]. This in large part was supported by 76,000 miles of pipeline and 141 operable petroleum refineries [23]. The United States accounts for approximately 25 percent of global gas production [24]. Natural gas in 2020 as measured by gross withdrawals and averaged 111.2 billion cubic feet per day (Bcf/d) [25], for which 38 percent (11.62 Tcf) was used for electricity in lieu of coal (higher GHG emissions) and both nuclear and renewables with much lower GHG emissions [26].

And it is just not the production and distribution side of fossil fuels that will be impacted by our sustainability transition. When you need to fill up your car with gas, you generally seek out one of the over 145,000 retail gas or convenience stores [27], such as 7-Eleven, BP, or Circle K. The dynamic implications are multifold. There will be implications for employment and state tax revenues due to much-reduced collections of gas tax and sales tax from products sold at these establishments. How will cities prepare for the eventual shuttering or re-imagining of these corner property establishments? And how will the US Environmental Protection Agency and state environmental agencies prepare for the potential abandonment, monitoring, and possible remediation of the over 540,000 underground storage tanks containing fuels spread across the United States [28]? The dynamics of the current sustainability transition come at a time of stress for the American farmer and rural America due to trade policies that have seen American agricultural exports to China fall from $15.8 billion in 2017 to $5.9 billion in 2018 and continue to remain depressed [29].

Both corn, which is used in ethanol production, and soy, an additive for biodiesel, are important economic drivers for rural America. Corn, primary grown in the Midwest, is the United States' largest crop, covering over

---

[3] Prior to the Russian invasion of the Ukraine.

91.7 million acres in 2019 – about 69 million football fields [30]. Forty percent of US corn is used to produce the renewable fuel additive ethanol [31]. In 2019 this amounted to over 15.8 billion gallons of fuel ethanol with an economic impact of more than 68,600 direct jobs, $43 billion to the GDP – a significant economic driver for rural America [32].

If I was an American farmer, working hard in rural parts of our nation and barely making a profit, what might my attitude be when my family's livelihood is placed at risk by a rapid decrease in corn-derived ethanol as those living primarily in heavily urbanized blue states along the coasts transition to EVs? How have our public and corporate policymakers considered actions that can both sustain and possibly even grow rural agriculture and related industries, new industries? The answer in many cases is that they have not.

In this book, I hope to raise awareness of these dynamics. I will lay out many of the exogenous factors that, coupled with the unprecedented rapid pace of the sustainable technology transition, are creating unique challenges and pressures that have the potential to result in unintended consequences to the environment, economy, and society, as well as risking our collective desired outcomes for the sustainability transition.

Some of these challenges are near-term, easier to quantify, and likely reversible. Other challenges from the transition have unknown implications and outcomes. Yet, each of these dynamics also provides opportunities, such as repurposing American agriculture and our legacy energy infrastructure for the development and production of a new generation of sustainable and carbon-SMART commodities and products to meet rapidly increased demand by manufacturers, brands, retailers, and consumers around the world. The United States can again be a manufacturing leader and create both jobs and wealth, not just in its cities but again in its forgotten rural regions.

However, this will take leadership, foresight, and in many cases an updated approach to corporate management and government policies. Even in times of heightened polarization, what I lay out I believe holds the promise of enabling conservatives and liberals, rural and urban, industry and government to come together to make the nation stronger and healthier.

While I outline many details of what has gone wrong and what could go wrong, this book is about possibilities and the promise of renewal in the United States (Figure 1.2). I hope you too see the opportunities. But most importantly, what I want to present is a way of thinking and managing at times of significant dynamics that impact policies, markets, and national security.

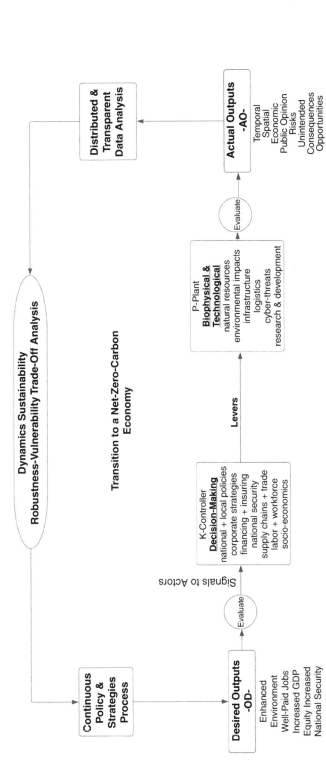

Figure 1.2 Dynamic sustainability Robustness–Vulnerability Tradeoff framework.

References

1. W. Clark and N. Dickson (2003). Sustainability Science: The Emerging Research Program. *Proceedings of the National Academy of Sciences*, 100(14): 8059–8061.
2. https://ca1-eci.edcdn.com/reports/ECIU-Oxford_Taking_Stock.pdf?mtime=20210323005817&focal=none.
3. www.gov.ca.gov/2020/09/23/governor-newsom-announces-california-will-phase-out-gasoline-powered-cars-drastically-reduce-demand-for-fossil-fuel-in-californias-fight-against-climate-change.
4. www.theverge.com/2020/11/17/21572312/uk-ban-combustion-engine-vehicles-sale-electric-cars.
5. www.bbc.com/news/business-59045100.
6. www.cnbc.com/2021/01/28/general-motors-plans-to-exclusively-offer-electric-vehicles-by-2035.html.
7. A. Brown (2020). Electric Cars Will Challenge State Power Grids. *The Washington Post*. www.washingtonpost.com/science/electric-cars-will-challenge-state-power-grids/2020/01/24/136a2a30-32e6-11ea-a053-dc6d944ba776_story.html.
8. US Department of Energy (2019). Summary Report on EVs at Scale and the U.S. Electric Power System. Report. www.energy.gov/sites/prod/files/2019/12/f69/GITT%20ISATT%20EVs%20at%20Scale%20Grid%20Summary%20Report%20FINAL%20Nov2019.pdf.
9. US EPA Inventory of US Greenhouse Gas Emissions and Sinks 1990–2020 (2022). www.epa.gov/ghgemissions/inventory-us-greenhouse-gas-emissions-and-sinks.
10. The White House (2021). Biden Administration Jumpstarts Offshore Wind Energy Projects to Create Jobs. www.whitehouse.gov/briefing-room/statements-releases/2021/03/29/fact-sheet-biden-administration-jumpstarts-offshore-wind-energy-projects-to-create-jobs.
11. US Department of Commerce – National Oceanic and Atmospheric Administration. NOAA (2021). Fisheries of the United States 2019.
12. LeMoult, C (2019). Seismic Testing Approval Process Raises Concern About Impact on Right Whales. WGBH Boston. www.wgbh.org/news/science-and-technology/2019/03/28/seismic-testing-approval-process-raises-concern-about-impact-on-right-whales.
13. US Department of Energy (2022). Rare Earth Permanent Magnets: US Department of Energy Response to Executive Order 14017, "America's Supply Chains."
14. Reuters (2019). U.S. Dependence on China's Rare Earth: Trade War Vulnerability. www.reuters.com/article/us-usa-trade-china-rareearth-explainer/u-s-dependence-on-chinas-rare-earth-trade-war-vulnerability-idUSKCN1TS3AQ.
15. S. Yu and D. Sevastopulo (2021). China Targets Rare Earth Export Curbs to Hobble US Defence Industry. *Financial Times*. February 16. www.ft.com/content/d3ed83f4-19bc-4d16-b510-415749c032c1.
16. US Department of Defense (2020). DOD Announces Rare Earth Element Awards to Strengthen Domestic Industrial Base. US DOD Press Release. November 17. www.defense.gov/News/Releases/Release/Article/2418542/dod-announces-rare-earth-element-awards-to-strengthen-domestic-industrial-base.

17. M. Rowe (2021). Dossier: Mining the Arctic. *Geographical*. August 6. https://geographical.co.uk/nature/polar/item/4113-dossier-mining-the-arctic.

18. United States Geological Survey (2008). Circum-Arctic Resource Appraisal: Estimates of Undiscovered Oil and Gas North of the Arctic Circle. USGS Fact Sheet 2008–3049. https://pubs.usgs.gov/fs/2008/3049.

19. J. Bermudez (2020). The Ice Curtain: Bringing Transparency to the Arctic. Center for Strategic and International Studies. March 23.

20. US Energy Information Administration (2021). United States Continued to Lead Global Petroleum and Natural Gas Production in 2020. www.eia.gov/todayinenergy/detail.php?id=48756.

21. American Petroleum Institute (2021). Impacts of the Natural Gas and Oil Industry on the U.S. Economy in 2019, prepared for the American Petroleum Institute by PwC, July.

22. US Energy Information Administration (2021). Oil and Petroleum Products Explained. May. www.eia.gov/energyexplained/oil-and-petroleum-products/use-of-oil.php.

23. Energy at Work. Upgrading America's Energy Infrastructure (2017). Business Roundtable. https://s3.amazonaws.com/brt.org/staging-qeOOpdhhbbqqq3/Energy-atWork-Full.pdf.

24. World Energy and Climate Statistics – Yearbook (2021). https://yearbook.enerdata.net/natural-gas/world-natural-gas-production-statistics.html.

25. US Energy Information Administration (2021). Natural Gas Explained. www.eia.gov/energyexplained/natural-gas/use-of-natural-gas.php#:~:text=The%20United%20States%20used%20about,of%20U.S.%20total%20energy%20consumption.

26. US Energy Information Administration (2021). Annual U.S. Natural Gas Production Decreased by 1% in 2020. www.eia.gov/todayinenergy/detail.php?id=46956#:~:text=U.S.%20natural%20gas%20production%E2%80%94asand%20oil%20prices%20in%202020.

27. NACS: The Association for Convenience and Fuel Retailing (2022). Convenience Stores Sell the Most Gas. March 10. www.convenience.org/Topics/Fuels/Who-Sells-Americas-Fuel.

28. US Environmental Protection Agency (2022). Underground Storage Tanks. www.epa.gov/ust#:~:text=Approximately%20542%2C000%20underground%20storage%20tanks,store%20petroleum%20or%20hazardous%20substances.

29. M. Chinn and B. Plumley (2020). What Is the Toll of Trade Wars on U.S. Agriculture? PBS in Partnership with EconoFact. January 16. www.pbs.org/newshour/economy/making-sense/what-is-the-toll-of-trade-wars-on-u-s-agriculture#:~:text=American%20agricultural%20exports%20to%20China,China%20deal%20promises%20some%20relief.

30. US Department of Agriculture (2021). Corn Is America's Largest Crop in 2019. www.usda.gov/media/blog/2019/07/29/corn-americas-largest-crop-2019.

31. US Department of Agriculture (2021). Feedgrains Sector at a Glance. Economic Research Service of the United States Department of Agriculture. www.ers.usda.gov/topics/crops/corn-and-other-feedgrains/feedgrains-sector-at-a-glance/#:~:text=Much%20of%20this%20growth%20in,percent%20of%20total%20corn%20use.

32. Renewable Fuels Association (2020). New Study: Despite Policy Challenges, Ethanol Industry Significantly Benefited Economy in 2019. February 10. https://ethanolrfa.org/media-and-news/category/news-releases/article/2020/02/new-study-despite-policy-challenges-ethanol-industry-significantly-benefited-economy-in-2019.

2

Global Trends

In the environment,
Every victory is temporary,
Every defeat permanent . . ..

Thomas Jefferson [51]

To get a better understanding of dynamic sustainability, it is important to first understand the socioeconomic and physical trends that are influencing global sustainability. We begin this exploration by examining three initial drivers: (1) population increases, (2) global affluence, and (3) technologies.

We can represent this using the IPAT mathematical notation [1]:

$I = P \times A \times T$

where:

I = impact (e.g., climate change)
P = population
A = affluence
T = technology

2.1 Population

In many minds the most important factor in regard to sustainability is not just that the world is getting bigger but that it is growing at an unprecedented pace. As shown in Table 2.1, our global population is anticipated to reach almost 10 billion people in 2050, up from 2.5 billion in a single century! There are a number of factors for this growth, including fertility rates as well as the fact that people are living longer (mortality rates) in large measure as a result of healthcare, food production, and the availability and ease of migration to avoid conflict and obtain employment.

Table 2.1 *World population by continent, 1950–2050, in thousands [3]*

	Oceania	North America	Europe	Latin America + Caribbean	Africa	Asia	World
1950	12,648	172,603	549,375	168,918	228,670	1,404,062	2,536,275
1960	15,825	204,807	605,925	221,051	285,142	1,700,463	3,033,213
1970	19,718	231,145	657,350	288,077	366,459	2,137,828	3,700,578
1980	23,005	254,414	694,207	364,284	480,012	2,642,489	4,458,412
1990	27,071	280,345	721,699	445,919	634,567	3,221,342	5,330,943
2000	31,229	312,845	727,201	525,795	817,566	3,730,371	6,145,007
2010	36,636	342,937	737,164	597,562	1,049,446	4,194,425	6,958,169
2020	42,384	369,159	743,390	664,474	1,352,622	4,623,454	7,795,482
2030	47,683	395,453	739,456	718,483	1,703,538	4,946,586	8,551,199
2040	52,572	417,193	728,823	757,027	2,100,302	5,154,419	9,210,337
2050	57,121	434,655	715,721	779,841	2,527,557	5,256,927	9,771,823

There is no consensus on just how much larger our planetary population will grow. Reaching one would be almost impossible given all the variables such as population limiters including pandemics and wars, as well as further technology advances that could extend population increases. The United Nations forecasts population plateauing to just under 11 billion (10.9 billion) by the end of this century [2]. What is also important to explore are the shifts in our global population. In 1950 we observe that Europe was the second most populous region with one-third of the population of the most populous region Asia, which includes both China and India. Jump to 2050 and the rapid growth in both Asia and the emergence of Africa become apparent, as is the lack of similar growth rates in both North America and Europe.

Additionally, two other factors are at play. One is the transitions of the most populous countries by 2050 (Figure 2.1) as India is poised to take over that role from China by 2027. Further, the United States by 2050 will move from the third most populous country to the fourth as Nigeria catapults to the third most populous ranking. The second population dynamic is that of rapid urbanization.

Not only is our population growing but most of the world's population is now also living in cities, as shown in Figure 2.2; and our big cities are becoming even bigger. In 1700 only 2 percent of the world's population lived in cities; even as recently as 1900, urban populations accounted for only 15 percent [4]. In 1950, there were seventy-eight cities around the world

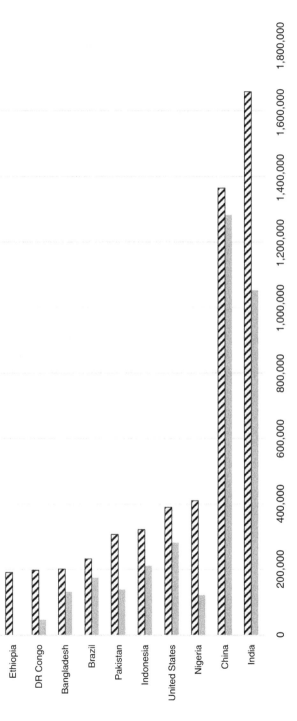

Figure 2.1 Ten most populous countries by 2050 and their growth from 1950 in thousands [3].

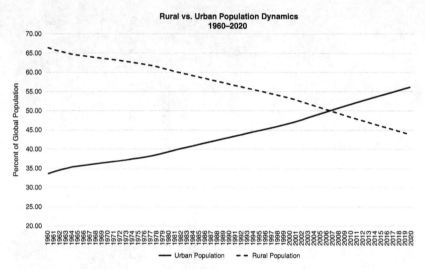

Figure 2.2 Rural versus urban global population trends [6].

that had populations greater than 1 million. However, by 2000 the figure had grown to 400, and by 2030 there are expected to be 662 cities with a population of at least 1 million [4].

The rapid pace of urbanization has generated a new term in our modern vocabulary: "megacities." These are cities with a population of at least 8 million. There were only two megacities in 1950 (Tokyo and New York City) and only ten by 1990. However, by 2035, it is projected that there will be forty-eight megacities in the world, which will host 15.52 percent of the world's urban population, with most of these cities (forty-one) located in developing countries [4]. Further, the expansion of urban land consumption is outpacing population growth by as much as 50 percent and is expected to add 1.2 million km² of new urban built-up area around the world by 2050 [5].

2.2 Affluence

In 2015, the global middle class numbered about 3 billion people who spent $33 trillion, amounting to two-thirds of the world's consumer spending [7]. According to a recent Credit Suisse Global Wealth Report (2021), the global middle class, defined as adults whose assets amount to between $10,000 and

$100,000, more than tripled to 1.7 billion in mid-2020 from just 507 million in 2000 [8]. The World Bank in 2022 reported that over the last forty years China has pulled over 800 million Chinese people out of extreme poverty,[1] contributing close to three-quarters of the total global reduction of people around the world living in extreme poverty [48].

In fact, China may reach 70 percent of its population being classified as middle class by 2030 and consuming nearly $10 trillion in goods and services. India is expected to overtake China as the world's most populous country by 2026 or sooner and may become the world's largest middle-class consumer market [50]. Combined, China and India will represent roughly two-thirds of the global middle-class population and 59 percent of middle-class consumption that is expected to tally $64 trillion by 2030. Together, they will be spending more than the combined middle-class spending in Europe and the USA in 2015 [9, 10].

As our global population has increased and as the global middle class expanded, we have witnessed and will continue to witness spending in the form of final consumption expenditure. Final consumption expenditure (formerly total consumption) is the sum of household final consumption expenditure (formerly private consumption) and general government final consumption expenditure (formerly general government consumption). Data are in constant 2000 US dollars [11] and are presented in Figure 2.3.

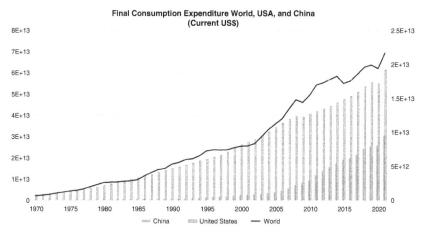

Figure 2.3 Growth of global final consumption expenditure between 1970 and 2020 in US dollars [12].

---

[1] The extreme poverty line equals incomes below $1.90 per day, as defined by the World Bank.

2.3 Technology

I continue to be amazed by the pace of technological innovations and advances. In 1990 there were only about 11 million mobile phone users around the globe. Yet, by 2022 that number had risen to an estimated 6.6 billion people or almost 84 percent of the world's population owning a smartphone [13]. Now consider all that can be done with that smartphone. It provides the opportunity to connect with individuals and, importantly in the context of this book, it allows you to reach companies around the globe, or rather it allows companies around the world to connect and advertise to you. In 2000 the total retail sales in the US were $2.98 trillion with less than 1 percent through e-commerce sales (0.9 percent). However, by 2020, of the $5.62 trillion in retail sales, e-commerce had jumped to 14 percent [14]. Adobe predicted global e-commerce sales to have reached $4.2 trillion in 2021 [15].

In addition to computers and telecommunications growing along with population and affluence, so have our options for mobility. In 1960 the number of vehicles globally per 1,000 population was forty-one. By 2002 that number had risen to 130 and the total number of vehicles around the world had increased from 122 million in 1960 to over 800 million by 2002, a 4.6 percent average annual growth rate [16]. In 2022, the number of vehicles is estimated to have reached approximately 1.46 billion, with 19 percent of those in the United States, lagging behind Asia, which has 531 million vehicles or over one-third of global vehicles. This is being fueled by the rapid growth of vehicle ownership in China, which in 2016 overtook the United States in total ownership but still lags in a per-capita ranking [17, 18].

Air travel, once the domain of the wealthy, has also grown to the masses. Globally, in 2000 air tourist spending was just under $350 billion and by 2018 (pre-COVID-19) it had reached $850 billion. In 2018, there were close to 4 billion origin–destination passenger journeys worldwide, with China providing the largest incremental increase in passenger trips – just under 50 million journeys – with the United States and India ranked second and third, respectively [19].

The 4.5 billion scheduled passengers carried in 2019 are expected to grow to about 10.0 billion by 2040. To accommodate this growth, Airbus reports that in 2019 almost 21,000 of its commercial aircraft were in service and this is expected to double to nearly 45,000 aircraft for both passengers and cargo by 2040. This means the industry will need to double by adding over 2 million new personnel, including 763,000 pilots [20, 21].

While you may intuitively consider transportation and electronics as part of a technology transition, you might not think of food in the same way. However, today's agriculture systems are heavily dependent on technological innovations and expansion spanning from automation and state-of-the-art satellite links to guide planting and tracking weather to the biosciences that provide more robust seeds.

As the global middle class has grown, so has our transition from a plant-based diet to a diet of greater meat consumption. Since 1990, the global consumption of meat has more than doubled, reaching 324 million metric tons in 2020. Between 1990 and 2020, the volume of poultry consumed worldwide increased from 34.6 million metric tons to more than 130 million metric tons. By weight, poultry is now the most consumed meat type world-wide [22]. As presented in Figure 2.4, China's economic growth and the growth of the middle class have played an important role in the population's desire for meat products in their diet. Certainly, the opening of China to foreign enter-prises played a major role too.

If, like me, you have spent any time in China, you will have quickly observed the number and size of Kentucky Fried Chicken (KFC) franchises in the country. KFC was the first foreign fast-food company in China and since 2017 KFC has become one of the most recognizable American brands in China, with over 5,600 restaurants in 1,200-plus cities providing for the parent company YUM China $5 billion in revenue in 2017. In fact, China is one of the few countries around the globe where KFCs outnumber McDonald's [24].

The trend for meat is part of a much bigger sustainability challenge. The total global food demand is expected to increase dramatically. One study by *Nature*

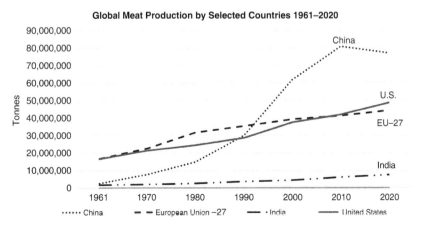

Figure 2.4 Meat production 1961 to 2020 for selected countries. Meat includes cattle, poultry, sheep/mutton, goat, pig meat, and wild game in million tons [23].

places this growth between 35 and 56 percent between 2010 and 2050 [25], while the Food and Agriculture Organization (FAO) estimates an even greater demand at 70 percent (worldwide total) to 100 percent (developing countries) between 2005 and 2050 [26]. This considers both feeding humans directly as well as the animals we consume. Animals are not efficient food converters. As an example, beef cattle generally need 8–10 kg of feed to produce 1 kg of meat. In terms of calories, for every 100 calories fed to animals in the form of edible crops, the return is only about 25 calories in the form of meat and dairy products [27].

2.4 Impacts

I have laid out the P, A, and T in the IPAT equation. Now we transition to the "I," which are the impacts. Clearly, the impact that has garnered the greatest attention is in regard to human-induced (anthropogenic) global climate change. Because of the rapid ascent on the focus to a net-zero carbon economy by government and industry, I have devoted an entire chapter to climate change (Chapter 3). However, global climate change is not the only impact and I provide a quick overview of some additional sustainability impacts. This listing is not extensive as there are numerous books that focus just on the numerous impacts and implications to our planet.

2.4.1 Forestry

More than half of the world's forests are found in only five countries (Russia, Brazil, Canada, the United States, and China). Globally, we are losing forests at a very high rate. According to scientists, since 1990 we have lost 420 million hectares (~1 billion acres) of forest mainly in Africa and South America. Agricultural expansion required to feed a growing and more affluent population is the main driver of deforestation and forest degradation, which also results in the loss of forest biodiversity. Large-scale commercial agriculture (primarily cattle ranching and cultivation of soya bean and oil palm) accounted for 40 percent of tropical deforestation between 2000 and 2010, and local subsistence agriculture for another 33 percent [28].

2.4.2 Land Conversions

Land-cover transitions are not caused only by agricultural practices. While deforestation has significant implications for carbon storage and sequestration as well as biodiversity, so does rapid urbanization, which is one of the most visible and irreversible forms of land-cover change [29]. We now know that most of us are living in cities and many of us experience the urban heat island effect where the temperatures in urban areas are increasingly becoming warmer in the daytime and mostly at night compared to the adjacent rural region (ΔTu-r).

This meso-scale[2] humanmade climate impact is a result of altering surface energy budgets through the removal of natural vegetation and replacing them with asphalt, concrete, and buildings, which, unlike vegetation, do not transpire and which have lower reflectivity (albedo) and higher heat storage capacity. In areas such as the Phoenix, Arizona metro area the urban heat island has been documented to be over 14°F at night. Beyond making it more uncomfortable and unsafe, it also requires more energy to power air-conditioning, alters aquatic life in urban ponds and lakes, intensifies storms, and impacts air quality and human health [30, 31].

2.4.3 Mineral Resources

As laid out earlier, we have become an urbanized planet and the rapid urbanization that will continue requires the consumption of a tremendous amount of resources to build and expand the cities where people will work and live.

That iPhone you own and the car you drive, as well as the house you live in, all require tremendous amounts of natural resources from biomass to metal ores. The minerals we consume in our consumer goods must be physically extracted from the earth and processed using large amounts of energy and chemicals. The global average of overall material demand per capita was 7.4 tons in 1970 and grew to 12.2 tons per capita in 2017. Since 1970, mineral resource extraction has more than tripled, including a fivefold increase in the use of non-metallic minerals[3] and a 45 percent increase in fossil fuel use. By 2060, global material is expected to reach 190 billion tons, up from 27 billion tons in 1970.

2.4.4 Water

Around the world, we consume water that is supplied in large measure from freshwater obtained through precipitation at a rate of almost 110,000 km^3 per year [32]. About 56 percent of this amount is evapotranspired by forests

---

[2] That is, 50 km^2 or less.
[3] This category includes rock phosphate, sand and gravel, limestone sulfur, nitrates, and so on.

and natural landscapes and 5 percent by rainfed agriculture. The remaining 39 percent or 43,000 km^3 per year is converted to surface runoff (feeding rivers and lakes) and groundwater recharge (feeding aquifers). Global water withdrawal for agriculture, industries, and municipalities increased sharply in the second half of the twentieth century; in fact, water withdrawal grew at a faster rate than human population. From 1970 to 2010, the growth rate of withdrawal grew from 2,500 km^3 per year to 3,900 km^3 per year [33]. When examining country measurements between 2000 and 2012, the global sum of water withdrawals is dominated by agriculture at 70 percent, mainly for irrigation (including livestock and aquaculture). Industry withdrawal accounts for 19 percent, with municipalities responsible for 11 percent [33]. The World Health Organization reports that 844 million people lack access to water [34].

2.4.5 Wastes

As a society, we produce a lot of wastes. On average we generate over 2.01 billion tonnes (2.21 billion tons) of municipal solid waste annually, enough to fill over 800,000 Olympic-sized swimming pools every year; this does not include hazardous and medical wastes as well as construction debris. This equates to a per-person per-day average of 0.74 kilograms (1.63 lb) with high-income countries generating about 34 percent, or 683 million tons, of the world's waste. It is anticipated that global waste is expected to grow to 3.4 billion tons by 2050, more than double population growth over the same period. Globally at least 33 percent of the world's waste – an extremely conservative estimate – is not managed in an environmentally safe manner, meaning the wastes can impact water supplies as well as pose air quality issues when burned.

Overall, there is a positive correlation between waste generation and income level. Daily per-capita waste generation in high-income countries is projected to increase by 19 percent by 2050 compared to low- and middle-income countries where it is expected to increase by approximately 40 percent or more. The United States with only 4 percent of the world's population generates 12 percent of the world's solid wastes. It is concerning that as our production and consumption of agriculture around the world grows, so does agriculture-related waste. In the United States, 30–40 percent of all food, worth US $48.3 billion, is thrown away each year. About half of the water used to produce this food also goes to waste since agriculture is the largest human use of water [35, 36, 37–41].

2.4.6 Oceans and Fisheries

Seventy-one percent of the earth's surface is covered by water and our oceans and fisheries help to sustain ourselves and our planet. However, our consumptive patterns and emissions of wastes and greenhouse gases are placing them at risk. According to the FAO [42], 87 percent of global fish stocks are either overexploited or fully exploited. Additionally, other studies place between 40 percent and 70 percent of fish stocks in European waters at an unsustainable level – either overfished or at their lower biomass limits [43, 44]. Recently, scientists have also observed mercury contamination has increased in some species (e.g., ~50 percent in swordfish), exceeding mercury consumption guideline thresholds (>1 mg/kg) and possibly impacting the capacity of fisheries and marine ecosystem to respond to the current climate-induced pollution sensitivity [45].

And for the fish population not over-harvested, they face another plight caused by humanmade wastes – our growing dependence on plastics. Each year we produce over 300 million tons of plastic and at least 14 million tons of plastic end up in our oceans every year. In fact, 80 percent of all marine debris is plastics that make their way to the surface and to deep-sea sediments, causing entanglement and death to marine life while also having an economic impact of at least $13 billion annually [46, 47].

2.5 Role of Consumerism

As briefly laid out, population, affluence, and technology working as part of a system have an impact on our environment. While we started this chapter with the IPAT equation, it should be clear by now that there is a very important factor not accounted for in this thinking. That is the role of you and I – the consumers of goods. What type of responsibilities come with our increase in our income and discretionary spending? A colleague of mine, Dr. Louis Lebel, who is a professor and researcher at Chiang Mai University in Thailand and the Stockholm Environment Institute, has written and developed a robust understanding of the coupled system between consumer demand and corporate production to meet the demand with interesting case studies of their implications.

The area of research is known as Production Consumption Systems. Lebel's book *Sustainable Production Consumption Systems* [50], as well as the works of others, bring to our attention that the focus on population and technology alone is not within itself sufficient to overcome our increasing environmental and social sustainability imperatives. They identify the need to develop strategies and policies for the increasingly important role of individual consumers' purchasing habits, as well as the social structures that drive consumerism and consumption upward. Satisfying this more ambitious objective will entail education including through social media as well as policy measures to reduce the volumes of production and consumption. Examples of production consumption systems are presented in Part II of this book where we explore the increased production of electric vehicles, which leads to increased consumption of electricity supplies that are yet to exist.

References

1. P. R. Ehrlich and J. P. Holdren (1971, March 26). Impact of Population Growth. *Science*, 171: 1212–1217. (See also the longer version by the same authors under the same title in Commission on Population Growth and the American Future [1972]. *Research Reports, vol. 3: Population, Resources, and the Environment*, Ronald G. Ridker (ed.). Washington, DC: US Government Printing Office, pp. 365–377.)
2. D. Adams (2021). How Far Will Global Population Rise? Researchers Can't Agree. *Nature*, 597: 462–465. doi: https://doi.org/10.1038/d41586-021-02522-6.
3. United Nations, Department of Economic and Social Affairs, Population Division (2018). World Urbanization Prospects: The 2018 Revision. https://population.un .org/wup/DataQuery.
4. Y.-M. Yeung, J. Shen, and G. Kee (2020). *Megacities: International Encyclopedia of Human Geography (2nd ed.)*. New York: Elsevier.
5. World Bank (2020). Urban Development. www.worldbank.org/en/topic/urbande velopment/overview#1.
6. M. Pesaresi, M. Melchiorri, A. Siragusa, and T. Kemper (2016). Atlas of the Human Planet: Mapping Human Presence on Earth with the Global Human Settlement Layer. Luxembourg: European Commission. https://ourworldindata .org/how-urban-is-the-world.
7. H. Kharas (2016). How a Growing Global Middle Class Could Save the World's Economy. Pew Trust. www.pewtrusts.org/en/trend/archive/summer-2016/how-a-growing-global-middle-class-could-save-the-worlds-economy.
8. Credit Suisse (2021). Global Wealth Report 2021. Zurich: Credit Suisse Research Institute.
9. C. Versace, L. E. Hawkings, and M. Abssy (2021, July 9). World Reimagined: The Rise of the Global Middle Class. www.nasdaq.com/articles/world-reimagined%3A-the-rise-of-the-global-middle-class-2021-07-09.
10. World Bank Group (2022). Four Decades of Poverty Reduction in China: Drivers, Insights for the World and the Way Forward. https://thedocs.worldbank.org/en/ doc/bdadc16a4f5c1c88a839c0f905cde802-0070012022/original/Poverty-Synthesis-Report-final.pdf.

11. World Bank (2022). Metadata Glossary. https://databank.worldbank.org/metadataglossary/all/series.
12. World Bank (2022). Final Consumption Expenditure (current US $). https://data.worldbank.org/indicator/NE.CON.TOTL.CD?end=2020&start=2000&view=chart.
13. A. Turner (2022). How Many Smartphones Are in the World? BankMyCell. www.bankmycell.com/blog/how-many-phones-are-in-the-world#:~:text=In%202022%2C%20the%20number%20of,91.54%25%20of%20the%20world's%20population.
14. How Much (2022). Charting Over 20 Years of Retail Sales and E-commerce in the US Retail Industry (Update). https://howmuch.net/articles/timeline-retail-sales-growth-US.
15. Forbes (2021). Global E-Commerce Sales to Hit $4.2 Trillion As Online Surge Continues. April 27. www.forbes.com/sites/joanverdon/2021/04/27/global-ecommerce-sales-to-hit-42-trillion-as-online-surge-continues-adobe-reports.
16. J. Dargay, D. Gately, and M. Sommer (2007, October). Vehicle Ownership and Income Growth, Worldwide: 1960–2030. *The Energy Journal*.
17. Hedges and Company (2022). How Many Cars Are There in the World in 2022? https://hedgescompany.com/blog/2021/06/how-many-cars-are-there-in-the-world.
18. Carsguide (2018). How Many Cars Are There Around the World? September 20. www.carsguide.com.au/car-advice/how-many-cars-are-there-in-the-world-70629.
19. International Air Transport Association (2019). Annual Review 2019. 75th Annual General Meeting, Seoul. June.
20. Air (2022). Commercial Aviation: Growth and Forecast 2021–2039. www.grupooneair.com/analysis-global-growth-commercial-aviation.
21. International Civil Aviation Organization (2019). Annual Report 2019. The World Air Transport in 2019. www.icao.int/annual-report-2019/Pages/default.aspx.
22. Statista (2022). Meat Consumption Worldwide, 2022. April 14. www.statista.com/statistics/274522/global-per-capita-consumption-of-meat/#:~:text=The%20global%20consumption%20of%20meat,most%20consumed%20meat%20type%20worldwide.
23. OurWorldInData (2022). Meat and Dairy Production. https://ourworldindata.org/meat-production.
24. N. Thomas (2018). How KFC Changed China and How China Changed KFC. *MacroPolo.* August 13. https://macropolo.org/analysis/how-kfc-changed-china-and-how-china-changed-kfc.
25. M. van Dijk, T. Morley, M. L. Rau et al. (2021). A Meta-Analysis of Projected Global Food Demand and Population at Risk of Hunger for the Period 2010–2050. *Nature Food*, 2: 494–501. https://doi.org/10.1038/s43016-021-00322-9.
26. Food and Agriculture Organization (2009). How to Feed the World 2050. High-Level Expert Forum. www.fao.org/fileadmin/user_upload/lon/HLEF2050_Global_Agriculture.pdf.
27. G. Silva (2018). Feeding the World in 2050 and Beyond – Part 1: Productivity Challenges. Michigan State University. www.canr.msu.edu/news/feeding-the-world-in-2050-and-beyond-part-1.

28. Food and Agriculture Organization and United Nations Environment Programme (2020). *The State of the World's Forests 2020: Forests, Biodiversity and People*. Rome: Food and Agriculture Organization.

29. J. Gao and B. C. O'Neill (2020). Mapping Global Urban Land for the 21st Century with Data-Driven Simulations and Shared Socioeconomic Pathways. *Nature Communications*, 11: 2302. https://doi.org/10.1038/s41467-020-15788-7.

30. J. Golden, A. Brazel, J. Salmond, and D. Laws (2006). Energy and Water Sustainability: The Role of Urban Climate Change from Metropolitan Infrastructure. *Engineering for Sustainable Development*, 1(1):55–70.

31. J. S. Golden, P. Guthrie, K. Kaloush, and R. Britter (2005). The Summertime Urban Heat Island Hysteresis Lag Complexity: Applying Thermodynamics, Urban Engineering and Sustainability Research. *Sustainable Engineering – A Journal of the Royal Institute of Civil Engineers*, 158(ES4):197–210.

32. International Resources Panel (2019). Global Resources Outlook 2019: Natural Resources for the Future We Want. www.resourcepanel.org/reports/global-resources-outlook.

33. Food and Agriculture Organization (2016). AQUASTAT. www.fao.org/nr/water/aquastat/data/query/index.html?lang=en.

34. World Health Organization and United Nations Children's Education Fund (2017). Progress on Drinking Water, Sanitation, and Hygiene: 2017 Update and SDG Baselines. Geneva. https://washdata.org.

35. S. Kaza, L. C. Yao, P. Bhada-Tata, and F. van Woerden (2018). What a Waste 2.0: A Global Snapshot of Solid Waste Management to 2050. Urban Development. Washington, DC: World Bank.

36. International Resources Panel (2018). The Weight of Cities: Resource Requirements of Future Urbanization. Nairobi: United Nations Environment Programme.

37. United Nations Environment Programme (2022). Think, Eat, Save. www.unep.org/thinkeatsave/get-informed/worldwide-food-waste.

38. World Bank (2022). What a Waste 2.0: A Global Snapshot of Solid Waste Management to 2050. https://datatopics.worldbank.org/what-a-waste/trends_in_solid_waste_management.html.

39. Center for Sustainable Systems (2021). The University of Michigan. Municipal Solid Waste. Factsheet. https://css.umich.edu/sites/default/files/Municipal%20Solid%20Waste_CSS04-15_e2021.pdf.

40. Visual Capitalist (2022). Visualizing the Global Landfill Crisis. March 2. www.visualcapitalist.com/visualizing-the-global-landfill-crisis.

41. World Bank (2018). What a Waste: An Updated Look into the Future of Solid Waste Management. www.worldbank.org/en/news/immersive-story/2018/09/20/what-a-waste-an-updated-look-into-the-future-of-solid-waste-management.

42. Food and Agriculture Organization (2012). *The State of the World Fisheries and Aquaculture*. Rome: Food and Agriculture Organization.

43. N. K. Dulvy, Y. Sadovy, and J. D. Reynolds (2003). Extinction Vulnerability in Marine Populations. *Fish and Fisheries*, 4: 25–64.

44. U. R. Sumaila and T. C. Tai (2020). End Overfishing and Increase the Resilience of the Ocean to Climate Change. *Frontiers in Marine Science*, 7: 523. doi: 10.1073/pnas.2008256117.

45. I. Issifu, J. J. Alava, V. W. Y. Lam, and U. R. Sumaila (2022). Impact of Ocean Warming, Overfishing and Mercury on European Fisheries: A Risk Assessment and Policy Solution Framework. *Frontiers in Marine Science*, 8: 770805. doi: 10.3389/fmars.2021.770805.

46. International Union for Conservation of Nature (2021). Marine Plastic Pollution. Technical Bulletin November 2021.

47. W. W. Y. Lau, Y. Shiran, R. M. Bailey et al. (2020). Evaluating Scenarios toward Zero Plastic Pollution. *Science*, 369: 1455–1461.

48. World Bank Group (2022). Four Decades of Poverty Reduction in China: Drivers, Insights for the World, and the Way Ahead. https://thedocs.worldbank.org/en/doc/ bdadc16a4f5c1c88a839c0f905cde802-0070012022/original/Poverty-Synthesis-Report-final.pdf.

49. J. Feng (2021). When Will India Overtake China in Population? *Newsweek*. May 11. www.newsweek.com/when-will-india-overtake-china-population-1590451.

50. L. Lebel, S. Lorek, and R. Daniel (2010). *Sustainable Production Consumption Systems: Knowledge, Engagement and Practice*. Dordrecht: Springer.

51. D. Evans (1997). *A History of Nature Conservation in Britain* (2nd ed.). London: Routledge.

3

Global Climate Change

The jury has reached a verdict. And it is damning. This report of the Intergovernmental Panel on Climate Change is a litany of broken climate promises. It is a file of shame, cataloguing the empty pledges that put us firmly on track towards an unlivable world.

We are on a fast track to climate disaster.

United Nations Secretary-General António Guterres,
speech in New York City, April 4, 2022 [25]

3.1 Climate Change

For those who seek an in-depth scientific overview of climate science and climate change, I suggest you explore chapter 1 of the Intergovernmental Panel on Climate Change (IPCC) Historical Overview of Climate Change [1]. However, for the sake of this abbreviated overview, in its simplest form, when we discuss climate change what scientists and policymakers are referring to are the long-term shifts in temperatures and weather patterns that are increasing global average temperatures. The climate challenge then can be framed as limiting total cumulative emissions of carbon dioxide (CO_2). As shown in this chapter, CO_2 is clearly not the only contributor to global warming but is considered the most important greenhouse gas (GHG).

While there are many different references to the scientific origins for climate change, most go back to Irish scientist John Tyndall who in 1859 showed the mechanisms causing climate change. He proved that gases including carbon dioxide and water vapor can absorb heat via radiation from a copper cube containing boiling water. This, in fact, was infrared radiation, which is similar to what is emitted from our earth's surface [2]. However, it is actually an

American scientist, Eunice Foote, who should be credited with our understanding of climate change. Three years prior to Tyndall, in 1856 Foote presented and was published on the absorption of thermal radiation by carbon dioxide and water vapor. Tyndall in his works three years later did not reference her works [3, 4]. Fast forward to March 1958 when C. David Keeling of the Scripps Institution of Oceanography started recording CO_2 in the atmosphere at Mauna Loa, Hawaii at a facility of the National Oceanic and Atmospheric Administration (NOAA). In 1974 NOAA also started to take CO_2 measurements at the site. This is the longest-running direct measurement of CO_2 in our atmosphere [5].

In 1997, the Kyoto Protocol framework was adopted but only entered into force in 2005 because of the political complexities of its adoption. The protocol does not stipulate absolute reductions by countries; rather, it only requires industrialized countries to commit to a transition to low-carbon emissions through country-specific targets, which each country reports on periodically. Developing countries were encouraged to voluntarily comply.

At the time, both China and India were exempted from the treaty. While President Clinton signed the treaty in 1997, it required authorization from Congress to go into effect. It was never sent to Congress as the United States senate in a majority vote made it clear that they would not ratify the US signing of the agreement.[1] In fact, in 2001, then-President Bush stated, 'I oppose the Kyoto Protocol because it exempts 80 percent of the world, including major population centers such as China and India, from compliance, and would cause serious harm to the US economy' [6, 7, 8].

Across the world, there was continued recognition that the Kyoto Protocol was not sufficiently addressing the increasing risks of global climate change in part because of the lack of significant GHG-contributing economies. Hence, in 2015, 196 parties agreed to the newly developed Paris Agreement[2] as part of the annual Conference of Parties (COP 21). Unlike Kyoto, which focused only on certain industrialized economies, the Paris Agreement requires both developed and developing countries to reduce their emissions. The Paris Agreement was also more aggressive and aimed to prevent the average global temperature from rising more than 2°C above preindustrial levels. The Kyoto Protocol was limited to six GHGs, while the Paris Agreement is focused on all anthropogenic GHGs. Finally, the goals of the Paris Agreement were set to be achieved between 2025 and 2030. President Obama signed the Paris Agreement in 2016, only to have President Trump formally withdraw in 2019. However, President Biden rejoined in February 2021 [9, 10, 11].

---

[1] See the Byrd-Hagel Resolution. [2] As of 2022. There were originally 175 parties.

In August of the same year, the IPCC published its sixth assessment report. Around the same time, the US NOAA and National Aeronautics and Space Administration (NASA) data provided some important new and reinforcing findings, including [1, 12, 13]:

1. 2019 and 2020 ranked among the top three warmest years in the history of our planet.
2. Earth's average land and ocean surface temperature in 2021 was 1.51°F (0.84°C) above the twentieth-century average.
3. Ocean heat content, which describes the amount of heat stored in the upper levels of the ocean, was at a record high in 2021, surpassing the previous record high set in 2020.
4. Between 3.3 billion and 3.6 billion people live in countries highly vulnerable to climate impacts.
5. Mortality from droughts, storms, and floods in 2010–2020 was fifteen times greater than in countries with very low vulnerability.
6. Our planet is currently facing a 1.1°C rise from global warming, but if it reaches 1.5°C, communities that depend on glacial and snow melt will face water shortages to which they cannot adapt.
7. The most important finding: human activities are the primary driver of our planet's climate change.

3.2 Climate Change Gases

Climate change is driven by a combination of factors, primarily anthropogenic GHG emissions measured in carbon dioxide equivalents (CO_2-eq). GHG emissions are primarily in the form of carbon dioxide (79 percent of all GHGs in the USA in 2020) and methane (10.9 percent of all GHGs in the USA in 2020) but also include nitrous oxide (7 percent) and fluorinated gases (3 percent) [14]. Each of these have a different intensity, which is why we measure in CO_2-eq.

3.2.1 Methane

Methane (CH_4) is one of the most powerful GHGs and traps heat twenty-eight times more effectively than CO_2 over a 100-year timescale; that is, it is twenty-eight times more potent than CO_2 [14]. The source of methane is not an exact science because of some variability. However, generally methane is produced under conditions where little to no oxygen is available. About 40 percent of

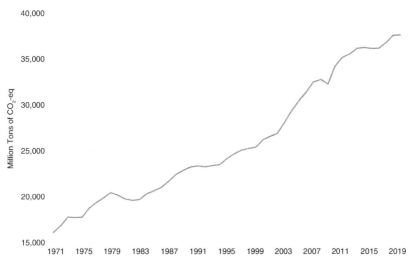

Figure 3.1 Annual CO_2 emissions in million tons CO_2-eq from energy [18].

global methane emissions are from natural sources, such as those produced by wetlands, including ponds, lakes, and rivers. The remaining 60 percent is from anthropogenic (human) activities. This includes agriculture (largest anthropogenic source) such as raising livestock, waste management, and agriculture practices, and of course our legacy energy systems, such as oil, gas, and coal extraction [15]. Methane is also released in our energy systems because of leaks in distribution and transportation such as in natural gas pipelines. In 2020, International Energy Agency estimates placed global annual global methane emissions at around 570 million tons (Mt) [15].

3.2.2 Carbon Dioxide

While methane is more potent, it is CO_2 that accounts for the largest source of GHG emissions, primarily as a result of producing energy through the burning of fossil fuels, such as oil, natural gas, and coal, as well as the use of biomass. It is also as a result of chemical processes such as when cement is manufactured and the chemical conversion process used in the production of clinker, a component of cement, in which limestone ($CaCO_3$) is converted to lime (CaO) [16]. In 2021, global CO_2 emissions from "energy-related" activities were 36.3 billion tons [17] (Figure 3.1).

3.3 Contributions to Greenhouse Gas Emissions

The 2022 report by the IPCC documents that the global energy sector accounted for 59 $GtCO_2$-eq or 34 percent of global GHG emissions. Electricity and heat generation were the largest subsectors contributing to those numbers. As presented in Figure 3.2, industry accounted for 14b$GtCO_2$-eq, while agriculture, forestry, and other land use accounted for 13 $GtCO_2$-eq and 8.7 $GtCO_2$-eq was from transport, with buildings contributing 3.3 $GtCO_2$-eq [19].

Back in 2001, the World Resources Institute and the World Business Council for Sustainable Development published their jointly developed Greenhouse Gas Protocol, which provides the GHG accounting platform for virtually every corporate GHG reporting program around the world [20]. Using this accounting standard, companies then submit their GHG emissions to the Carbon Disclosure Project (CDP), which is a not-for-profit that began by working with the financial sector to persuade companies to report on their emissions. In 2008 only 634 suppliers actually disclosed to CDP. By 2021 over 210 major buyers with a combined purchasing power of $5.5 trillion and almost 600

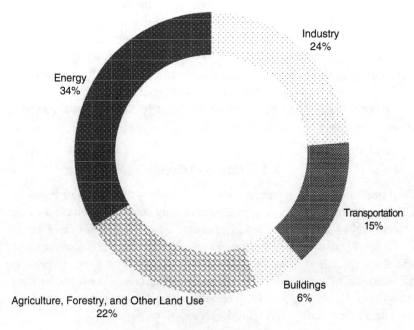

Figure 3.2 Sources of CO_2 by sector globally in 2014 [19].

investors with assets over $110 trillion were working with CDP, requesting annual carbon emissions from over 27,000 suppliers. Firms submit to CDP by late July of each year and their reports are scored by the end of September the same year [21].

When firms as well as cities undertake their carbon accounting, they do so by acquiring data from operations under their direct control, as well as data that are indirectly controlled by their operations. These are grouped into three different scopes.

Scope 1 emissions are direct GHG emissions. This includes emissions if the facility combusts their own fuels in a stationary source such as a boiler or furnace. It also includes combustion of fuels in company-owned/-controlled mobile sources like trucks, trains, ships, and cars. It also includes fugitive emissions from, say, leaks in refrigeration equipment. This information can be obtained from fuel purchase receipts and pre-established emission factors, which are readily available from government and non-governmental organization sources [22].

Scope 2 emissions are most associated with electricity purchased. While the company has direct control of the amount of electricity purchased, it does not directly control the fuels used to generate the electricity, such as coal, natural gas, and renewables. However, companies can invest in on-site renewable electricity generation and/or purchase renewable energy credits to lower their GHG emissions. Again, information can be easily obtained from purchasing records of electricity purchases. Either the utility or the regional/national government will have the emission factors for electricity for a specific region based on the average fuels used to generate the electricity [22].

Scope 3 emissions are a big and broad category of indirect emissions. Scope 3 has historically been an optional reporting scheme. However, as is further detailed in this book about the global efforts to achieve net-zero carbon, scope 3 emissions do not just play an important role but in fact play a critical role if organizations are to achieve net-zero carbon emissions [22]. Tackling scope 3 emissions is a very difficult process as it requires firms to obtain GHG emissions data from all of their suppliers, or at least those who account for the greatest impact. Examples of scope 3 are as follows.

Upstream. Capital goods purchased, transportation and distribution, waste generation, business travel, employees commuting to work, and purchased goods ranging from office supplies to large commodities needed in manufacturing, as well as any leased assets of the company. Consider a company like Walmart or Amazon. Consider how many suppliers they have, which run into the hundreds of thousands. Now consider trying to acquire GHG emission data of the goods they purchase as well as the logistics upstream to bring those products from overseas factories to domestic distribution centers or stores. And each of those suppliers, which are all name brands like Levis, Nike, Procter and Gamble, and Unilever, all have thousands of their own suppliers.

Downstream. Now consider the product after it arrives at the store. It may require shipment if purchased online, so it will have to travel to another distribution center by rail, air, or truck and eventually to your home. How do you use the product? Is it a computer that uses energy and for how long? How do you dispose of the computer? Is it recycled or landfilled? All of these datapoints are part of scope 3 emissions. All are necessary to understand if we are to identify hotspots and develop alternatives and strategies to mitigate the climate impacts.

So now we come back to Figure 3.2. If we take the IPCC emissions by major sector and break them down by direct and indirect emissions of subsectors globally for 2019, we can see what parts of the economy are contributing and how much of the total, as depicted in Figure 3.3.

Switching from a global perspective to one specific to the United States, as presented in Figure 3.4, we see the role that transportation plays and why the transition to electric vehicles plays such an important role in the movement to a net-zero-carbon economy.

Each of these sectors identified in both the global and US context are heavily coupled with the energy sector, which makes decoupling and the transition to sustainable energy sources an imperative. The IPCC [19] reports that if we are to avoid a 2°C increase compared to 2019 levels, global emissions must peak before 2025, then fall by 43 percent by 2030. Given our current levels, global consumption of coal must decrease by 95 percent, oil by 60 percent, and natural gas by 45 percent, all by 2050 as compared to

OTHER ENERGY 12%	TRANSPORT 15%	BUILDINGS 16%	AGRICULTURE, FORESTRY, & LAND USE 22%	INDUSTRY 34%
Petroleum refining–1.1%	Inland shipping–0.3%	Residential–11%	Land-use/Land-use change forestry–11%	Cement process–2.6%
Coal mining fugitive emissions–2.2%	Domestic aviation–0.4%	Non-residential–5.9%	Enteric fermentation–5%	Waste–3.9%
Oil and gas fugitive emissions–4.4%	Other–0.9%	Other–0.1%	Managed soils and pasture–2.5%	Chemicals–6.3%
Other (energy systems)–4.7%	International aviation–1.1%		Rice cultivation–1.7%	Metals–7.8%
	Road–10%		Synthetic fertilizer application–0.75%	Other industry–13%
			Manure mgt–0.70%	
			Biomasss burning–0.1%	

Figure 3.3 Total anthropogenic direct and indirect greenhouse gas emissions for 2019 based on 59 $GtCO_2$-eq. Adapted from IPCC [19].

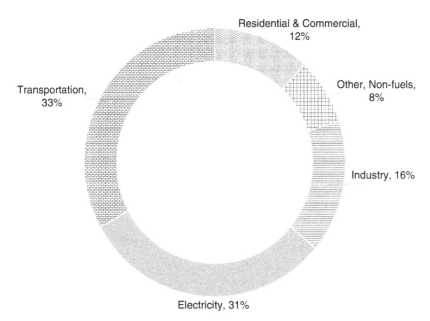

Figure 3.4 Sources of CO_2 by sector in the United States in 2020 [14].

2019, in order to meet the goals established in the Paris Agreement [10]. This clearly speaks to the pressures that are accelerating the pace of the transition to a net-zero-carbon economy.

3.4 Who and What Is Responsible

The issue of responsibility is complex. In Chapter 2 we explored the way in which society's increasing consumptive patterns are driving a similar response and demand to increase manufacturing, which is reliant on extraction of natural resources and consumption of energy. Additionally, climate change is an issue that is compounded over time as the build-up of GHGs accumulates in our atmosphere and the natural carbon sinks are impaired.

When you examine Figures 3.1 to 3.4, what should quickly get your attention is how the rise of economic growth and industrialization are major drivers of GHG emissions. As the United States and European Union (EU-27) member economies grew in the later part of the twentieth century, so too did their CO_2 emissions. As we have entered the twenty-first century, expanding economies in India and most notably China are on the rise to the extent that China, with the

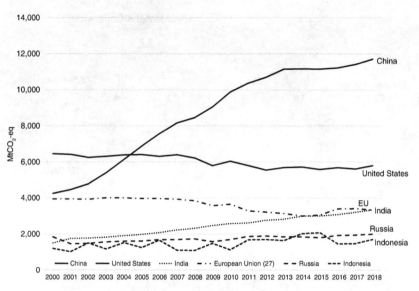

Figure 3.5 World's top emitters of greenhouse gas, 2000–2018 [23].

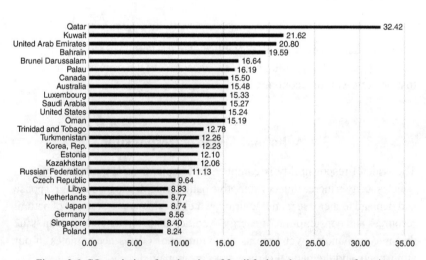

Figure 3.6 CO_2 emissions from burning of fossil fuels and cement manufacturing in metric tons per capita in 2018 by the World Bank [24].

world's second largest economy, is the world's largest polluter of CO_2. In fact, as presented in Figure 3.5, of the five largest emitters of GHG, China's emissions continue to rise while the USA and EU are declining.

Another way to think through who contributes to climate change is to explore emissions based on population. We already know that India will soon be the most populous country, surpassing China. And there is variability in each country based on their gross domestic product, economic and industrial base, and other related factors. However, in Figure 3.6 we see that oil- and gas-producing countries have a very high per-capita basis.

References

1. Intergovernmental Panel on Climate Change (2022). *Summary for Policymakers.* Cambridge: Cambridge University Press.
2. *The Conversation* (2020). John Tyndall: The Forgotten Co-founder of Climate Science. https://theconversation.com/john-tyndall-the-forgotten-co-founder-of-climate-science-143499.
3. E. Foote (1856). Circumstances Affecting the Heat of the Sun's Rays. *The American Journal of Science and Arts*, 22: 382–383.
4. R. Jackson (2019). Eunice Foote, John Tyndall and a Question of Priority. The Royal Society. *Notes and Records*, 74: 105–118. http://doi.org/10.1098/rsnr.2018.0066.
5. National Oceanic and Atmospheric Administration (2022). Global Monitoring Laboratory. Earth System Research Laboratories. https://gml.noaa.gov/ccgg/trends.
6. United Nations (2022). What Is the Kyoto Protocol? https://unfccc.int/kyoto_protocol.
7. CNN (2022). Kyoto Protocol Fast Facts. Updated April 7, 2022. www.cnn.com/2013/07/26/world/kyoto-protocol-fast-facts/index.html#:~:text=The%20United%20States%20has%20not,were%20exempted%20from%20the%20treaty.
8. J. Hovi, D. F. Sprinz, and G. Bang (2012). Why the United States Did Not Become a Party to the Kyoto Protocol: German, Norwegian, and US Perspectives. *European Journal of International Relations*, 18(1): 129–150. doi: 10.1177/1354066110380964.
9. Natural Resources Defense Council (2021). Paris Climate Agreement: Everything You Need to Know. www.nrdc.org/stories/paris-climate-agreement-everything-you-need-know#sec-whatis.
10. Obama Foundation (2022). The Best Possible Shot to Save the One Planet We've Got. www.obama.org/paris-climate-agreement.
11. National Public Radio (2021). U.S. Officially Rejoins Paris Agreement on Climate Change. www.npr.org/2021/02/19/969387323/u-s-officially-rejoins-paris-agreement-on-climate-change.
12. National Oceanic and Atmospheric Administration (2022). NOAA National Centers for Environmental Information, State of the Climate: Global Climate Report for Annual 2021. www.ncdc.noaa.gov/sotc/global/202113.
13. National Aeronautics and Space Administration (2022). Global Climate Change: Vital Signs of the Planet. Evidence. https://climate.nasa.gov/evidence.

14.   United States Environmental Protection Agency (2022). Overview of Greenhouse Gas Emissions. www.epa.gov/ghgemissions/overview-greenhouse-gases.

15.   International Energy Agency (2020). Methane Tracker 2020, Paris. www.iea.org/reports/methane-tracker-2020.

16.   M. Gibbs, P. Soyka, and D. Conneely (2000). CO_2 Emissions from Cement Production. Background Papers: IPCC Expert Meetings on Good Practice Guidance and Uncertainty Management in National Greenhous Gas Inventories. www.ipcc-nggip.iges.or.jp/public/gp/bgp/3_1_Cement_Production.pdf.

17.   International Energy Agency (2022). Global Energy Review: CO_2 Emissions in 2021, Paris. www.iea.org/reports/global-energy-review-co2-emissions-in–2021–2.

18.   International Energy Agency (2021). GHG Emissions from Energy. https://iea.blob.core.windows.net/assets/d755e4d6-9572-4549-9421-7d2bc377cd2f/WORLD_GHG_Documentation.pdf.

19.   Intergovernmental Panel on Climate Change (2021). Sixth Assessment Report. Working Group III. Chapter 2: Emissions Trends and Drivers. https://report.ipcc.ch/ar6wg3/pdf/IPCC_AR6_WGIII_FinalDraft_Chapter02.pdf.

20.   S. Russell (n.d.). Looking Back on 15 Years of Greenhouse Gas Accounting. Greenhouse Gas Protocol. https://ghgprotocol.org/blog/looking-back-15-years-greenhouse-gas-accounting.

21.   Carbon Disclosure Project (2022). CDP Leadership Presentation and Interview at Syracuse University, April 20.

22.   World Business Council for Sustainable Development and World Resources Institute (2004). The Greenhouse Gas Protocol. A Corporate Accounting and Reporting Standard, revised ed. https://ghgprotocol.org/sites/default/files/standards/ghg-protocol-revised.pdf.

23.   Climate Watch (2022). Data Explorer. www.climatewatchdata.org/data-explorer/historical-emissions?historical-emissions-data-sources=cait&historical-emissions-gases=all-ghg&historical-emissions-regions=All%20Selected&historical-emissions-sectors=total-including-lucf%2Ctotal-including-lucf&page=1.

24.   World Bank (2022). CO_2 Emissions (Metric Tons Per Capita). https://data.worldbank.org/indicator/EN.ATM.CO2E.PC.

25.   United Nations (2022). Secretary-General Warns of Climate Emergency, Calling Intergovernmental Panel's Report "a File of Shame," While Saying Leaders "Are Lying," Fuelling Flames. April 4. https://press.un.org/en/2022/sgsm21228.doc.htm.

PART II

Net-Zero-Carbon Transitions

Now that we have a better understanding of the drivers that are occurring on our planet and throughout our society, it is time to explore the net-zero-carbon transitions. This will span how corporations are reacting to new technologies such as electric vehicles, energy transitions, and biobased transitions.

4

Corporate Net-Zero-Carbon Transitions

Today, we announced a comprehensive plan to accelerate action related to climate change. P&G has also set a new ambition to achieve net zero greenhouse gas (GHG) emissions across its operations and supply chain, from raw material to retailer, by 2040 as well as interim 2030 goals to make meaningful progress this decade.

Procter and Gamble, September 14, 2021 [1]

The net-zero-carbon economy[1] has become a phrase that has taken over today's business vernacular. It has taken on a life of its own. The rate at which governments and especially businesses around the world are committing to it in some form outpaces the systems and knowledge currently in place to achieve it on a mass scale. While many of us can intuitively work out what net-zero carbon means in the abstract, the real-world implications for agricultural systems, global supply chains, financial and insurance markets, and manufacturing systems are not well understood and quantified. Yet, both companies and governments alike are making these commitments in rapid succession in large measure due to necessity as businesses have lacked the urgency to address climate change, and as a response to shareholders and the investment community who are pulling companies toward climate neutrality.

The transition to the net-zero-carbon economy can be traced back to Allen and Frame in 2005. Allen, a professor of geosystem science at Oxford, and his colleague Professor David Frame, who directs the New Zealand Climate Research Institute at Victoria University, gave a presentation at the 2005 United Nations Framework Convention on Climate Change in Montreal, Canada, where they stated "that the 1992 convention's goal of stabilizing atmospheric concentrations of greenhouse gases – which for carbon dioxide

---

[1] Net-zero refers to balancing the quantity of emissions put into the atmosphere with the quantity taken out.

meant 50%–80% reductions in global emissions by 2100 – was unlikely to be enough to stop global warming. Warming was primarily determined by cumulative carbon dioxide emissions, so to halt warming we would need to reduce annual CO_2 emissions to net zero" [2, 3].

Ten years later in 2015, at the Council of Parties (COP 21) held in Paris, the net-zero-carbon transition was initialized into Article 4.1 of the Paris Agreement, which states that the world should aim "to achieve a balance between anthropogenic emissions by sources and removals by sinks of greenhouse gases in the second half of this century" [4].

4.1 Recent Drivers for a Net-Zero-Carbon Transition

According to McKinsey [5], up to $5 trillion annually will be invested in sustainability by 2025 – "the largest capital reallocation in history." Investors and shareholders are becoming increasingly sophisticated in regard to climate risks and opportunities to deploy technologies and services to reduce these risks. This has recently manifested itself in the form a major regulatory proposal by the US Securities and Exchange Commission (SEC)[2] to add a new subpart to Regulation S-K, 17 CFR 229.1500–1507 ("Subpart 1500 of Regulation S-K"), that would require public companies to provide detailed reporting of their:

1. Climate-related risks
2. Greenhouse gas (GHG) emissions
3. Net-zero transition plans.

The proposed rule [6] follows similar disclosure requirements in the European Union, Hong Kong, Japan, the UK, and so on. These follow voluntary guidelines that were issued in 2021 by the Task Force on Climate-Related Financial Disclosures[3] chaired by Michael Bloomberg and which over 2,600 companies in 89 countries around the world have already endorsed.

In addition to the company risking significant civil penalties for false or misleading statements in the SEC filing, and potentially criminal actions if the case is referred to law enforcement, a company's certifying officers can be held personally liable for any untrue statement of material fact or material omission necessary to ensure that statements contained in the reports or other statements to the SEC are not misleading [7].

---

[2] March 21, 2022. [3] www.fsb-tcfd.org.

The rule would require large companies to disclose information by filing year 2024, while smaller firms would have an extra year. The disclosures must cover both scope 1 and scope 2 emissions, as detailed later in this chapter. The SEC would allow an additional year for companies to add the more difficult scope 3 (supply chain and value chain) emissions.

While the SEC would require quantification and disclosure by public companies, what about private firms or suppliers based in other countries not regulated by the SEC? Simply put, there will be considerable pressure on them to provide detailed data to public firms, especially manufacturers, brands, and retailers.

4.2 What Does It Mean to Be Net-Zero?

The first thing you need to know is that net-zero does not mean the elimination of all carbon emissions. Rather, net-zero provides organizations more flexibility and fewer constraints in making clear progress to meet the scientific needs as laid out in the Paris Agreement and subsequent research findings that have come to light on climate change. Think of net-zero as an old-fashioned scale with two pans – one on each side – and a measurement device in the middle. On the pan to the left, you would place all of the GHG emissions from your organization (scopes 1, 2, and 3). They would weigh down the pan when all piled up on top of each other. On the right pan, you would place all the efforts you have implemented to lighten the load of the left pan.

This could include eliminating portions of your scope 1, 2, and 3 emissions, such as reducing transportation emissions, switching to lower-carbon biobased feedstocks, and making your buildings more energy efficient. However, the pan on the left (the scale with your total emissions) is still lower and heavier than the pan on the right. So, you decide to purchase carbon credits in some form (planting trees, investing in renewable energy projects to offset that difference). Once you add those credits to the pan on the right, the scale is balanced. That is a simple way to understand net-zero carbon (Figure 4.1).

4.3 Science-Based Targets

Rather than take an ad hoc or best guess strategy for implementing carbon reductions, organizations are now applying science-based targets. The Science-Based Targets Initiative (SBTi) was founded in 2015 as a partnership between the Carbon Disclosure Project, the United Nations Global Compact, the World

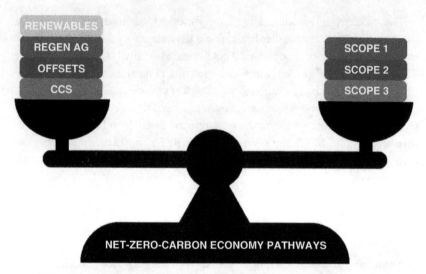

Figure 4.1 Balancing greenhouse gas emissions with various net-zero-carbon pathways.

Resources Institute, and the World Wide Fund for Nature. Their focus is on the private sector. Emissions reductions targets adopted by companies to reduce GHG emissions are considered "science-based" if they are in line with the level of decarbonization required to keep the global temperature increase below 1.5°C compared to preindustrial temperatures, as described by the Intergovernmental Panel on Climate Change (IPCC) [8].

Science-based targets provide companies a roadmap on how much and how quickly they will need to reduce their GHG emissions and are assessed and validated by third parties. Since 2019, more than 600 companies from across the world have committed to making changes in line with the SBTi's goal, which represents $13 trillion in market capitalization [9].

4.4 Scopes 1, 2, and 3 GHG Emissions

The first step an organization must undertake in order to reduce their carbon footprint is to quantify their current GHG emissions, or more realistically their recent past of GHG emissions. This is primarily because an organization will need to acquire past invoices and reports. An easy example to understand is that we typically receive our utility bill for the electricity, energy, and water we consumed the prior month. Carbon accounting is just that: accounting. So, one will need to obtain the data in units that can be used to calculate the various GHG emissions as presented in Chapter 3. The accounting for GHG emissions is structured into three different scopes, as presented in Figure 4.2.

4.4.1 Scope 1 Emissions

The Greenhouse Protocol provides various guidelines on the differences in GHG scopes, which are primarily used in my descriptions here [10].

Scope 1 emissions are "direct" emissions, meaning they are in direct control of the organization. Emissions in scope are some of the most straightforward to address as they refer to the direct emissions controlled directly by a business. These emissions are most frequently associated with the energy consumed to heat buildings and boilers and that used as fuel for company-owned vehicles. Scope 1 emissions are broken down into four areas that include the following.

1. **Stationary combustion**. This includes such things as boilers for heating buildings, gas furnaces, and gas-fired combined heat and power (CHP) plants. More of the common fuels used in stationary combustion include natural gas, liquified petroleum gas (LPG), diesel, and kerosene.

   Reduction Strategies
   The most prevalent approach to reducing stationary combustion scope 1 emissions is to reduce the demand for the use of stationary combustion. Second, an organization should stop or significantly reduce the use of fossil fuels and transition to renewable electricity and/or renewable energy sources, as well as alternative technologies such as geothermal energy heat pumps, air-source heat pumps, and solar water heating systems as examples.

2. **Mobile combustion**. Generally, this represents fuels combusted for the vehicles (cars, vans, trucks) owned or leased by an organization. This will include gasoline, diesel, and cleaner burning alternatives such as LPG, liquefied natural gas (LNG) and biofuels, bio-diesel, and bio-ethanol. As discussed later in this book, we are witnessing the rapid transition from internal combustion fossil fuels to electric vehicles (EVs) and plug-in hybrids (PHEVs). This will result in the increased use of EVs. This will result in an organization's GHG emissions captured in scope 1 to switch to scope 2 emissions, described later.

   Reduction Strategies
   In many ways, both the government's and the automotive manufacturing sector's rapid transition to EVs (with electricity being provided by renewable energy sources) in itself will lead to significant reductions in scope 1 GHG emissions from mobile sources.

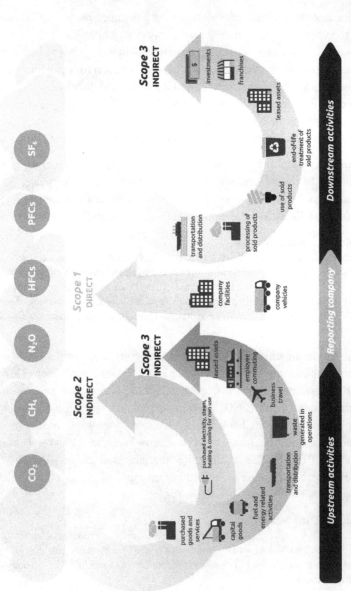

Figure 4.2 Scopes of greenhouse gas emissions. Image courtesy of World Resources Institute through their Creative Commons license [10].

3. **Fugitive emissions**. Fugitive emissions are in fact emissions that "escape," similar to a fugitive of the law. These include leaks of GHGs from refrigeration and air-conditioning units. Refrigerant gases are generally extremely potent GHGs, some of which are thousands of times more damaging than carbon dioxide (CO_2).

Reduction Strategies
For most businesses, this will require the leadership of facilities and maintenance personnel as well as the chief financial officer. In many cases, the elimination and replacement of outdated equipment should be undertaken as well as the deployment of monitoring equipment such as at valve locations.

4. **Process emissions**. Releases into the atmosphere during industrial processes; for example, CO_2 produced as part of cement manufacturing is a process emission.

Reduction Strategies
Organizations, especially manufacturing companies, continually strive to reduce the costs of operations. Process engineers need to incorporate reductions in wastes, energy use, and water use, such as lean manufacturing (aka Manufacturing 4.0).

4.4.2 Scope 2 Emissions

Scope 2 emissions are "indirect" emissions from the organization but not under the direct control of the company such as the type of energy source used by the local utility to provide electricity. There are four main forms of energy tracked under scope 2 emissions, which are as follows:

1. **Electricity.** This is generally the largest contributor to scope 2 emissions but not for overall GHG emissions by an organization (see scope 3). This area encompasses the electricity your organization purchases, including at multiple company-owned or -leased facilities. The significant impact is electricity generated as thermoelectric power plants that use and burn fossil fuels such as coal or natural gas. Electricity travels through distribution lines and can come from multiple power plants given electricity demand at the time needed.
Consider a power plant that uses solar in part of its electricity mix but, due to clouds and the lack of back-up battery storage, the utility has a gap between electricity demand versus electricity power generation. Hence, the utility will dispatch from multiple power plants such as natural gas power plants, which can quickly be turned on and off versus coal. So, in essence, an organization does not know the exact energy mix of renewables versus

different types of fossil fuels. Therefore, utilities generally provide an average electricity fuel mix that can be used to calculate GHG emissions based on the consumption of electricity in kWh or MWh.

2. **Steam**. Producing steam requires the heating of water and thus requires an energy source to produce the heat via a boiler or thermal power plant. Many times the steam is produced outside of the company's control, which makes this a scope 2 indirect GHG emission.

3. **Heat**. For heat to be considered a scope 2 GHG emission rather than scope 1, the heat is generally delivered by a local district heat network rather than produced on-site.

4. **Cooling**. For example, chilled water provided by a third party will fall into a scope 2 emission.

Scope 2 Reduction Strategies

The "nega-watt" should be the first strategy deployed. The nega-watt is a euphemism that describes the strategy to eliminate electricity usage at every possible turn. The utility industry uses the term DSM (demand-side management), meaning to develop strategies to reduce demand of electricity, thus providing reductions in operating costs as well as GHG emissions. In addition, organizations can install renewables on-site to reduce non-renewable purchases of electricity.

An organization can also enter into a corporate power purchase agreement, which is a long-term contract between the owner of a renewable energy plant and the company that will consume the renewable electricity. As part of this agreement, the electricity can be delivered physically via a public electricity grid. Another related option is a power purchase agreement (PPA) where a developer finances a large-scale (usually) renewable installation on the customer's property and the customer agrees to a long-term contract to purchase the electricity – which is usually at a lower rate than the utility would charge for the electricity. However, as of August 2021, only fifteen states in the USA having enacted legislation to authorize and regulate PPAs [11].

4.4.3 Scope 3 Emissions and the Supply Chain

Scope 3 emissions are "indirect" emissions but those that the organization impacts through its value chain. Scope 3 emissions include all sources not within an organization's scope 1 and 2 boundary. It should be understood from an accounting standpoint that scope 3 emissions for one organization are the scope 1 and 2 emissions of another organization. This double accounting is intentionally designed into the GHG Protocols. Scope 3 emissions are also referred to as value chain emissions, which include both the supply chain (upstream) and the customers/consumers of the organization (downstream).

Scope 3 emissions are very important, if not critical, for efforts to reduce GHG emissions. A Carbon Trust report indicated that for most companies, Scope 3 emissions represent from 65 percent to 95 percent of a company's broader carbon impact [12, 13]. In fact, eight supply chains account for more than 50 percent of global emissions. Those sectors are (1) food; (2) construction; (3) fashion; (4) fast-moving consumer goods; (5) electronics; (6) automotive; (7) professional services; and (8) freight [14].

There are fifteen categories of scope 3 business emissions pursuant to the GHG Protocols. The eight upstream are as follows [15].

Upstream

1. **Business travel:** Travel by air, rail, subway, light rail, taxis, buses, and private vehicle usage for business.
2. **Employee commuting**: This includes emissions released from employees commuting to and from work. Such emissions can be reduced by encouraging public transportation, cycle-to-work schemes, and introducing remote work.
3. **Waste generation**: This includes solid[4] non-hazardous, hazardous, and medical waste disposal in landfills, waste treatment facilities, incinerators, and so on.
4. **Purchased goods and services**: These include all the upstream emissions (cradle to grave) from the production of goods and services. There are clear guidance distinctions between products and goods that are production-related (e.g., materials, equipment, and components) and products and goods that are non-production-related (e.g., furniture and information technology systems).
5. **Transportation and distribution**: This includes supplier and customer transportation by land, sea, and air. This category also includes third-party warehousing.
6. **Fuel and energy-related activities**: Energy related to the production of fuel and the energy purchased and consumed by the reporting organization that is not already accounted for in scopes 1 and 2.
7. **Capital goods**: Purchased goods that are used to manufacture a product, provide a service, or that are used for storing, selling, and delivering merchandise need to have their emissions accounted for. This means accounting for emissions from cradle to grave of purchased goods in the year of acquisition.

---

[4] In the United States under US Code of Federal Regulations, Title 40: Protection of Environment, solid wastes include liquids.

8. **Upstream leased assets:** This includes emissions from the operation of assets that are leased by the reporting company, in the reporting year, and not already included in the reporting company's scope 1 or 2 inventories. These are leased assets involved in upstream activities.

Downstream

9. **Investments**: According to GHG accounting, investments will fall under five categories: equity investments, debt investments, project finance, managed investment, and client services. This category is mainly relevant to larger financial institutions.
10. **Downstream distribution and transportation:** This category includes emissions that occur in the reporting year from the transportation and the distribution of sold products in vehicles and facilities not owned or controlled by the reporting company.
11. **Processing of sold products**: This includes emissions from the processing of sold intermediate products by third parties. Intermediate products are those that require further processing, transformation, and inclusion in another product before use.
12. **Franchises**: Companies that operate under a franchise (paying a fee to the franchisor) should consider reporting emissions associated with the franchisor's operations (i.e., scope 1 and 2 emissions of the franchisor).

> There are considerations and variables such as: How much control does the franchisor have of the individual franchises? Does the franchise own the building? For a fast-food franchise, maybe they own the building or perhaps they lease the building. They may even only be leasing a small space such as at an airport or sports stadium where they have no control over the lighting, air conditioning, heating, and so on.

13. **Downstream leased assets:** This takes into account the emissions from the operation of assets that are leased by the reporting company in the reporting year and not already included in the reporting company's scope 1 or 2 inventories. These are leased assets involved in upstream activities.
14. **Use of sold products:** This refers to the products that are sold to the consumer and measures emissions that result from product usage. These emissions may vary considerably. Consider the issues of a fairly basic product – laundry detergent. The "use phase," which is when the customer uses the product, has so many variables.

   • How far a distance does the consumer have to travel to purchase the product?

- Does the consumer use hot or cold water or a variation?
- Does the consumer wash a full load and how large? (That is, the volume of clothes would that be based on the size of the washing machine.)

These are just some of the variables let alone issues driven by the manufacturer such as concentration, chemicals use, type of packaging, and can the packaging be recycled, etc.

15. **End-of-life retirement:** This is reported similarly as waste generated from operations. To report emissions from end-of-life retirement, companies must assess how products are disposed of. You can see how such reporting can be difficult as the disposal of a product is usually dependent on the consumer. Yet, this category will encourage firms to design recyclable products to limit landfill disposal.

4.5 Carbon Credits and Carbon Offsets

As companies seek to eliminate their GHG emissions and meet their net-zero-carbon commitments, they will need to find transitional pathways because the deployment of new technologies and organizational strategies, including locating low-carbon suppliers and renewable electricity and energy sources, will take time. Therefore, organizations will need to offset some of their GHG emissions for the near and mid-term future (see Figure 4.1).

What are carbon offsets? They are tradable rights and/or certificates linked to activities that lower the amount of CO_2 in the atmosphere by lowering CO_2 emissions, or sequestering CO_2, by taking CO_2 out of the atmosphere and storing it in such a way that eliminates leakage [15]. Current ways to do this in the marketplace include the development of new renewable energy projects, agricultural practices that increase the carbon that can be stored in soils, reforestation, and so on.

Carbon removal is easier to calculate than carbon avoidance. Carbon removal has carbon physically taken out of the atmosphere and sequestered using either a nature-based project such as forestry or agriculture or an engineered solution such as injecting CO_2 deep into rock or soil. Carbon avoidance offsets are focused on future emissions and are activities that reduce future emissions by preventing carbon releases into the atmosphere. This could include renewable energy projects or stopping the conversion of grasslands to croplands and limiting timber harvest levels, as well as projects that reduce emissions from deforestation and forest degradation (REDD projects) in developing countries.

Carbon offsets are measured as credits and must be verifiable emission reductions from certified climate action projects and adhere to a rigorous set of criteria to pass verification by third-party organizations and a review by a panel of experts such as Verra or Gold Standard [16].

4.5.1 Carbon Markets

A recent Bloomberg research study [17] indicates that an oversupplied voluntary market would produce prolonged growth in prices. On the opposite end of the spectrum, a carbon-removals-only scenario could cause a pricing surge of as much as 3,000 percent by 2029.

As Bloomberg notes, the market for carbon offsets is highly dependent on worldwide regulatory efforts to hold countries accountable for their climate impacts where an oversupplied voluntary market would produce prolonged growth in prices, as opposed to a carbon-removals-only scenario. "The price of offsets could rise significantly, creating a $190 billion market as early as 2030" [17]. As of January 2022, the Global Emissions Offset CBL futures[5] on the New York Mercantile Exchange traded at $7.53 a ton with contracts expiring in July 2025 at $8.89.

How might this change? Bloomberg estimates that for voluntary markets, offsets will be unsustainably cheap as supply grows. If left unregulated, supply will flourish and prices will grow slowly over time to $47 a ton in 2050. "While low prices may be desirable for offsets buyers, other investors such as developers, banks and brokers will find little incentive to support the market" [17]. A carbon-removal scenario has the strongest future outlook as companies would only be allowed to purchase credits from the removal of CO_2 to meet their net-zero-carbon commitments, which would result in a projected increase of 2,975 percent, to $224 a ton, in 2029 before tapering off to settle at $120 in 2050. Either way, carbon pricing will soon cover a fifth of the world's emissions [18].

Companies have multiple pathways to acquire carbon credits.

- Purchase at the source by investing in the project on their own.
- Invest with a project development firm such as Carbonfund.org or TerraPass.[6]

[5] CBL is a global exchange platform for transacting energy and environmental commodity products, such as carbon, renewable energy, water, and natural gas. They connect buyers and sellers to trade multiple environmental products on one screen. See https://xpansiv.com/cbl.
[6] The author is not endorsing or promoting any specific developer-organizations and individuals should conduct their own due diligence.

- Buy Emission Reduction Purchase Agreements, which are upfront payment for carbon credits to be delivered when they are generated.
- Purchase the carbon offsets through a broker. Firms should choose their broker carefully and ensure a clear understanding on the fees or mark-up fees by the broker.
- Buy carbon credits in a market exchange.

4.6 Net-Zero-Carbon Commitments: A Lack of Transparency

A *Financial Times* article [19] penned by the co-lead of Net-Zero Tracker[7] in 2022 shared that 91 percent of country targets, 79 percent of city targets, 78 percent of regional targets, and 48 percent of listed company targets failed to specify if offsets will be used in their net-zero plans.

Similarly, of the companies with a public net-zero target that will incorporate some form of carbon offsets, 66 percent have failed to specify conditions on the use of offset credits and failed to provide sufficient information so that shareholders, non-governmental organizations, or the general public can evaluate the validity of the offset. Interestingly, according to Net-Zero Tracker, 10 percent of companies have committed to avoid offsetting altogether.

4.6.1 Decarbonization in Practice

4.6.1.1 Consumer Products Manufacturing

Dating back to 1860, London-based Unilever is one of the world's largest companies, ranking 175 in the global Fortune 500 and producing over 400 of some of the best-known brands including Dove, Ben & Jerry's, Seventh Generation, and Knorr [20].

In 2021, Unilever's chairman Nils Andersen and its chief executive officer Alan Jope jointly issued the company's Climate Transition Action Plan to their shareholders [21]. In the document the company places their annual value chain GHG emissions (scopes 1, 2, and 3, excluding indirect use-phase emissions) at approximately 32 million tons of CO_2eq. The company declares that emissions from their own manufacturing facilities, offices and labs, data centers, warehouses, and distribution centers make up only 2 percent of their total GHG

---

[7] https://zerotracker.net/about.

footprint. The remaining emissions are derived from their scope 3 indirect emissions. The breakdown is shown in Figure 4.3.

However, because Unilever does not calculate indirect use-phase emissions, the distribution of Unilever GHG emissions may in fact be closer to that represented in Figure 4.4. Why is this? One has to take into account the product portfolio that Unilever produces.

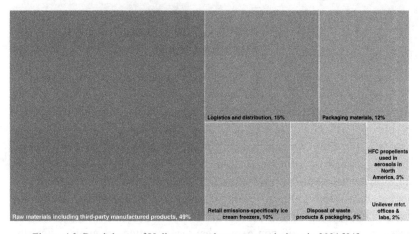

Figure 4.3 Breakdown of Unilever greenhouse gas emissions in 2021 [21].

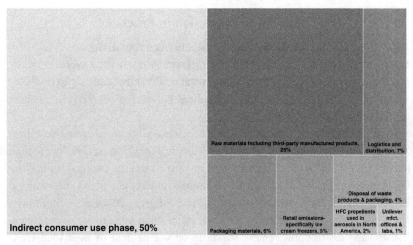

Figure 4.4 Possible role of indirect consumer use phase in Unilever greenhouse gas emissions in 2021 [21].

It contains laundry detergents and soaps, which often require heated water. The food product portfolio is used in different ways by consumers who use energy to heat and cook food products or electricity to refrigerate prior to and after initial use. Thus, the company would have to make very unreliable assumptions on how consumers use and dispose of their products. Further, the regions where consumers are located vary greatly, which means the energy sources – that is, renewable energy mixes – vary widely. Hence, most consumer product manufactures and brands focus on reducing the upstream indirect GHG emissions as well as formulating their products to reduce carbon burdens, such as cold-water detergents and/or packaging that can be reused in the circular economy.

References

1. Procter and Gamble (2021). P&G Accelerates Action on Climate Change toward New Zero GHG Emissions by 2040. September 14. https://us.pg.com/blogs/net-zero-by-2040.
2. M. Allen, D. Frame, C. Huntingford et al. (2009). Warming caused by cumulative carbon emissions towards the trillionth tonne. *Nature*, 458: 1163–1166. https://doi.org/10.1038/nature08019.
3. M. Allen (2021). The World Has Made More Progress on Climate Change Than You Might Think – Or Might Have Predicted a Decade Ago. *The Conversation*. November 15. https://theconversation.com/the-world-has-made-more-progress-on-climate-change-than-you-might-think-or-might-have-predicted-a-decade-ago–171787.
4. United Nations Framework Convention on Climate Change (2015). The Paris Agreement. https://unfccc.int/files/meetings/paris_nov_2015/application/pdf/par is_agreement_english.pdf.
5. McKinsey and Company (2022). Understanding the SEC's Proposed Climate Risk Disclosure Rule. June 3. www.mckinsey.com/business-functions/strategy-and-corporate-finance/our-insights/understanding-the-secs-proposed-climate-risk-disclosure-rule.
6. US Securities and Exchange Commission (2022). The Enhancement and Standardization of Climate-Related Disclosures for Investors. www.sec.gov/rules/proposed/2022/33-11042.pdf.
7. US Securities and Exchange Commission (n.d.). Existing Regulatory Protections Unchanged by either H.R. 3606 or S.1993. www.sec.gov/info/smallbus/acsec/ongoinginvestorprotections.pdf.
8. Science Based Targets (2016). Definition of Science Based Targets and Eligibility Criteria. https://sciencebasedtargets.org/resources/legacy/2017/01/EligibilityCriteria.docx.pdf.
9. United Nations (2022). Climate Action. www.un.org/en/climate-action/science-based-emissions-targets-heighten-corporate-ambition.

10. World Resources Institute (2022). Greenhouse Gas Protocol: Corporate Value Chain (Scope 3) Accounting and Reporting Standards: Supplement to the GHG Protocol Corporate Accounting and Reporting Standard. https://ghgprotocol.org/sites/default/files/standards/Corporate-Value-Chain-Accounting-Reporing-Standard_041613_2.pdf.
11. Energy Link (2021). Which States Allow Power Purchase Agreements (PPAs)? www.ysgsolar.com/blog/power-purchase-agreements-state-state-ysg-solar.
12. CNBC (2021). Climate Experts Are Worried about the Toughest Carbon Emissions for Companies to Capture. August 18. https://tinyurl.com/3z69h9nj.
13. Deloitte (2022). Scope 1, 2 and 3 Emissions: What You Need to Know. www2.deloitte.com/uk/en/focus/climate-change/zero-in-on-scope-1-2-and-3-emissions.html.
14. World Economic Forum (2021). Net-Zero Challenge: The Supply Chain Opportunity. Insight Report in collaboration with the Boston Consulting Group. January. www3.weforum.org/docs/WEF_Net_Zero_Challenge_The_Supply_Chain_Opportunity_2021.pdf.
15. GHG (2013). Greenhouse Gas Protocol Technical Guidance for Calculating Scope 3 Emissions (v1). https://ghgprotocol.org/sites/default/files/standards/Scope3_Calculation_Guidance_0.pdf.
16. Massachusetts Institute of Technology (2020). Carbon Offsets. MIT Climate Portal. https://climate.mit.edu/explainers/carbon-offsets.
17. Bloomberg (2022). Carbon Offsets Price May Rise 3,000% by 2029 under Tighter Rules. March 2. www.bloomberg.com/professional/blog/carbon-offsets-price-may-rise-3000-by-2029-under-tighter-rules.
18. *The Economist* (2020). The Great Disrupter: Climate Change Is about to Upend the Corporate World. Firms Must Reach. September 19. www.economist.com/special-report/2020/09/17/the-great-disrupter.
19. *Financial Times* (2022). The Carbon Offset Market Is Falling Short. Here's How to Fix It. May 4. www.ft.com/content/32b1a051-7de6-4594-b31b-753e78aefde1.
20. Fortune (2022). Global 500. https://fortune.com/company/unilever/global500.
21. Unilever (2021). Climate Transition Action Plan. https://assets.unilever.com/files/92ui5egz/production/bbe89d14aa9e0121dd3a2b9721bbfd3bef57b8d3.pdf/unilever-climate-transition-action-plan-19032021.pdf.

5

The Electric Vehicle Transition

General Motors (GM) Will Sell Only Zero-Emission Vehicles by
2035 . . . The move, one of the most ambitious in the auto industry, is
a piece of a broader plan by the company to become carbon neutral by
2040.

New York Times, *January 28, 2021 [1]*

5.1 First There Was the Death of the Horse and Carriage

While many Americans think of Henry Ford and the Ford Model T as the start
of the automobile, history tells us that in actuality it was Carl Benz who on
January 29, 1886 applied for a patent for his vehicle powered by a gas engine.[1]
He was ultimately granted the patent – number 37435 and the three-
wheeled vehicle made its first public appearance in July 1886 as Motor Car
model no. 1 [2].

Before there was either the Benz Motor Car model no. 1 or the Ford Model T,
around the world the horse and carriage dominated the transportation industry.
The era lasted around 300 years, spanning from the late seventeenth century
until the early twentieth century. In the United States, the real height of the
carriage era lasted less than a century, from about 1850 to 1910 [3]. However, in
one decade, cars replaced horses (and bicycles) as the standard form of
transport for people and goods in the United States. In 1907 there were
140,300 cars registered in the USA and 2,900 trucks.

---

[1] Note that Nicolas-Joseph Cugnot, a French military engineer, built a steam-powered tricycle for
hauling artillery in 1769.

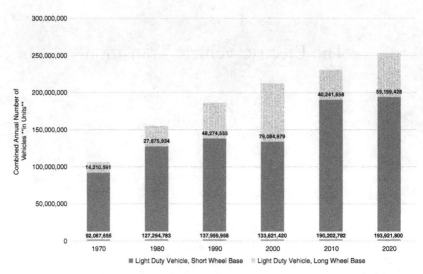

Figure 5.1 Growth of registered vehicles excluding motor buses in the United States, 1970 to 2020 [7].

Ten years later in 1917, there had been a 33-fold increase in the number of cars registered, to almost 5 million, and a 134-fold increase in the number of commercial, agricultural, and military vehicles, to almost 400,000 [4].

Fast forward to the 2020s and we see how the internal combustion engine (ICE) vehicle has continued to enjoy increased demand. In the United States, with a total population of approximately 331.5 million [5], an astonishing 276 million vehicles were registered in 2020 with a rapid increase since 1960, as presented in Figure 5.1. Only the tiny European country of San Marino with a population of 33 million and 1,263 cars per 1,000 residents in 2020 [6] had a higher per capita of cars than the United States in 2020. Nowhere in the world is the ICE vehicle more associated with a single country.

5.2 Tesla: The Great Disruptor

Today, when we think of electric vehicles (EVs), we think of Tesla. It is the most well-known automotive brand that has all of us witnessing another unprecedented disruption to mobility with the rapid transition away from the ICE to an all-electric vehicle.

Tesla was founded in 2003 by Martin Eberhard, a Californian who received his degrees from the University of Illinois in computer science and electrical engineering, and fellow Californian, Marc Tarpenning, a University of California–Berkeley graduate in computer sciences. The pair founded NuvoMedia, one of the first e-book readers, which was acquired in 2000 by Gemstar-TV Guide International for $187 million – another Silicon Valley success story [8, 9].

However, Elon Musk would soon enter the picture and forever change the company, the global automotive industry, and its vast supply chain and financial markets. Musk was born and raised in South Africa to a reportedly wealthy family in the mining industry. Later at college age he moved to Canada and then attended the University of Pennsylvania and obtained degrees in both physics and economics. He then moved to Silicon Valley where he thrived and created an incredible career. He made his fortune as a forward-thinking and risk-taking start-up entrepreneur. In fact, he may be the only person who has built four billion-dollar companies – PayPal, Tesla, SpaceX, and Solar City [10, 11].

Musk's interest in EVs dated back to 2003 when he was thirty-two years old after test driving tzero, an electric car. Tzero was designed and built in very small numbers by AC Propulsion out of San Dimas, California. In fact, only three were built and only one survived. According to Musk, he wanted to be part of the future EV transition but since SpaceX was in its early stages and consuming his time, he did not want to start from ground zero. The leadership of AC Propulsion did not have any intentions to mass produce but suggested that Musk meet with the leadership of a new start-up called Tesla. So, in 2004, Musk, who had just received a windfall from eBay's $1.5 billion purchase of PayPal (which Musk cofounded), made a $6.5 million investment in Tesla's series A funding round, thus becoming the largest shareholder in Tesla [12, 13, 14].

In 2008 Musk took over the role as chief executive officer with different variations of stories by those in leadership at Tesla at the time. Some say it was a pure power play, while others state it was a necessary step. No matter the reason, the results of his leadership are clear and undeniable. In 2009 the Tesla Roaders started production and on June 29, 2010, Tesla Motors went public with an initial public offering share price of $17 per share [10].[2]

As discussed in Chapter 1, in 2020 Tesla had the highest market value of any automotive manufacturer in the world. Since 2020, both EV and battery indices have outpaced those of the top ten automakers, as well as the broader market benchmark [15]. Yet they certainly are still not even close to the production numbers of vehicles manufactured and sold, as presented in Figure 5.2.

---

[2] As of May 27, 2022, if you invested $10,000 in Tesla stock in 2010 at its price of $17/share and after its 5-for-1 stock split in 2020, your investment would be worth $1.39 million – a 13,800 percent increase in value.

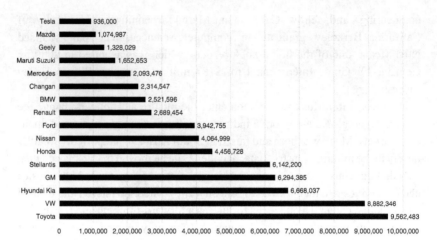

Figure 5.2 Annual global sales of all types of passenger vehicles for 2021 [16, 17].

In 2021, global EV sales remained a small but quickly growing portion of global automotive sales, even though they doubled year over year in rising to 6.6 million (Table 5.1). In the United States EV sales represented 4.4 percent of the domestic sales, with California, Washington, DC, Oregon, Hawaii, Colorado, and Washington state leading in sales. Of the total EV sales in the USA, 630,000 were plug-in battery and hybrid electric cars, twice as many as the year before, while in Europe 2.3 million EVs were sold [18, 19]. This all occurred when the average gas price in the United States at the beginning of 2021 was $2.25 per gallon [20], well below the post-Russian invasion of Ukraine[3] that drove gas prices in California to $6.37 per gallon [21] and over $8.00 per gallon[4] in Switzerland ($8.30), the Netherlands ($8.33), Greece ($8.36), Denmark ($8.47), the UK ($8.50), Finland ($8.52), Norway ($9.10), and Iceland ($9.30) [22].

5.3 Growth and Adoption

So how large will the EV market get? The International Energy Agency (IEA) estimates that by 2030 the EV stock across all modes except two-/three-wheelers will reach between 145 million and 300 million globally, accounting for 60 percent of new car sales compared to 4.6 percent in 2020. The higher estimate of 300 million is using the net-zero emissions by 2050 scenario [23].

---

[3] February 24, 2022. [4] Converting liters to gallons and exchange rates at the time.

Table 5.1 *Snapshot of recent automotive company commitments [26]*

BYD announced that it would only produce battery electric vehicles (BEVs) and plugin hybrid electric vehicles (PHEVs) from April 2022 onward.

Dongfeng plans to electrify 100% of its new models of main passenger car brands by 2024.

Fed Ex with 87,000 vehicles is transitioning its fleet to EV and will only buy EVs after 2025 and be a completely electric fleet by 2040.

Ford expects one-third of its sales to be fully electric by 2026 and 50% by 2030 and to move to all-electric in Europe by 2030.

General Motors aims for 30 EV models and for installed BEV production capacity of 1 million units in North America by 2025 and for carbon neutrality in 2040.

Lexus aims to achieve 100% BEV sales globally in 2035.

Mercedes announced that from 2025, all newly launched vehicles will be fully electric.

Toyota announced the roll-out of 30 BEV models and a goal of reaching 3.5 million annual sales of electric cars by 2030.

US Government Fleet – by 2035, the Biden administration wants the entire federal fleet to purchase EVs only, with light-duty vehicles making the shift by 2027.

Volkswagen announced that all-electric vehicles would exceed 70% of European and 50% of Chinese and US sales by 2030, and that by 2040 nearly 100% should be zero-emission vehicles.

Volvo committed to becoming a fully electric car company by 2030.

US auto executives surveyed by KPMG indicated they believe that 52 percent of all new car sales in the USA will be EVs by 2030 [24]. The Edison Electric Institute estimated in 2021 that there will be 22 million EVs on US roads by 2030, requiring over 100,000 fast-chargers [25].

As of August 2022, a total of fourteen states in the USA have adopted California's Zero-Emission Vehicle (ZEV), which was designed to accelerate the commercialization of battery-electric, plug-in hybrid, and fuel-cell EVs. The regulations across the states require that a certain percentage of the vehicles delivered for sale in a state are ZEVs. Vehicle manufacturers receive credits for each delivered vehicle based on the type of vehicle, range, and other factors. Each year, manufacturers must meet a ZEV credit amount that is based on average annual sales [27, 28].

From a manufacturing perspective, in 2021 Tesla had the highest-selling EV model, the Tesla Model 3 with over 500,000 units sold. Close behind was Wuling HongGuang's Mini EV[5] made in partnership with General Motors,[6] which is a very small microcar and sells for about $5,000 new [29, 30] versus

---

[5] Not available outside of China. [6] A reported 44 percent ownership stake.

the Tesla Model 3 with a starting price of over $46,000. While Tesla is the current industry leader, it is doubtful that it will retain that position moving forward as the entire and much larger industry transitions to EVs. In part, the race to the top will be fueled by access to important and much more competitive supply chains, especially batteries and critical earth elements as well as adoption rates in countries. While the next chapter will focus on batteries and minerals, it is important to understand adoption rates.

The Boston Consulting Group [31] analyzed adoption rates considering market, rapidly declining battery costs, tougher government regulation, and the introduction of new EV models by an expanding manufacturing base/capacity. Their analyses identified that while 78 percent of all light vehicles sold in 2019 globally were internal combustion (gasoline), 15 percent diesel and about 2 percent battery-electric, those numbers get flipped by 2035. Their analysis shows that by 2035 battery-electric global sales will jump to 45 percent of the market (54 percent in the USA, 58 percent in China, and 62 percent in the European Union), and another 43 percent of EV designs; that is, plugin hybrid electric vehicles (PHEVs), hybrid electric vehicles (HEVs), and mild hybrid electric vehicles (MHEVs). Meanwhile, by 2035 global sales of gasoline cars will drop from 78 percent to 11 percent, while diesel will increase to 26 percent from 15 percent primarily based on renewable (biobased) diesel increases to meet national-level net-zero-carbon commitments. Several original equipment manufacturers will start exiting the highest-volume ICE programs.

In 2021, Norway led the world with the higher percentage of new passenger car registrations being EVs (BEV and PHEV) with 64.5 percent. This was followed by Germany with 13.6 percent, China[7] at 12.7 percent, the UK at 11.6 percent, France at 9.8 percent, Italy at 4.6 percent, Spain at 2.8 percent, the USA at 2.6 percent, and Japan at 0.9 percent [32].

5.3.1 Hydrogen Fuel Cells

With all this realized and anticipated growth in EVs, some may be asking about hydrogen fuel-cell cars and their market penetration and growth. There certainly has been significant press about the hydrogen revolution in the past. Toyota, the world's largest automobile manufacturer, placed its bet on hydrogen fuel cells dating back to 1992, and gained progress in 2014 with the development of the Mirai sedan [33]. Toyota made a bet in 1992 that hydrogen would outperform sales of EVs. However, by at least 2010 it should have been obvious that EVs would dominate, so the reasons for Toyota's continued pursuit of hydrogen are not transparent.

---

[7] A doubling of EV registrations from 2020.

As will be discussed further in Chapter 8, if hydrogen is to be part of the net-zero-carbon economy, it has to be "green" hydrogen; that is, electrolysis through the use of renewable energy sources. That is not currently cost-effective. Further, in the marketplace, hydrogen refueling stations in the USA are almost non-existent, with a total of forty-eight (of which forty-seven are located in California). Conversely, there are almost 50,000 battery EV charging stations at the time of writing and likely many more by the time you are reading this book.

In part, the rapid expansion is a result of the Biden Administration's funding and incentive programs passed in 2022 [34]. Secondly, the sustainability value of hydrogen is that the byproduct of green hydrogen is that the combustion produces water; however, a small amount of engine metal burns as well, resulting in about 2 percent of the emissions of a gasoline engine. The exhaust also contains traces of nitrogen oxide, while EVs do not pollute in operation. Finally, the average costs of hydrogen for a light-duty fuel-cell EV (passenger car) in California is $16.51 per kilogram, which is not competitive with electricity costs or even gasoline [35].

5.4 Will EVs Have an Impact on Climate Change?

In the United States, which has had a slower EV adoption than other countries, EVs still were able to displace over 500 million gallons of gasoline in 2020, up from 12 million in 2012 [36]. Globally, 13.1 billion liters[8] gasoline equivalent were displaced worldwide, up from less than 23[9] million liters gasoline equivalent in 2010 [18]. That amounts to about 3 percent of global demand or about one-fifth of Russia's pre-invasion of Ukraine oil exports. The IEA believes that oil displacement from the global EV fleet will increase to 3.4 million barrels a day under the Sustainable Development Scenario.

This converts to 5.2e+10 US gallons per year (52 billion gallons per year). In the United States, gasoline is the most consumed petroleum product and in 2021 it consumed on average 8.8 million barrels (369 million gallons/day), which equals 44 percent of the total US petroleum consumption[10] [37]. Again, this is all before the invasion of the Ukraine by Russia and the resulting energy crisis, which in the mid-term will likely prove to have an even greater economic impact on oil-producing countries as consumers, companies, and countries accelerate the EV transition.

---

[8] That is, 3.43 billion gallons.   [9] That is, 6.07 million gallons.
[10] Other uses include lubricants, asphalt, jet fuel, heating oil, and so on.

And while there continue to be strong expectations about the EV transition, there has also been much in the news in the United States, mainly in op-ed pieces that question or discount the potential positive impact of EVs in addressing climate change. Much of this has been focused on the embedded emissions that come with the manufacturing of the vehicle and all the components. Additionally, some point out that the individuals who can currently afford to purchase EVs are favoring larger SUV-type vehicles.

However, a 2022 study led by researchers at the University of Michigan [38] found that light-duty, battery-electric vehicles result in 64 percent lower cradle-to-grave environmental life-cycle analysis (LCA) greenhouse gas (GHG) emissions than ICE vehicles on average across the United States. Specifically, in the lifetime of an EV versus the lifetime of an ICE vehicle, an EV provides GHG emission benefits of approximately 45 tons CO_2eq for sedans, 56 tons CO_2eq for SUVs, and 74 tons CO_2eq for pickup trucks.

The researchers also show that the carbon emissions from manufacturing processes used to produce lithium-ion batteries for EVs do not offset the carbon savings from operating an EV, a major argument by those opposed to EVs. Yet, the true answer for the climate value of EVs is dependent on one major variable. That is, what is the energy source for the electricity being used to charge the EV batteries?

This is reinforced by a 2019 IEA report that found that when modeling the life cycle of electric versus ICE vehicles, BEVs provided GHG emission reductions of between 20 and 30 percent relative to conventional ICE vehicles on a global average. The life-cycle assessment modeling covered the manufacturing, consumer use, and end-of-life of both types of vehicles [39]. These benefits increase in countries that have a higher utilization of renewable energy sources where BEV life-cycle emissions are around 45–55 percent lower.

What these stories tell us is that it would make absolutely no sense to move forward with the EV transition if in fact the electricity being used was from coal or natural gas. Rather, domestically and globally, we will need to significantly increase our generation of renewable electricity from wind, solar, and even nuclear. Even the hope of green hydrogen is dependent on sufficient renewables to power the electrolysis process.

So just how much in GHG savings might EVs provide? According to the IEA, by 2030 in the Stated Policies Scenario (STEPS)[11] the global EV fleet will reduce GHG emissions by more than one-third compared to an equivalent ICE,

---

[11] The STEPS provides a more conservative benchmark for the future because it does not take it for granted that governments will reach all their announced goals.

meaning 230 Mt CO_2-eq in 2030 for EVs compared to ICE vehicle emissions at 350 Mt CO_2eq, providing 120 Mt CO_2-eq of net savings.

For the Sustainable Development Scenario[12] the wheel-to-wheel GHG emissions from the EV fleet in 2030 are expected to be lower than in the STEPS, reflecting that the increase in the number of EVs is counterbalanced by less carbon-intense power generation. The Sustainable Development Scenario delivers 410 Mt CO_2-eq in net savings. To put this in perspective, "fossil" CO_2 emissions (not CO_2-eq) in 2020 for the UK were 313.8 Mt CO_2 and 386.4 Mt CO_2 for Australia, while China's fossil CO_2 emissions were 11,680 Mt, by far the greatest emitter of fossil CO_2 emissions [40]. However, another important variable is the use of petroleum for non-transportation fuels.

5.5 Costs of EVs

There are a number of drivers of the EV transition and many variables that will influence the rate and success of the transition, including policies, incentives, costs of the vehicles and energy sources, supply chains, the range of vehicles, and the availability of charging stations.

One generalized approach examined the manufacturer's suggested retail prices versus the vehicles' range in miles to derive the vehicles' retail cost per mile of range.[13] The EV market is making great strides in growing the range of the vehicles per full charge and thus are becoming less expense in inflation-adjusted terms. The median EV costs $554 per mile of range in 2012 and dramatically lowered to $214 in 2021, a 61 percent improvement. Tesla reached $173 per mile in 2021, down from $352 in 2012. However, this is still higher than that of internal gas combustion vehicles, which came in at $104 per mile, as shown in Figure 5.3 [41]. The actual purchase costs for the manufacturer, the dealer, and ultimately the consumer for EVs continue to come down.

5.5.1 Manufacturing Costs

EVs currently and for the expected near-term (i.e., 2035) will remain more expensive to produce than internal combustion passenger vehicles primarily due to the costs of the large battery storage, something an ICE car does not need

---

[12] In this scenario, all current net-zero pledges are achieved in full and there are extensive efforts to realize near-term emissions reductions; advanced economies reach net-zero emissions by 2050, China around 2060, and all other countries by 2070 at the latest.

[13] There are many variables, including differing vehicle capabilities, so this is highly generalized.

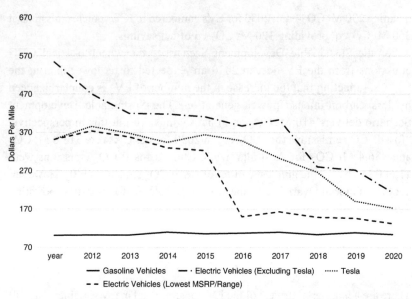

Figure 5.3 Vehicle's retail cost per mile of range calculated by a vehicle manufacturer's suggested retail price divided by its range [41].

to worry about (Figure 5.4). An EV can have up to 70 percent different components than an ICE vehicle. An EV simply has one moving part – the motor – while gas-powered vehicles can have hundreds of moving parts. The vehicle drive components of an EV are the charger, the battery pack, the controller, and the motor. The gasoline car has the gas tank, the engine, the carburetor, smog controls (EVs have no tailpipes), the starter, the water pump, the exhaust system, the gas pump, the oil pump, and the generator [42].

As presented in Figure 5.5, the battery costs in EVs can run from 25 percent to 40 percent of the total vehicle costs, depending on the model and supply chain. The current battery technology is composed of lithium-ion batteries. Of this, it is important to note that the cathode is approximately 50.5 percent of the battery's costs [44].

5.6 Total Costs of Ownership

For the individual consumer, one of the questions to answer is if owning an electric vehicle is less expensive than owning an internal combustion (gasoline/ diesel) vehicle. A 2020 study [45], which was prior to the dramatic increase in

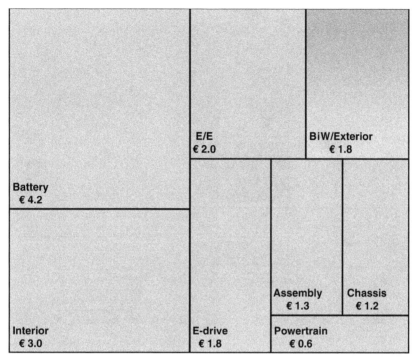

Figure 5.4 Electric vehicle cost by 2030 in thousands of Euros [43]. BiW = Body-in-White; E/E = electrical/electronics.

gasoline prices and 2022 inflation, compared both luxury and mid-sized ICE and EV new vehicles in California, Florida, and New York state. The analyses explored high mileage and low mileage for three-year, seven-year, and ten-year periods that incorporated:

- acquisition vehicle costs including financing or lease costs and a home charger
- subsidies at the federal and state level
- driving distance 12,000 miles/year and 40,000 miles per year
- energy costs including fuels and electricity
- maintenance costs
- residual values.

The results were consistent in that the overall costs of ownership for ICE vehicles are estimated to be two to three times more than the electricity cost of EVs charged at home and the maintenance costs for ICE vehicles are twice those of EVs. Subsidies have limited impact on total costs of ownership. Fuel

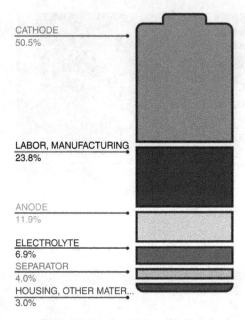

CATHODE
50.5%

LABOR, MANUFACTURING
23.8%

ANODE
11.9%

ELECTROLYTE
6.9%
SEPARATOR
4.0%
HOUSING, OTHER MATER...
3.0%

Figure 5.5 Cost breakdown of lithium-ion batteries for electric vehicles [44].

costs, residual value, and maintenance dominate total costs of ownership in the advantage of EVs over ICEs. Clearly, there are a number of variables that are still in play that will continue to affect the total costs of ownership over time.

References

1. *New York Times* (2021). General Motors (GM) Will Sell Only Zero-Emission Vehicles by 2035. January 28. www.nytimes.com/2021/01/28/business/gm-zero-emission-vehicles.html#:~:text=General%20Motors%20said%20Thursday%20that,trucks%20and%20sport%20utility%20vehicles.
2. Mercedes Benz (2022). 1885–1886. The First Automobile. https://group.merce des-benz.com/company/tradition/company-history/1885-1886.html#:~:text=On%20January%2029%2C%201886%2C%20Carl,1.
3. Park City (2012). Introduction: Transportation in America and the Carriage Age. https://parkcityhistory.org/wp-content/uploads/2012/04/Teacher-Background-Information.pdf.
4. *Scientific American* (2017). The Motor Vehicle. www.scientificamerican.com/article/the-motor-vehicle-1917-slide-show.
5. US Census (2022). Quick Facts. www.census.gov/quickfacts/fact/table/US/PST045221.

6. World Bank (2022). Data. https://data.worldbank.org/indicator/SP.POP.TOTL?locations=SM.

7. US Department of Transportation (2022). Number of U.S. Aircraft, Vehicles, Vessels, and Other Conveyances. Bureau of Transportation Statistics. www.bts.gov/content/number-us-aircraft-vehicles-vessels-and-other-conveyances.

8. CNN (2000). Gemstar Gobbles Up Two E-book Companies. January 20. www.cnn.com/2000/books/news/01/20/ebook/index.html.

9. Tesla (2022). About Tesla. www.tesla.com/about.

10. Motley Fool (2022). If You Invested $10,000 in Tesla in 2020, This Is How Much You Would Have Today. May 27. www.fool.com/investing/2022/12/21/if-invested-10000-tesla-stock-ipo-how-much-today.

11. International Energy Agency (2022). Global EV Outlook 2022. www.iea.org/reports/global-ev-outlook–2022.

12. CNBC (2020). Elon Musk: "I Really Didn't Want to Be CEO of Tesla" – Here's How He Says It Happened. www.cnbc.com/2020/01/30/elon-musk-i-really-didnt-want-to-be-ceo-of-tesla.html.

13. Finance (2022). A Deep Dive into Elon Musk's Investments: The Makings of a Billionaire. www.toptal.com/finance/venture-capital-consultants/elon-musks-investments#:~:text=As%20with%20X.com%2C%20he,in%20its%20Series%20A%20round.

14. CNBC (2020). Elon Musk: CEO Is a "Made-Up Title," So He's Tesla's "Technoking" Instead. www.cnbc.com/2021/12/07/elon-musk-ceo-is-made-up-title-prefers-tesla-technoking.html.

15. BBC (2021). Tesla Surpasses $1 Trillion Valuation after Hertz Order. October 25. www.bbc.com/news/business-59045100.

16. Tesla (2022). Tesla Q4 2021 Vehicle Production and Delivery. Press Release. https://ir.tesla.com/press-release/tesla-q4-2021-vehicle-production-deliveries.

17. F&I Tools (2022). Worldwide Car Sales. www.factorywarrantylist.com/car-sales-by-manufacturer.html.

18. International Energy Agency (2022). Global EV Outlook 2022. www.iea.org/reports/global-ev-outlook–2022.

19. Alliance for Automotive Innovation (2022). Get Connected. Electric Vehicle Quarterly. Q4 Report. www.autosinnovate.org/posts/papers-reports/Get%20Connected%20EV%20Quarterly%20Report%20Q4.pdf.

20. Energy Information Agency (2022). Retail Gasoline Prices Rose across the United States in 2021 As Driving Increased. *Today in Energy.* January 5. www.eia.gov/todayinenergy/detail.php?id=50758#:~:text=Rising%20crude%20oil%20prices%20and,average%20nominal%20price%20since%202014.

21. Statista (2022). Weekly Retail Prices of Regular Gasoline in the United States As of June 7, 2022 by State. www.statista.com/statistics/204160/retail-prices-of-motor-fuel-in-the-united-states-in-2011-by-state.

22. Global PetrolPrices (2022). Gasoline Prices in Europe, US Gallons 25 July 2022. www.globalpetrolprices.com/gasoline_prices/Europe.

23. International Energy Agency (2021). Electric Vehicles. www.iea.org/reports/electric-vehicles.

24. CNBC (2021). Auto Executives Say More Than Half of U.S. Car Sales Will Be EVs by 2030, KPMG Survey Shows. www.cnbc.com/2021/11/30/auto-execu

tives-say-more-than-half-of-us-car-sales-will-be-evs-by-2030-kpmg-survey-shows.html.

25. Utility Dive (2021). Major US Utilities Plan Nationwide Charging Network, Anticipating 22 M EVs by 2030. December 8. www.utilitydive.com/news/major-us-utilities-plan-nationwide-charging-network-anticipating-22m-evs-b/611150/#:~:text=The%20coalition%20is%20led%20by,more%20than%20100%2C000%20fast%20chargers.

26. Dynamic Sustainability Lab (2022). Policies Driving the EV Transition in the United States. Bulletin No. 20220305. www.dynamicslab.org.

27. California Air Resources Board (2022). States That Have Adopted California's Vehicle Standards under Section 177 of the Federal Clean Air Act. ww2.arb.ca.gov/resources/documents/states-have-adopted-californias-vehicle-standards-under-section-177-federal.

28. California Air Resources Board (2022). Zero-Emission Vehicle Program. ww2.arb.ca.gov/our-work/programs/zero-emission-vehicle-program/about.

29. Statista (2022). Best Selling Plug-In Electric Vehicle Models Worldwide in 2021. www-statista-com.libezproxy2.syr.edu/statistics/960121/sales-of-all-electric-vehicles-worldwide-by-model.

30. Wired (2022). This Chinese EV Sells at Just Over $5,000. So We Tried It. www.wired.com/story/review-wuling-hongguang-mini-ev.

31. Boston Consulting Group (2021). Why Electric Cars Can't Come Fast Enough. April 20. www.bcg.com/publications/2021/why-evs-need-to-accelerate-their-market-penetration.

32. Statista (2022). Electric Mobility: Norway Leads the Charge. February 15. www.statista.com/chart/17344/electric-vehicle-share.

33. CNBC (2022). After Toyota's Mirai, the Japanese Auto Giant Zeroes in on Hydrogen Buses and Heavy-Duty Trucks. May 17. www.cnbc.com/2022/05/18/toyota-ramps-up-efforts-to-look-at-potential-of-hydrogen-vehicles.html.

34. The White House (2022). Fact Sheet: Biden-Harris Administration Proposes New Standards for Electric Vehicles. June 9. www.whitehouse.gov/briefing-room/statements-releases/2022/06/09/fact-sheet-biden-harris-administration-proposes-new-standards-for-national-electric-vehicle-charging-network.

35. California Energy Commission (2019). Joint Agency Staff Report on Assembly Bill 8: 2019 Annual Assessment of Time and Cost Needed to Attain 100 Hydrogen Refueling Stations in California. Publication number: CEC-600–2019–039.

36. US Department of Energy (2021). Light Duty Plug-In Electric Vehicles Displaced 500 Million Gallons of Gasoline in the U.S. in 2020. FOTW #1203. September 13.

37. Energy Information Agency (2022). Oil and Petroleum Products Explained. www.eia.gov/energyexplained/oil-and-petroleum-products/use-of-oil.php.

38. M. Woody, P. Vaishnav, G. Keoleian et al. (2022). The Role of Pick-Up Truck Electrification in the Decarbonization of Light Duty Vehicles. *Environmental Research Letters*, 17.

39. International Energy Agency (2019). Global EV Outlook 2019. www.iea.org/reports/global-ev-outlook-2019.

40. M. Crippa, D. Guizzardi, E. Solazzo et al. (2021). GHG Emissions of All World Countries – 2021 Report, EUR 30831 EN, Publications Office of the European Union, Luxembourg.

41. Federal Reserve Bank of Dallas (2022). Electric Vehicles Gain Ground but Still Face Price, Range, Charging Constraints. February 22. www.dallasfed.org/research/economics/2022/0222.

42. Idaho National Lab (2022). How Do Gasoline and Electric Vehicles Compare? Advanced Vehicle Testing Activity. https://avt.inl.gov/sites/default/files/pdf/fsev/compare.pdf.

43. *Financial Times* (2020). Electric Car Costs to Remain Higher Than Traditional Engines. www.ft.com/content/a7e58ce7-4fab-424a-b1fa-f833ce948cb7.

44. Dynamic Sustainability Lab (2022). Lithium Battery Manufacturing and the EV Transition. www.dynamicslab.org/_files/ugd/8e5fe6_3f8fcddd2b4d483883845efe3adf3bae.pdf.

45. Avicenne Energy (2020). North American Automotive EV vs ICE Total Cost of Ownership. https://nickelinstitute.org/media/8d993d0fd3dfd5b/tco-north-american-automotive-final.pdf.

6

Electric Vehicle Charging Networks

> If we are to meet the target of 290 million charging points by 2040, we'll
> need $500 billion in public–private investment.
>
> *Frank Mühlon, 2021 chief executive officer of ABB (the world's*
> *largest electric vehicle charging company by revenue) [1]*

I just finished my annual commute from our winter and spring home in the
research triangle of North Carolina to our summer and fall home in the Finger
Lakes, New York state. My wife and I and our dogs fill the car and we make the
eleven-hour/650-mile drive in a single day in our hybrid. With a range of over
500 miles on a full tank, we only need to make one fueling stop for our trip.
Notwithstanding running inside the gas station for the bathroom and/or iced
tea, the refueling will take less than five minutes at the most. And we can find
multiple gas station options every few miles for the most part in rural areas and
locate a gas station every couple of blocks in the city.

However, if I was to drive a battery-electric vehicle (EV), I would likely have
a range between 100 and 300 miles,[1] and if I was driving any non-Tesla EV,
I would have a limited number of available fast-charging stations. While one
obvious impact is that the limited ranges and charging station availability are
a current concern of consumers interested in purchasing an EV, there are even
more impactful issues.

6.1 Range and Charge Characteristics

The first characteristic is the mileage range of battery EVs. Going back to 1975
in the United States, the average fuel economy for a sedan vehicle[2] class had
a rating of 13.5 miles per gallon (mpg), which by 2021 had risen to 31.7 mpg. In

---

[1] See Table 6.1. [2] This does not include SUV or crossovers with larger fuel capacity.

a non-scientific review of vehicle specifications, I have comfort in stating that a 14.5-to-16-gallon fuel tank size is an appropriate volume to use [2, 3]. Given a 15-gallon capacity, the average range would be 475.5 miles. How does

Table 6.1 *2022 mileage range for every battery-electric vehicle sold in the United States in 2022 [4]*

Rank	2022 Make and Model	Mileage Range
32	Mazda MX-30	100
31	Mini Cooper SE	114
30	Porsche Taycan Cross Turismo	215
29	Audi e-tron	222
28	Volvo XC40 Recharge	223
27	Volvo C40 Recharge	226
26	Nissan Leaf	226
25	Porsche Taycan	227
24	Jaguar 1-Pace	234
23	Audi e-tron GT	238
22	Kia Niro EV	239
21	Audi Q4 e-tron	241
20	Chevrolet Bolt EUV	247
19	Hyundai Kona Electric	258
18	Chevrolet Bolt EV	259
17	Polestar 2	270
16	Volkswagen ID.4	275
15	BMW i4	301
14	Hyundai Ioniq 5	303
13	Ford Mustang Mach-E	305
12	Kia EV6	310
11	Rivian R1T	314
10	Rivian R1S	316
9	Ford F-150 Lightning	320
8	BMW ¡X	324
7	GMC Hummer EV	329
6	Tesla Model Y	330
5	Tesla Model X	348
4	Mercedes EQS	350
3	Tesla Model 3	358
2	Tesla Model S	405
1	Lucid Air	520
	Mean	279.6
	Median	272.5

this compare to the current EV models? As presented by Table 6.1, it is clear that the current battery technology in EVs falls short with an average of 279 miles.

Table 6.2 *Characteristics of electric vehicle charging stations in the United States, not accounting for incentives, offsets and rebates [5, 6, 7]*

	Level 1	Level 2	Level 3 (Direct Current Fast Charge)
Location	Home standard 120-volt wall outlet	Public locations or home purchased unit	Public and commercial locations
Power (kW)	1	3 to 20 avg. 6	50.
	120 Volt	240 volt	480-volt DC
Apx. Charging Time (Empty Battery)	20 hours for 124 miles and 43 hours for 250 miles	5 hours for 124 miles and 11 hours for 250 miles	30 minutes for 124 miles and 1 hour for 250 miles
Non-Tesla Connector Type	SAEJ1772 EV Plug	SAEJ1772 EV Plug	CHAdeMO and SAE Combo **not Interchangeable
Tesla Charging Stations	SAEJ1772 EV Plug	Tesla Vehicles Only	Tesla Vehicles Only
Average Costs Including Installation	$600–$1,000	$2,370–56,700	apx. $40,000 per single port
Number of Charging Locations and Ports in the USA in 2022	115,000 individual charging ports	41,000 stations providing 91,000 ports	6,000 with 23,000 charging ports

The second characteristic has to do with the time to charge a battery EV as compared to gasoline-powered vehicles. In the United States there are three different types of charging stations, as presented in Table 6.2.

As of August 2022,[3] there are just over 53,000 EV charging stations and 139,122 charging ports in the United States. The company with the largest EV charging network in the United States is ChargePoint (CHPT). The company has over 30,000 charging stations with over 47,000 individual charging ports, most of which are Level 2 chargers [8]. Tesla, the next closest rival, has fewer than 6,000 station locations and about 25,000 charging ports. However, the majority of Tesla's charging ports (at ~1,300 Supercharger stations) are Superchargers (13,000 DC Fast Chargers).

---

[3] For an interactive map, see https://afdc.energy.gov/fuels/electricity_locations.html#/find/nearest?fuel=ELEC.

However, Tesla in its domestic US strategy has developed an extensive charging network and it does not offer access to its high-speed supercharging network to non-Tesla owners. Yet, because of more consumer-friendly regulations in European countries, Tesla is required to provide access and, in fact, it has rolled out access in thirteen European Union countries. Electrify America has about 750 stations and 3,300 fast-charging ports. ChargePoint and EVgo both have over 1,700 DC Fast-Charging ports each, though ChargePoint has about 1,700 total fast-charging locations to EVgo's 840 [7, 9, 10].

Clearly, this is an insufficient domestic volume. However, on June 9, 2022, the White House released its plans for the rapid expansion of a nationwide EV charging network by proposing to build 500,000 new EV charging stations across the country by 2030 – less than eight years' time. In conjunction, the US Department of Transportation and US Department of Energy issued a Notice of Proposed Rulemaking to develop a set of minimum requirements for projects funded under the National Electric Vehicle Infrastructure (NEVI) Program and all public EV chargers funded by the federal government. The NEVI formula program authorized $5 billion in formula funding to states to build charging infrastructure [13]. The purpose of the NEVI Formula Program is to "provide funding to States to strategically deploy electric vehicle charging infrastructure and to establish an interconnected network to facilitate data collection, access, and reliability" [14]. To be effective, the EV charging infrastructure deployed under this program must provide a seamless customer experience for all users through a convenient, reliable, affordable, and equitable national EV charging network. Importantly, the standards are designed to apply nationwide regardless of the operator or type of vehicle being charged.

As one example of the funds distribution, the New York State Department of Transportation will receive approximately $175 million through NEVI over five years. The NEVI program requires funds to be invested within one travel mile of designated EV corridors, with charging stations no more than 50 miles apart. For the State of New York, their designated corridors include many of the state's most-traveled interstate and state highways [15].

6.2 Alliances

Across the country, Tesla is the only automotive brand that owns and operates its own proprietary charging network, as discussed earlier. However, other automakers have recently announced significant investments and plans for large national networks. However, they are primarily based on partnerships with existing networks, which offer a multitude of Level 2 stations and some DC Fast-Charging stations [7].

6.2.1 Electrify America, Volkswagen, and Siemens

Reston, Virginia-based Electrify America[4] provides both home and commercial charging solutions and is one of the few networks that can charge at speeds of up to 350 kW, though some charging ports only offer 50 kW speeds. In addition, not all EVs are capable of accepting the maximum power level. That said, Electrify America is also the only comprehensive DC Fast-Charging network that allows people to take a non-Tesla EV on a road trip virtually anywhere in the USA, and from coast to coast.

Over a ten-year period (made up of four thirty-month "cycles"), Electrify America plans to invest $2 billion in zero-emission vehicle infrastructure, access, and education programs in the United States. In the wake of the Volkswagen (VW) scandal in 2016 related to VW pleading guilty to falsifying emission standards on its diesel-fueled vehicles in the USA, the company reached a consent decree with the government in the amount of $4.3 billion, including $2 billion to promote EVs.

In 2017 VW rolled out the Electrify America brand in the United States. In its 2021 annual report issued in 2021, the company indicates that it ended 2021 with 799 ultra-fast-charging stations open or constructed nationwide with 41.4 GW hours delivered and enabling 145.4 million electric miles of driving, equating to the avoidance of 5.7 million gallons of gasoline. It installed on average 3.4 ultra-fast-charging stations per week nationwide in 2021. In June 2022, VW agreed to sell a minority stake in Electrify America to Siemens AG for $450 million, which values the company at $2.45 billion [16, 17, 18, 19, 20].

6.2.2 EVgo, General Motors, and Pilot

On July 14, 2022 a joint announcement by General Motors (GM), Pilot Travel Centers,[5] and EVgo announced a partnership to build 2,000 charging stalls at up to 500 Pilot Flying J sites across the nation at 50-mile intervals on US highways. The stations will be capable of offering charging speeds of up to 350 kW, which can give an EV about 100 miles of range in about 10 minutes. EVgo

[4] EVgo listed on Nasdaq.
[5] Majority ownership by Berkshire Hathaway to take effect by 2023: www.usatoday.com/story/money/markets/2017/10/03/warren-buffett-berkshire-hathaway-pilot-flying-j-truck-stops/726378001.

and GM had previously announced a joint effort to build 3,250 fast chargers in American urban cities and suburbs by 2025. The move for GM is connected to its plans to manufacture only electric passenger vehicles by 2035 and its pledge to have 30 EV models for sale globally by 2025, and to invest over $750 million to build a fast-charging network [19, 20].

6.2.3 Ford: Addressing EV Charging Complaints

Ford has taken a different tack. The company launched the BlueOval Charge Network.[6] Rather than invest in manufacturers and retailers of fast-charging stations, Ford has partnered with existing charging providers including ChargePoint, SemaCharge, FLO, EVgo, Electrify America, and others, excluding Tesla. On FordPass software, a driver can locate a fast-charging station from the network of over 19,500 charge points and 63,000 plugs [21].

However, Ford has undertaken an effort that is likely even more impactful. Because the EV charging industry is nascent and rapidly growing, it comes with a tremendous amount of consumer complaints ranging from fast-charging stations down to difficulties with phone apps and software to pay or use the system. PlugShare[7] is a widely used website that allows users to map out locations of EV chargers. It is also a platform for which consumers can comment about the different locations and their experiences through its "Checkins" section when you click on a specific charging location.

Here you will find some very common experiences of issues with the equipment or software. As all major automotive manufacturers rapidly build up and transition to EVs, they cannot afford to have consumers facing continued poor charging experiences. So, in response, Ford has created "Charge Angels" who travel across the country in their Ford Mach-Es and test EV charging station equipment. Ford staff will diagnose any problems and communicate those results to the station owner. If the station does not correct the issues, then Ford will not direct its customers there anymore through its BlueOval program [22].

References

1. McKinsey (2021). The Future of EV Charging Infrastructure: Executive Perspectives. www.mckinsey.com/business-functions/operations/our-insights/the-future-of-ev-charging-infrastructure-executive-perspectives.

---

[6] The Ford car logo is a blue oval. [7] www.plugshare.com.

2. Toyota (2022). What Is the 2022 Toyota Camry Gas Tank Size? www.genemes
    sertoyota.com/gas-tank-size-of-the-2022-toyota-camry/#:~:text=Each%
    202022%20Camry%20with%20an,fuel%20tank%20is%20equipped%20instead.
3. Honda (2022). 2022 Honda Accord Gas Tank Size. www.sterlingmccallhonda
    .com/2022-honda-accord-gas-tank-size.
4. Car and Driver (2022). EVs with Longest Driving Range, Ranked. June 7. www
    .caranddriver.com/shopping-advice/g32634624/ev-longest-driving-range.
5. Climatebiz (2022). Cost of an EV Charging Station: What You Can Expect.
    June 25. https://climatebiz.com/cost-of-an-ev-charging-station.
6. Future Energy (2021). How Much Do EV Charging Stations Cost? July 1. https://
    futureenergy.com/how-much-do-ev-charging-stations-cost.
7. US News (2022). A Comprehensive Guide to U.S. Public EV Charging Networks.
    April 22. https://cars.usnews.com/cars-trucks/ev-charging-stations#:~:text=be
    come%20the%.
8. US Department of Energy (2022). Alternative Fuels Data Center: Alternative
    Fueling Station Locator. https://afdc.energy.gov/stations/#/analyze?country=
    US&fuel=ELEC&ev_levels=all&access=public&access=private.
9. CNET (2022). Tesla Will Let Other EVs Use Supercharger Stations Later in 2022.
    July 7. www.cnet.com/roadshow/news/tesla-will-let-other-evs-use-supercharger-
    stations-later-in-2022.
10. Tesla (2022). Non-Tesla Supercharger Pilot. www.cnet.com/roadshow/news/
    tesla-will-let-other-evs-use-supercharger-stations-later-in-2022.
11. US Department of Transport (2022). Bipartisan Infrastructure Law: National
    Electric Vehicle Infrastructure Formula Program Fact Sheet. www.fhwa.dot
    .gov/bipartisan-infrastructure-law/nevi_formula_program.cfm.
12. US Department of Transport (2022). Memorandum: The National Electric
    Vehicle Infrastructure (NEVI) Formula Program Guidance from Chief Counsel
    to Division Administrators. February 10. www.fhwa.dot.gov/environment/alter
    native_fuel_corridors/nominations/90d_nevi_formula_program_guidance.pdf.
13. State of New York (2022). National Electric Vehicle Infrastructure (NEVI)
    Program. www.nyserda.ny.gov/All-Programs/ChargeNY/Charge-Electric/
    Charging-Station-Programs/National-Electric-Vehicle-Infrastructure-Program.
14. Electrify America (2022). Investing in an Electric Future. www.electrifyamerica
    .com/our-plan.
15. US Environmental Protection Agency (2023). Volkswagen Clean Air Act Civil
    Settlement. February 27. www.epa.gov/enforcement/volkswagen-clean-air-act-
    civil-settlement.
16. US Department of Justice (2017). Volkswagen AG Agrees to Plead Guilty and
    Pay $4.3 Billion in Criminal and Civil Penalties; Six Volkswagen Executives and
    Employees Are Indicted in Connection with Conspiracy to Cheat U.S. Emissions
    Tests. Press Release on January 11. www.justice.gov/opa/pr/volkswagen-ag-
    agrees-plead-guilty-and-pay-43-billion-criminal-and-civil-penalties-six.
17. Electrify America (2022). National Annual Report Summary 2021. https://media
    .electrifyamerica.com/assets/documents/original/869-2021AnnualReport
    SummaryEPAvF.pdf.

18. *Wall Street Journal* (2022). Volkswagen Sells Stake in Electrify America to Siemens. June 28. www.wsj.com/articles/volkswagen-sells-stake-in-electrify-america-to-siemens-11656424395.

19. Detroit Free Press (2022). GM, Partners to Build 2,000 EV Chargers at Nearly 500 Pilot Flying J Travel Centers. July 14. www.freep.com/story/money/cars/general-motors/2022/07/14/gm-electric-vehicle-charging-stations-pilot-travel-centers-ev-go/10058051002.

20. Cision PR Newswire (2022). GM and Pilot Company to Build Out Coast-to-Coast EV Fast Charging Network. www.prnewswire.com/news-releases/gm-and-pilot-company-to-build-out-coast-to-coast-ev-fast-charging-network-301586678.html.

21. Ford (2022). What is the BlueOval™ Charge Network for Ford Electric Vehicles? www.ford.com/support/how-tos/fordpass/blueoval-charge-network/what-is-the-blueoval-charge-network-for-electric-vehicles.

22. E&E News (2022). EV Charging Stations Are Annoying. Ford Wants to Fix Them. January 4. www.eenews.net/articles/ev-charging-stations-are-annoying-ford-wants-to-fix-them.

7

Legacy Energy Transitions

> Going forward, the foundation's endowment will not invest in any
> fossil-fuel-related industries.
>
> *Darren Walker, president of the Ford Foundation, October 18, 2021,*
> *announcing that one of the world's largest private foundations would*
> *divest from fossil fuels [1]*

7.1 Legacy Energy

The transition to a net-zero-carbon economy is completely contingent on
decoupling from fossil fuel consumption that has seen incredible growth in
consumption since the beginnings of the Industrial Revolution. It was further
exasperated by global population growth and the expansion of the global
middle class, as presented in Figure 7.1.

It is important to understand how each of these fossil fuel energy sources is
used. In 2021, the United States consumed 97.3 quadrillion[1] British thermal
units (Btu) [3]. A Btu it is defined as the amount of heat required to raise the
temperature of one pound of water by 1°F [4]. To contextualize 1 Btu, think of it
as the energy of a single match burned down that you might use in the kitchen or
camping to start a fire [5]. While this is a lot of energy, China consumed almost
twice as much in 2021, the majority of which were fossil fuels [6].

As presented in Figure 7.2, petroleum represented the largest source of
energy consumed in the United States with almost 70 percent being deployed
for transportation and only 1 percent for electricity. Natural gas is more
versatile and is primarily split between industrial use (40 percent) and

---

[1] Quadrillion is a number equal to 1 followed by fifteen zeros.

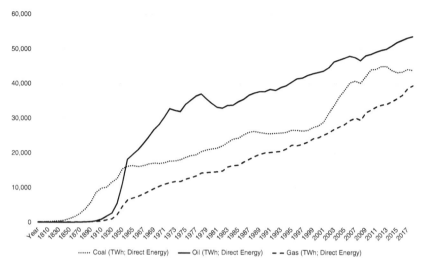

Figure 7.1 Global fossil fuel consumption, 1800–2017, by fossil fuel source, measured in terawatt-hours (TWh) [2].

electricity (32 percent). Fifty-nine percent of renewables is used for electricity while coal at 90 percent and nuclear (100 percent) feed electricity generation.

As presented, industrial uses include agriculture such as herbicides and pesticides, mining including both oil and gas extraction, and combined-heat-and-power (CHP) generators used for creating electricity and construction. Petroleum products include aviation gasoline, motor gasoline, jet fuel, kerosene, distillate fuel oil, residual fuel oil, petrochemical feedstocks, special naphthas, lubricants, waxes, petroleum coke, asphalt, road oil, still gas, and miscellaneous products and excludes biofuels blended with petroleum products. Petroleum products are obtained from the processing of crude oil, natural gas, and other hydrocarbon compounds.

Electricity shows both retail sales, which is the amount of electricity sold to customers and not re-sale, and electrical system energy loses, the amount of energy lost during the generation, transmission, and distribution of electricity, including plant and uses that are unaccounted for. Electrical system energy losses are calculated as the difference between total primary consumption by the electric power sector and the total energy content of electricity retail sales. Generally, losses most frequently happen in the generation phase at power plants as a thermodynamically necessary feature of steam-electric and combustion (gas) turbines as well as transmission and distribution of electricity from power plants to end-use consumers [3].

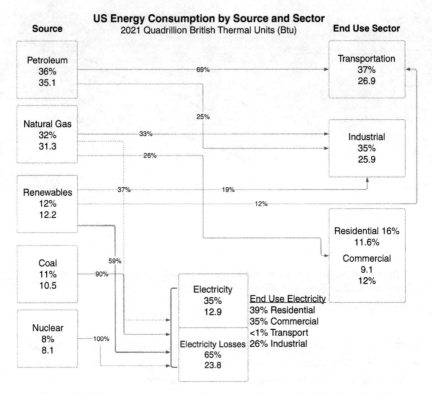

Figure 7.2 US energy consumption by source and sector for 2021 showing only primary uses. Adapted from US Energy Information Agency monthly energy review [3].

In this chapter we will explore the historical use of oil, coal, and natural gas and how the net-zero-carbon and sustainability transitions will impact their future.

7.2 Oil

An abrupt transition to renewable energy will cause society to pay a high price.

Darren Woods, chief executive officer of Exxon Mobile,
during a CNBC interview in 2022 [7]

As was presented in Chapter 3, the fossil fuel energy sector is the major contributor of greenhouse gas emissions and the impacts that follow. In some ways our current climate crisis origins can be traced back to a group of drillers near the town of Beaumont in southeast Texas, who discovered on a salt dome formation on January 10, 1901 the first producing oil field, which marked the birth of the modern petroleum industry.

The Gladys City Oil, Gas, and Manufacturing Company, formed in August 1892, began exploration on the site but on that January day the mud began bubbling, and after several minutes of quiet, mud, then gas, then oil spurted out to a height over 100 feet high and from a depth of 1,139 feet. Ten days later the well was capped and produced an estimated 100,000 barrels a day. Within a year, more than 1,500 oil companies had been chartered, and oil became the dominant fuel of the twentieth century and an integral part of the Industrial Revolution and the American economy [8, 9].

The companies who provide us with these fossil fuels comprise some of the largest public corporations, including Exxon Mobil (US), BP (UK), Total Energies (France), Chevron (US), Marathon (US), and Shell (UK) [10]. In 2018, prior to COVID-19, the oil and natural gas industry in the United States supported 10.3 million jobs and nearly 8 percent of the nation's gross domestic product (GDP) [11]. And while most of the public and non-governmental organization (NGO) focus has been on these public corporations, it is actually the nationally owned oil companies (NOCS)[2] that have the biggest impacts and that possess some of the greatest risks moving forward in large measure because of the lack of pressures placed upon them and their unsustainable economic impact on these resource-dependent countries.

For example, the petroleum sector in Saudi Arabia[3] accounts for approximately 45 percent of the Kingdom's GDP and 90 percent of export earnings. Other fossil fuel countries are equally dependent, such as Iraq, Venezuela, Kuwait, Qatar, and Nigeria [12]. More recently, attention has been directed toward Russia's economy before and after its invasion of Ukraine. Russia, too, is heavily energy dependent. Russian exports[4] of energy in 2021 (primarily crude oil and oil products) accounted for almost 50 percent of total exports, equating to 14 percent of the Russian GDP [13].

Most of these resource-dependent economies are home to the NOCS, which produce three-fifths of the world's crude oil and half of the world's natural gas as compared to just over a tenth by large publicly traded international oil firms.[5]

---

[2] Nationally owned oil companies include Qatar Energy, ADNOC (United Arab Emirates), Saudi Aramco, Rosneft (Russia), Gazprom (Russia), China National Petroleum Corporation, Kuwait Petroleum Corporation, Petroleos de Venezuela, Nigerian National Petroleum Corporation, and National Iranian Oil Company.
[3] 2016 report. [4] The total impact is higher when considering domestic use of oil and natural gas.
[5] The rest is from independent companies.

Table 7.1 *Top ten consuming and producing oil countries in 2021 [17]*

Top 10 Largest Oil-Consuming Countries in 2021		
Country	Million Barrels Per Day	Share of the World Total
United States	20.54	20%
China	14.01	14%
India	4.92	5%
Japan	3.74	4%
Russia	3.70	4%
Saudi Arabia	3.18	3%
Brazil	3.14	3%
Canada	2.63	3%
South Korea	2.60	3%
Germany	2.35	2%
Total top 10	60.81	61%
World total	100.23	
Top 10 Largest Oil-Producing Countries in 2021		
Country	Million Barrels Per Day	Share of the World Total
United States	18.88	20%
Saudi Arabia	10.84	11%
Russia	10.78	11%
Canada	5.54	6%
China	4.99	5%
Iraq	4.15	4%
United Arab Emirates	3.79	4%
Brazil	3.69	4%
Iran	3.46	4%
Kuwait	2.72	3%
Total top 10	68.82	72%
World total	95.57	

The NOCS possess two-thirds of the global reserves of discovered oil and natural gas [14].

In 2017 China became the world's largest importer of oil, importing 11.8 million barrels per day as compared to the United States at 9.1 million barrels per day [15]. The two top suppliers of oil to China are Saudi Arabia (17.4 percent) and Russia ($35.8 billion – 15.6 percent) [16]. While China imports the most oil, the United States remains the world's largest consumer of oil, as presented in Table 7.1, showing the world's ten largest consuming countries and producers of oil in 2021.

7.2.1 A Barrel of Oil

A barrel of crude oil is measured in gallons – specifically, 42 gallons. While many might think all of that goes to produce transportation fuels, this would be wrong. About 19.2 gallons or 42.7 percent of a barrel is refined to produce motor gasoline. Another 12.3 gallons or 27.4 percent is used to produce diesel fuel. Jet fuel takes up another 5.8 percent and heavy fuels such as those used by cargo ships come from 2.25 gallons or 5 percent [18].

Asphalt, which we use for our roads, consumes about 4 percent of the crude, while light fuel, which many use in their homes to produce heat, uses about 1.3 gallons. Two percent or 0.9 gallons are hydrocarbons that provide propane and butane, which is essential to many of our rural communities that are not connected to power grids or natural gas pipelines [19]. Finally, a little over 10 percent of the crude from that 42-gallon barrel of oil is used as a petrochemical feedstock, which we use in so many products spanning paints, pens, and consumer goods products. Petrochemicals are also used for our health as they are part of what is used to manufacture analgesics, antihistamines, antibiotics, antibacterials, rectal suppositories, cough syrups, lubricants, creams, ointments, salves, and many gels, and those petroleum-based pro-cessed plastics are used in heart valves and other medical devices and equip-ment [20, 21].

7.2.2 Oil Transitions

There is no consensus on the exact timing of the oil peak but almost all energy companies agree that the industry is facing a fall-off on global demand, with some indicating that the peak may have recently been achieved and demand will continue to erode. In its 2020 annual report, BP anticipates a high penetra-tion of electric vehicles (EVs). By 2050, they predict that EVs will account for between 80 and 85 percent of the stock of passenger cars in a rapid and net-zero scenario and for light- and medium-duty trucks 70–80 percent in a rapid and net-zero scenario [22]. And while property continues to increase the global middle class, thus driving short-term increased demand for oil, BP states in their 2020 annual report:

> The structure of energy demand is likely to change over time: declining role of fossil fuels, offset by an increasing share of renewable energy and a growing role for electricity. These changes underpin core beliefs about how the structure of energy demand may change. A transition to a lower carbon energy system is likely to lead to fundamental restructuring of the global energy system, with a more diverse energy mix, greater consumer choice, more localized energy markets, and increasing levels of integration and competition. These changes underpin core beliefs about how the

global energy system may restructure in a low-carbon transition. Demand for oil falls over the next 30 years. The scale and pace of this decline is driven by the increasing efficiency and electrification of road transportation. The outlook for natural gas is more resilient than for oil, underpinned by the role of natural gas in supporting fast growing developing economies as they decarbonized and reduce their reliance on coal, and as a source of near-zero carbon energy when combined with carbon capture use and storage (CCUS). [22]

However, exactly when oil demand will significantly decline depends on variables such as the economic outlook for the forecasted period, climate policies, population growth, the penetration rate of EVs, energy efficiency gains, carbon prices, and the rate of deployment of renewable energy sources.

7.3 Natural Gas

We must become independent from Russian oil, coal and gas. We simply cannot rely on a supplier who explicitly threatens us. We need to act now to mitigate the impact of rising energy prices, diversify our gas supply for next winter and accelerate the clean energy transition. The quicker we switch to renewables and hydrogen, combined with more energy effi-ciency, the quicker we will be truly independent and master our energy system.

Ursula von der Leyen, European Commission president, 2022 [23]

You cannot discuss oil without mentioning natural gas. First, natural gas deposits are often located near oil deposits. And like oil, natural gas is described as a fossil fuel. However, many, including governmental agencies around the world, consider natural gas as a transitional energy source. This is because natural gas has lower greenhouse gas emissions than coal, so it can assist governments' transitions away from coal to renewables while acting as an interim energy source. Second, it can be used to scale up hydrogen as a cleaner energy source [24, 25]. The growth of natural gas in the United States is attributable to horizontal drilling technology development and hydraulic fracturing techniques in shale since 2005 [26].

While oil is primarily a transportation energy source, thus why EVs play an essential role in a net-zero-carbon transition, natural gas is primarily an electric power energy source used in the current and near-term to transition away from coal. According to the Energy Information Agency (EIA), in 2021 in the United States 30.28 trillion cubic feet (Tcf) of natural gas was consumed, the equiva-lent of about 31.35 quadrillion British thermal units (quads) and 32 percent of US total energy consumption as follows [26].

- Electric power (37 percent) 11.27 Tcf, which provided about 32 percent of the US electric power sector's primary energy consumption.
- Industrial use (33 percent) 10.04 Tcf, which is used for process heating and as a raw material or feedstock to produce chemicals, fertilizer, and hydrogen. Texas consumes the largest share in the United States at 15.2 percent, followed by California (6.8 percent) and Louisiana (6 percent).
- Residential (15 percent) 4.65 Tcf, which is used for heating and cooking primarily.
- Commercial (11 percent) 3.26 Tcf, used for heating and refrigeration as well as cooking and so on.
- Transportation (3 percent) 1.05 Tcf, such as compressed natural gas found in bus fleets.

In 2019, the United States was the world's largest producer of energy from natural gas at 35.18 (quad) quadrillion Btu followed by Russia at 25.71 quad; third was Iran at 8.86 quad [27]. The largest natural gas reserves in 2020 were [28]:

- Russia: 1,341 trillion cubic feet or 19 percent of the world's total reserves
- Iran: 1,131 trillion cubic feet or 16 percent of the world's total reserves
- Qatar: 872 trillion cubic feet or 12 percent of the world's total reserves
- Turkmenistan: 688 trillion cubic feet or 9.8 percent of the world's total reserves
- United States: 455 trillion cubic feet or 6.5 percent of the world's total reserves

While not having the largest reserves, the United States boasts some of the best technological advances and capital investments so that in less than a decade, the USA went from projections of energy shortages to being the largest producer of oil and natural gas in the world.[6] In part because of the invasion of Ukraine by Russia, the United States became the world's largest exporter of liquified natural gas (LNG) in the first half of 2022, exporting on average 11.2 billion cubic feet per day (Bcf/d) [29, 30]. Of course, none of this would have occurred in part because of US policy. In 1975, following the 1973 Arab oil embargo, the US Congress passed legislation to largely prohibit the export of oil as "consistent with the national interest," although a few broad exemptions, like exports to Canada, were allowed to protect against very high energy costs that resulted from the embargo [31].

---

[6] The USA surpassed Russia in 2011 to become the world's largest producer of natural gas and surpassed Saudi Arabia in 2018 to become the world's largest producer of petroleum per the US EIA, August 20, 2019, Energy Today.

However, in 2015, Congressional leaders agreed to remove the ban in large part because of the rapid increase in US oil and natural gas production. In a bipartisan compromise, rare in today's climate, the Senate voted 65–33 and the House of Representatives voted 316–113. The legislation approved lifting the ban and providing five-year extensions of tax breaks to boost renewable energy development as part of a $1.8 trillion government spending and tax relief bill that President Barack Obama quickly signed into law [32, 33].

7.3.1 Natural Gas Transitions

In 2021, congressional democrats including senators Markey (D-MA), Merkley (D-OR), Wyden (D-OR), and Warren (D-MA), along with independent senator Sanders (I-VT), introduced a legislative bill called Block All New (BAN) Oil Exports Act to reinstate the ban on exporting American crude oil and natural gas in an effort to address climate change [34]. Given the essential and humanitarian needs of those in Europe who face natural gas scarcity as Russia reduces exports resulting from the invasion of Ukraine, it is highly unlikely this legislation will advance.

More broadly, natural gas will increase in demand in large part due to economics and climate change policies. The European Union, which has committed to carbon neutrality by 2050 and reductions of greenhouse gas emissions by 55 percent by 2030, has formally adopted natural gas and some forms of nuclear as "sustainable sources of energy" in general[7] [35]. In large measure this is because natural gas is relatively clean burning as compared to coal. According to the EIA [36], approximately 117 pounds of CO_2 are produced per million British thermal units (MMBtu) equivalent of natural gas compared with more than 200 pounds of CO_2 per MMBtu of coal.

While domestic and inter-land distribution of natural gas is effective through pipelines, non-land transportation, which is what is required if the United States is to further support Europe through exports, has significant hurdles. First, LNG is highly flammable and is shipped at negative 260°F condensed into a liquid. Offloading of ships at ports is risky and requires significant safety precautions. Newer tanker ships generally have double hulls, separated by six feet of seawater, and protect four gas membranes (i.e., tanks) [37].

In 2006, there were five LNG terminals in the United States [38], all designed to import LNG, with a capacity of around 4 billion cubic feet per day. As of 2022, there are eight operating LNG export terminals in the United States, with three currently under construction, twelve approved by the

---

[7] Generally for use in generating electricity as well as heating and cooling.

Federal Energy Regulatory Commission but not under construction, and nine projects with pending applications or in pre-filing [39]. Further, LNG shipping is usually done through a long-term contract, not on a spot-business such as the quick pivot to Europe in 2022. The government through the US Department of Energy Office of Fossil Energy has also been required to grant authority to US companies to export to countries that do not have free trade agreements with the USA[8] [40].

Once a supplier obtains approval and can transport the LNG, they need a terminal and there are bottlenecks. There have been at least eight reported shipborne LNG terminals known as floating storage and regasification units, or FSRUs, announced over the past three months from the Netherlands to Germany and Estonia. And even though their installation can be fairly rapid, they have to be connected to existing grids and backed up by agreements for round-the-clock supply. And some countries lack the port infrastructure, such as Hungary and Bulgaria [41].

7.4 Coal

> Coal is the single largest source of global carbon emissions, and
> this year's historically high level of coal power generation is a worrying
> sign of how far off track the world is in its efforts to put emissions into
> decline towards net zero.
>
> *Fatih Birol, executive director at the International Energy*
> *Agency, 2021 [42]*

Coal is the oldest form of non-renewable energy, with archeologists having found evidence that it was used between 100 and 2000 AD in England by the Romans. James Watt famously used coal to produce steam power for engines that accelerated the Industrial Revolution and heavy dependence on coal. Today, coal remains an abundant non-renewable energy source and the United States has more coal reserves than any other country in the world, containing one-fourth of the world's total reserves [43, 44].

As presented in Table 7.2, China continues to be the leading coal-consuming country. In fact, while other industrialized countries showed decreased consumption of coal between 2010 and 2021, China increased its consumption by 18.3 percent. And this trend is not expected to slow. China planned to build

---

[8] The US International Trade Administration indicates that the USA currently has fourteen free trade agreements with twenty countries, but no European Union countries have a free trade agreement with the USA. See www.trade.gov/free-trade-agreements.

Table 7.2 *Top ten coal-consuming countries in 2010 and 2021 and the percentage in change of consumption [48]*

Country	2021 Amount in Mt	2010 Amount in Mt	Percentage Change 2010 to 2021
China	4,102	3,350	18.3%
India	1,024	684	33.2%
United States	497	954	−92.0%
Russia	214	212	0.9%
South Africa	188	193	−2.7%
Japan	182	184	−1.1%
Germany	164	232	−41.5%
Indonesia	138	67	51.4%
Turkey	124	95	23.4%
South Korea	117	120	−2.6%
Poland	112	134	−19.6%
Australia	92	133	−44.6%

forty-three new coal-fired power plants and eighteen new blast furnaces in 2021 and is building more than half of the world's new coal power plants, with more than 52 percent of the 176 gigawatts of coal capacity under construction in 2021 [45, 46]. Driven by fast-growing electricity demand and the resilience of heavy industry, China's power generation, including district heating, accounts for one-third of global coal consumption. China's overall coal use is more than half of the global total [47].

Consumption patterns are correlating to coal production patterns. China in 2024 will be producing 50 percent or more of all the coal being produced in the world. The next closest is India, with a growing economy and population at 12 percent, as presented in Table 7.3 [47].

The top three coal exporters in the world in 2020 were (1) Indonesia, exporting 405 Mt; (2) Australia, 390 Mt; and (3) Russia, 212 Mt [48]. In the United States the Powder River Basin, which is located in Wyoming, produces more than 40 percent of American coal. China and India combined in 2021 to represent 28.17 million short tons (India 15.36 and China 12.81) or 33 percent of the total US exports of coal [49].

7.4.1 Coal Transitions

However, as has been presented, coal production and consumption in the United States has precipitously dropped. But not, as some argue, because of direct climate commitment actions. Rather, utilities have realized the cost

Table 7.3 *World coal production in 2021 and 2024 projections [47]*

Location	Coal Production (2021)	2024 Projections		Change (2021–2024)
		Coal Production	Share	
China	3,925 Mt	3,982 Mt	50%	+57 Mt
India	793 Mt	955 Mt	12%	+162 Mt
Indonesia	576 Mt	570 Mt	7%	(−) 6 Mt
United States	528 Mt	484 Mt	6%	(−) 44 Mt
Australia	470 Mt	477 Mt	6%	+7 Mt
Russia	429 Mt	445 Mt	5%	+ 16 Mt
European Union	329 Mt	247 Mt	3%	(−) 82 Mt
Rest of the world	839 Mt	855 Mt	11%	+ 16 Mt

efficiencies of building and operating natural gas power plants as well as lower costs from renewables, as will be discussed in Section 7.5. The impacts have been significant. More than half of the US coal mines operating since 2008 have closed, from 1,435 coal mines in 2008 to 671 in 2017 [50].

7.5 Discussion

There are strong market signals that oil as a primary energy source primarily used for transportation is in peril in the longer term. The industry is pinning much of its hopes on petrochemical growth, especially plastics[9] [51]. Plastics represent a small percentage of oil and natural gas demand around the world [52] and growing public and private policies are rapidly moving away from plastics. Just one example is the Coca-Cola company, which, like Pepsi and Nestlé, who are some the largest consumers of plastics for their packaging, has repeatedly been the target of NGOs and named top plastic polluters as published in major media outlets, garnering consumer and retailer attention [53, 54]. However, these brands are taking steps, as are other sectors, to reduce or eliminate plastics. As this book was being written, Coca-Cola announced the deployment of a paperboard packaging system to replace plastic ring-holders for multipacks as it also continues to move toward recycled and plant-based plastic bottles [55]. More than ninety countries have established (or have imminent plans to establish) either bans or fees on single-use plastic bags or other products [56]. These trends will be in direct competition with the oil industries' stated growth of plastics through 2040.

[9] See Chapter 9.

Natural gas will likely to continue to play an important role in the net-zero-carbon transition as a transitional and lower CO_2-eq and lower-cost energy source as compared to coal. Both of these trends are positive to meet climate change reduction targets. However, as stated by the International Energy Agency [48] in 2022,

> the evidence indicates a widening gap between political ambitions and targets on one side and the realities of the current energy system on the other. This disconnect has two clear implications: climate targets are getting further out of reach, and energy security is at risk because, while investments in fossil fuels are shrinking, funding for clean energy and technologies is not expanding quickly enough. This should be concerning not only for policymakers and industry, but all stakeholders.

In the next few chapters, we will explore whether progress on renewable energy and biobased energy transitions will be large enough and quick enough.

References

1. US News (2021). Ford Foundation to Divest Millions from Fossil Fuels. October 18. www.usnews.com/news/us/articles/2021-10-18/ford-foundation-to-divest-millions-from-fossil-fuels.
2. H. Ritchie, M. Roser, and P. Rosado (2020). Energy. https://ourworldindata.org/energy.
3. Energy Information Agency (2022). Monthly Energy Review. July 26. www.eia.gov/energyexplained/us-energy-facts/images/consumption-by-source-and-sector.pdf.
4. Energy Information Agency (2022). Units and Calculators Explained. www.eia.gov/energyexplained/units-and-calculators/british-thermal-units.php.
5. Energy Vanguard (2016). Heat Is a BTU-tiful Thing. February 8. www.energyvanguard.com/blog/heat-is-a-btu-tiful-thing.
6. Statista (2022). Primary Energy Consumption Worldwide in 2021, by Country. July 5. www.statista.com/statistics/263455/primary-energy-consumption-of-selected-countries/#:~:text=China%20is%20the%20largest%20consumer,such%20as%20oil%20and%20coal.
7. CNBC (2022). Exxon Mobil CEO Cautions against an Abrupt Energy Transition, Warning Underinvestment Leads to High Gas Prices. June 26. www.cnbc.com/2022/06/26/exxon-mobil-ceo-darren-woods-on-energy-transition-gas-prices.html.
8. Lamar University (n.d.). Spindletop Gladys City Boomtown. www.lamar.edu/spindletop-gladys-city/spindletop-history.html.
9. History (2018). Oil Industry. www.history.com/topics/industrial-revolution/oil-industry.
10. Offshore Technology (2021). Top 10 Highest-Earning Oil Companies in 2021. July 27. www.offshore-technology.com/analysis/top-10-highest-earning-oil-gas-companies-2021-2020.

11. American Petroleum Institute (2018). Oil and Natural Gas: Supporting the Economy, Creating Jobs, Driving America Forward. www.api.org/-/media/Files/Policy/Taxes/DM2018-086_API_Fair_Share_OnePager_FIN3.pdf.

12. World Economic Forum (2016). Which Economies Are Most Reliant on Oil? www.weforum.org/agenda/2016/05/which-economies-are-most-reliant-on-oil.

13. OENB (2022). The Russian Economy and World Trade in Energy: Dependence of Russia Larger Than Dependence on Russia. www.oenb.at/dam/jcr:c7d95c7b-c469-4834-ac94-98554c5e6f5f/2022-04-15-russian-economy-and-world-trade-in-energy.pdf.

14. *The Economist* (2022). Nationally Determined Contributors. July 30.

15. H. Reale, E. Bingham, and K. Greenberg (2020). Where Does China Get Its Oil? Columbia University Energy Policy. www.energypolicy.columbia.edu/sites/default/files/file-uploads/Where%20Does%20China%20Get%20Its%20Oil_%20-%20The%20Wire%20China.pdf.

16. World's Top Exports (2022). Top 15 Crude Oil Suppliers to China. www.worldstopexports.com/top-15-crude-oil-suppliers-to-china.

17. Energy Information Agency (2022). What Countries Are the Top Producers and Consumers of Oil? www.eia.gov/tools/faqs/faq.php?id=709&t=6.

18. Canadian Association of Petroleum Producers (2022). Uses for Oil. www.capp.ca/oil/uses-for-oil.

19. Energy Information Agency (2011). Beyond Natural Gas Electricity: More Than 10% of US Homes Use Heating Oil or Propane. www.eia.gov/todayinenergy/detail.php?id=4070#:~:text=Across%20the%20country%2C%20propane%20use,share%20is%20greater%20than%2090%25.

20. J. Hess, D. Bednarz, J. Bae, and J. Pierce (2011). Petroleum and Health Care: Evaluating and Managing Health Care's Vulnerability to Petroleum Supply Shifts. *American Journal of Public Health*, 101(9): 1568–1579. https://doi.org/10.2105/AJPH.2011.300233.

21. D. Bednarz (2022). Medicine after Oil. *Orion*. https://orionmagazine.org/article/medicine-after-oil/#:~:text=Petrochemicals%20are%20used%20to%20manufactureand%20other%20esoteric%20medical%20equipment.

22. BP (2020). Energy Outlook 2020 Edition. www.bp.com/content/dam/bp/business-sites/en/global/corporate/pdfs/energy-economics/energy-outlook/bp-energy-outlook-2020.pdf.

23. European Union (2022). REPowerEU: Joint European Action for More Affordable, Secure and Sustainable Energy. Press Release, March 8. https://ec.europa.eu/commission/presscorner/detail/en/IP_22_1511.

24. International Energy Forum (2021). 4 Reasons Natural Gas Is a Critical Part of the Energy Transition. September 20. www.ief.org/news/4-reasons-natural-gas-is-a-critical-part-of-the-energy-transition#:~:text=Natural%20gas%20is%20also%20frequently,a%20future%20climate%2Dneutral%20economy.

25. International Energy Agency (2019). The Role of Gas in Today's Energy Transitions. www.iea.org/reports/the-role-of-gas-in-todays-energy-transitions.

26. Energy Information Agency (2022). Natural Gas Explained. www.eia.gov/energyexplained/natural-gas/use-of-natural-gas.php#:~:text=Most%20U.S.%20natural%20gas%20use,other%20uses%20for%20natural%20gas.&text=The%

20electric%20power%20sector%20usesand%20produce%20useful%20thermal%20output.

27. Energy Information Agency (n.d.). Total Energy Production from Natural Gas, 2019. www.eia.gov/international/rankings/country/USA?pid=4413&aid=1&f=A&y=01%2F01%2F2019&u=0&v=none&pa=287.

28. NS Energy. Profiling the Top Five Countries with the Biggest Natural Gas Reserves. March 15. www.nsenergybusiness.com/features/biggest-natural-gas-reserves-countries/#:~:text=1.,of%20the%20world's%20total%20reserves.

29. Reuters (2022). U.S. Becomes Top LNG Exporter in the First Half of 2022l. July 25. www.reuters.com/business/energy/us-becomes-top-lng-exporter-first-half-2022-eia-2022-07-25.

30. Energy Information Agency (2022). Today in Energy. July 25. www.eia.gov/todayinenergy/detail.php?id=53159

31. *New York Times* (2015). Oil Industry Gaining in Push for the Repeal of U.S. Ban on Petroleum Exports. October 5. www.nytimes.com/2015/10/06/business/energy-environment/oil-industry-gaining-in-push-for-repeal-of-us-ban-on-petroleum-exports.html.

32. Reuters (2015). Congress Kills U.S. Oil Export Ban, Boosts Solar, Wind Power. December 18. www.reuters.com/article/us-usa-fiscal-oil/congress-kills-u-s-oil-export-ban-boosts-solar-wind-power-idUSKBN0U121U2015121.

33. *Wall Street Journal* (2015). Congressional Leaders Agree to Lift 40-Year Ban on Oil Exports. December 16. www.wsj.com/articles/congressional-leaders-agree-to-lift-40-year-ban-on-oil-exports-1450242995.

34. Senator Markey (2021). Proposed Bill for the 117th Congress. www.markey.senate.gov/imo/media/doc/ban_oil_exports.pdf.

35. CNBC (2022). Europe Will Count Natural Gas and Nuclear As Green Energy in Some Circumstances. July 6. www.cnbc.com/2022/07/06/europe-natural-gas-nuclear-are-green-energy-in-some-circumstances-.html.

36. Energy Information Agency (2021). Natural Gas Explained. www.eia.gov/energyexplained/natural-gas/natural-gas-and-the-environment.php.

37. Energy Information Agency (n.d.). Total Energy Production from Natural Gas, 2019. www.eia.gov/international/rankings/country/USA?pid=4413&aid=1&f=A&y=01%2F01%2F2019&u=0&v=none&pa=287.

38. NS Energy. Profiling the Top Five Countries with the Biggest Natural Gas Reserves. March 15. www.nsenergybusiness.com/features/biggest-natural-gas-reserves-countries/#:~:text=1.,of%20the%20world's%20total%20reserves.

39. Reuters (2022). U.S. Becomes Top LNG Exporter in the First Half of 2022. July 25. www.reuters.com/business/energy/us-becomes-top-lng-exporter-first-half-2022-eia-2022-07-25.

40. Energy Information Agency (2022). Today in Energy. July 25. www.eia.gov/todayinenergy/detail.php?id=53159.

41. Bloomberg (2022). Europe's Plan to Replace Russian Gas Stumbles on LNG Bottlenecks. May 23. Anna Shiryaevskaya. www.bloomberg.com/news/articles/2022-05-23/europe-s-plan-to-replace-russian-gas-stumbles-on-lng-bottlenecks.

42. International Energy Agency (2021). Coal Power's Sharp Rebound Is Taking It to a New Record in 2021, Threatening Net Zero Goals. Press Release, December 17.

www.iea.org/news/coal-power-s-sharp-rebound-is-taking-it-to-a-new-record-in-2021-threatening-net-zero-goals.

43. *Guardian* (2015). James Watt and the Sabbath Stroll That Created the Industrial Revolution. May 29. www.theguardian.com/technology/2015/may/29/james-watt-sabbath-day-fossil-fuel-revolution-condenser.

44. US Department of Energy (n.d.). Fossil Energy Study Guide. www.energy.gov/sites/prod/files/ElemCoalStudyguide.pdf.

45. *Time* (2021). China Is Planning to Build 43 New Coal-Fired Power Plants. Can It Still Keep Its Promise to Cut Emissions? Amy Gunia. August 20. https://time.com/6090732/china-coal-power-plants-emissions.

46. New Scientist (2022). China Is Building More Than Half of the World's New Coal Power Plants. Adam Vaughan. April 26. www.newscientist.com/article/2317274-china-is-building-more-than-half-of-the-worlds-new-coal-power-plants.

47. International Energy Agency (2021), Coal 2021. www.iea.org/reports/coal–2021.

48. International Energy Agency (2021). Coal Information: Overview. www.iea.org/reports/coal-information-overview.

49. Energy Information Agency (2022). How Much Coal Does the United States Export and to Where? www.eia.gov/tools/faqs/faq.php?id=66&t=2.

50. CNBC (2022). How the Fossil Fuel Industry Is Pushing Plastics on the World. January 29. www.cnbc.com/2022/01/29/how-the-fossil-fuel-industry-is-pushing-plastics-on-the-world-.html.

51. *LA Times* (2019). Oil Giants Bet Their Future on Plastic – Just in Time for a Plastic-Trash Crackdown. June 6. www.latimes.com/business/la-fi-oil-plastic-petroleum-environment-20190606-story.html.

52. Vox (2020). Big Oil's Hopes Are Pinned on Plastics. It Won't End Well. October 28. www.vox.com/energy-and-environment/21419505/oil-gas-price-plastics-peak-climate-change.

53. *Guardian* (2020). Coca-Cola, Pepsi and Nestle Named Top Plastic Polluters for Third Year in a Row. December 7. www.theguardian.com/environment/2020/dec/07/coca-cola-pepsi-and-nestle-named-top-plastic-polluters-for-third-year-in-a-row.

54. Reuters (2022). Coca-Cola, Criticized for Plastic Pollution, Pledges 25% Reusable Packaging. February 15. www.reuters.com/business/sustainable-business/coca-cola-criticized-plastic-pollution-pledges-25-reusable-packaging-2022-02-10.

55. Bevnet (2022). Liberty Coca-Cola Beverages Unveils New Paper Packaging to Replace Plastic Rings, First of Its Kind in the U.S. August 9. www.bevnet.com/news/supplier-news/2022/liberty-coca-cola-beverages-unveils-new-paper-packaging-to-replace-plastic-rings-first-of-its-kind-in-the-u-s.

56. Environmental Health News (2021). The US Falls Behind Most of the World in Plastic Pollution Legislation. www.ehn.org/plastic-pollution-2655191194.html.

8

Renewable Energy Transitions

Breakthrough Energy Catalyst, a private-public fund backed
by Microsoft billionaire Bill Gates, is planning to help invest up to
$15 billion into clean tech projects across the U.S., the U.K. and the
European Union.

CNBC, 2022 [1]

Renewables are set to account for almost 95% of the increase in global
power capacity through 2026, with solar PV alone providing more than
half.

International Energy Agency, 2021 [2]

8.1 Renewables 101

There seems to be more and more importance placed on the role of renewable
energy, especially in our use of electricity, as shown in Figure 8.1.

Let us start with a basic definition of renewable energy. The US Energy
Information Agency defines renewable energy as "energy from sources that are
naturally replenishing but flow-limited; renewable resources are virtually inex-
haustible in duration but limited in the amount of energy that is available per
unit of time" [4]. They list the following as examples:

1. Biomass

   a. Wood and wood waste
   b. Municipal solid waste
   c. Landfill gas and biogas
   d. Biofuels

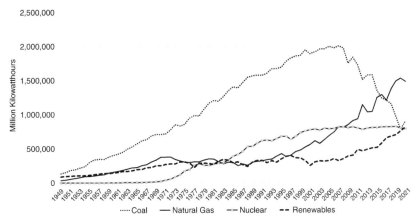

Figure 8.1 Annual US electricity generation from all sectors 1949–2021 in million kilowatt-hours (MkWh) [3].

2. Hydropower
3. Geothermal
4. Wind
5. Solar

Each of these renewable energy sources produces energy with much lower carbon emissions than do fossil fuels such as oil, coal, and natural gas [4]. However, none of these renewable energy sources is carbon neutral or carbon negative for their life cycle without some form of additional technology like carbon sequestration or with carbon offsets. In part this is due to their embedded carbon such as the mineral extraction and manufacturing energy required to produce the technologies to produce energy like photovoltaic cells or wind turbines. Distribution and transportation are yet another reason. Transportation and distribution can also contribute to carbon emissions of renewables. However, and importantly, renewables generally have significantly lower overall greenhouse gas emissions than their fossil fuel counterparts, as presented in Table 8.1.

Given the carbon reduction benefits by these renewable energy sources and what was discussed in Chapter 3, it is clear why there is tremendous global focus on increasing the utilization of renewable energy sources for fuels and electricity to combat climate change. But just how much new renewable energy generation will be required and at how fast a pace? As presented in Figure 8.2, we can see global growth since 2000 and short-term growth projections.

Table 8.1 *Median published life-cycle emissions factors for electricity generation technologies by life-cycle phase (g CO_2-eq/kWh) [5]*

	Generation Technology	One-Time Upstream	Ongoing Combustion	Ongoing Non-combustion	One-Time Downstream	Total Life Cycle
RENEWABLES	Biomass	NR	N/A	NR	NR	52.0
	Photovoltaic	~28	N/A	~10	~5	43.0
	Concentrating solar power	20.0	N/A	10.0	0.53	28.0
	Geothermal	15.0	N/A	6.9	0.12	37.0
	Hydropower	6.2	N/A	1.9	0.004	21.0
	Ocean	NR	N/A	NR	NR	8.0
	Wind	12.0	N/A	0.7	0.34	13.0
STORAGE	Pumped storage hydropower	3.0	N/A	1.8	0.07	7.4
	Lithium-ion battery	32.0	N/A	NR	3.40	33.0
	Hydrogen fuel cell	27.0	N/A	2.5	1.90	38.0

TRANSITION SOURCES	Nuclear	2.0	N/A	12.0	0.70	13.0
	Natural gas	0.8	389.0	71.0	0.02	486.0
NON-RENEWABLE	Oil	NR	NR	NR	NR	840.0
	Coal	<5	1,010.0	10.0	<5	1,001.0

Note: I classify nuclear and natural gas as transitional versus the National Renewable Energy Laboratory, which lists them as non-renewable. This is done in terms of a net-zero-carbon economy transition.

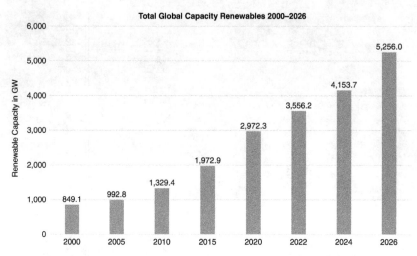

Figure 8.2 Growth of global renewables capacity from 2000 to 2026 with 2026 including additional 455 GW as part of the accelerated case [63].

In May 2021, the International Energy Agency (IEA) released the world's first comprehensive study of what is necessary to transition to a net-zero energy system[1] by 2050, while "ensuring stable and affordable energy supplies, providing universal energy access, and enabling robust economic growth" [6]. Their analysis included underlying policy realities, including that nation-level pledges for net-zero emissions cover around 70 percent of global emissions and lack near-term "policies and measures" and that, at best, current pledges would leave around 22 billion tons of CO_2 emissions around the globe in 2050. Their recommendations and pathway are intended to overcome these gaps as well as to incorporate the realities of anticipate economic growth around the world by 2030, which is determined to be 40 percent larger than 2021 but with 7 percent less energy consumption.

Given these parameters, the IEA places the greatest emphasis on the timeline between 2021 and 2030. Their modeling and analyses resulted in the following recommendations [6]:

1. Scaling up solar and wind rapidly through 2030, reaching annual additions of 630 GW of solar photovoltaics (PV) and 390 GW of wind by 2030, four times the record levels set in 2020.
2. For solar PV, this is equivalent to installing the world's current largest solar park roughly every day.

---

[1] Important to note is that this is for the energy system and not the entire anthropogenic system.

3. Hydropower and nuclear, the two largest sources of low-carbon electricity today, provide an essential foundation for energy transitions.
4. Electric vehicles (EVs) go from around 5 percent of global car sales to more than 60 percent by 2030.

And by 2050 the IEA states:

1. In the net-zero pathway, global energy demand in 2050 is around 8 percent smaller than today, but it serves an economy more than twice as big and a population with 2 billion more people.
2. Instead of fossil fuels, the energy sector is based largely on renewable energy. Two-thirds of total energy supply in 2050 is from wind, solar, bioenergy, geothermal, and hydro energy. Solar becomes the largest source, accounting for one-fifth of energy supplies. Solar PV capacity increases twenty-fold between now and 2050, and wind power eleven-fold.
3. Fossil fuels that account for four-fifths of total energy supply in 2021 decline to slightly over one-fifth by 2050. Fossil fuels that remain in 2050 are used in goods where the carbon is embodied in the product such as plastics, in facilities fitted with carbon capture utilization and storage, and in sectors where low-emissions technology options are scarce.
4. Electricity accounts for almost 50 percent of total energy consumption in 2050. It plays a key role across all sectors – from transport and buildings to industry – and is essential to produce low-emission fuels such as hydrogen. To achieve this, total electricity generation increases over two and a half times between today and 2050.
5. Almost half the reductions come from technologies that are currently at the demonstration or prototype phase. In heavy industry and long-distance transport, the share of emissions reductions from technologies that are still under development today is even higher.
6. The biggest innovation opportunities concern advanced batteries, hydrogen electrolysers, and direct air capture and storage. Together, these three technology areas make vital contributions to the reductions in CO_2 emissions between 2030 and 2050.

8.2 Financing Energy Transitions

If you are someone who pays attention to their retirement investments, you no doubt have had at least some focus on how the race to a net-zero carbon economy is influencing the market and government investments. Prior to the

US Inflation Reduction Act (2022) and the Bipartisan Infrastructure Bill (2021), China was by far the leader in energy transition investments. In 2021, the top ten countries in investment accounted for nearly three-quarters of the global total, as presented in Table 8.2. Relatedly, renewables and EVs drove much of the increase in investment in the energy transition.

The Inflation Reduction Act (IRA)[2] in the United States has various aspects specifically designed to propel the United States into a leading role in the net-zero-carbon economy transition. First, there are incentives, specifically tax incentives, including for renewable energy production, investments in clean energy technology manufacturing and grants and loans for energy transmission projects. Incentives are expanded for certain social justice projects including

Table 8.2 *World's top ten countries investing in the energy transition in 2021 and the change in the top investments from 2020 [7]*

	Country	2021 Energy Transition Investment (US$)	% of World Total
1	China	$266B	35.20%
2	US	$114B	15.10%
3	Germany	$47B	6.20%
4	UK	$3 lB	4.10%
5	France	$27B	3.60%
6	Japan	$26B	3.40%
7	India	$14B	1.90%
8	South Korea	$13B	1.70%
9	Brazil	$12B	1.60%
10	Spain	$11B	1.50%
	Total	$561B	74.30%

	Technology/Sector	Total Investment in 2021 (US$)	% Change from 2020
1	Renewable energy	$365.9B	6.80%
2	Electrified transport	$273.2B	76.70%
3	Electrified heat	$52.7B	10.70%
4	Nuclear	$31.5B	6.10%
5	Sustainable materials	$19.3B	141.30%
6	Energy storage	$7.9B	−6.00%
7	Carbon capture and storage	$2.3B	−23.30%
8	Hydrogen	$2. 0B	33.30%
	Total	$754.8B	26.80%

[2] Signed into law on August 16, 2022 by President Biden.

offering clean energy to low-income communities. A $27 billion Greenhouse Gas Reduction Fund appropriation was made for the development of the first national green bank, similar to what exists in some states such as New York [8] of which 60 percent of the funds must go to disadvantaged communities for projects like solar. States can also have access to $4 billion to provide to rebate programs for homeowners including apartments on energy-saving projects [9]. Additionally, the IRA will provide [10]:

1. $10 billion investment tax credit for new manufacturing facilities that make clean tech such as EVs, wind turbines, and solar.
2. Production tax credits for green-tech manufacturing.
3. $500 million to use the Defense Production Act to accelerate processing of critical minerals for renewables, batteries, EVs, and so on.
4. $2 billion in grants to help automaker facilities transition to clean vehicle production.
5. Up to $20 billion in loans to construct new manufacturing facilities for clean vehicles.

Meanwhile, the $1 Trillion Bipartisan Infrastructure Deal[3] provides [11]:

1. $65 billion to upgrade the electric transmission grid.
2. $3 billion for smart communities technologies.
3. $500 million for five clean energy demonstration projects.
4. $3 billion in grants processing and refining raw products into materials for advanced and another $3 billion to on-shore battery manufacturing and recycling into the US through R&D and demonstration projects.
5. $7.5 billion over five years to build out a national EV charging infrastructure including supporting support building a network of 500,000 EV chargers along highway corridors and within communities.
6. $355 million in grant funding for demonstration and pilot projects for energy storage, advanced reactors, carbon capture technologies, and direct air capture technologies.
7. $500 million grant program over five years for efficiency building codes in public schools, and $120 million to boost energy efficiency in manufacturing and industrial facilities.
8. $3 billion for funding advanced nuclear demonstration projects. The law also authorizes the Department of Energy to implement a $6 billion credit program over five years to subsidize and thereby prevent certain existing nuclear facilities from closing prematurely due to economic factors.

---

[3] Signed into law on November 15, 2021 by President Biden.

9. The Large-Scale Carbon Storage Commercialization program will provide
    $2.5 billion in funding for the development of new or expanded commer-
    cial large-scale carbon sequestration projects and related carbon dioxide
    transport infrastructure, including funding for the feasibility, site charac-
    terization, permitting, and construction phases of development.
10. $1 billion in financial assistance over four years to rural or remote areas for:
    (i) improving cost-effectiveness of energy generation, transmission, or
    distribution systems; (ii) siting or upgrading transmission and distribution
    lines; (iii) reducing greenhouse gas emissions from energy generation by
    rural or remote areas; (iv) providing or modernizing electric generation
    facilities; (v) developing microgrids; and (vi) increasing energy efficiency.

8.3 Comparing Renewables

Cost is one of the most important factors for both institutional users such as
utilities to determine feasibility for implementation. As presented in Figure 8.3,
the price per MWh in 2019 for the levelized cost[4] for on-shore wind was the
least expensive.

However, cost is not the only factor. The capacity factor (Cf) is another
important consideration. The Cf is the ratio of the electrical energy produced by
a generating unit for the period of time considered to the electrical energy that
could have been produced at continuous full power operation during the same
period [13]. In basic terms, capacity factor is how the energy industry measures
the reliability of a power plant because it measures how long a power plant
operates during a specified period of time.

In regard to renewables, consider that the sun does not shine for twenty-four
hours, hence solar has a lower Cf without the addition of battery storage. Offshore
wind offers the highest Cf of all renewables, close to the most efficient gas-fired
power plants with new offshore wind projects delivering capacity factors ranging
from 40 to 50 percent;[5] floating wind projects like Hywind Scotland delivered
a record-breaking average capacity factor of 57 percent in its third year of
operation to March 2020. The daily generation profile for offshore wind also
reflects greater consistency, with around half of the hourly fluctuation typically
seen in solar PV [14].

---

[4] The average total cost of building and operating the energy asset per unit of total electricity
     generated over an assumed lifetime.
[5] Utilizing 5 MW turbines.

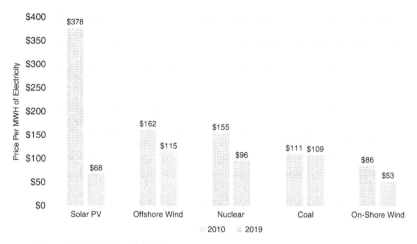

Figure 8.3 Global weighted average of the levelized costs of energy (LCOE) without subsidies, adjusted for inflation [12].

8.4 Solar Energy

Solar panels are also known as photovoltaic panels or systems. Their origins date back to the French physicist Alexandre Edmond Becquerel (1820–1891), who discovered the photovoltaic effect where an electric current with two plates of platinum or gold immersed in an acid, neutral, or alkaline solution are exposed in an uneven way to solar radiation [15]. Albert Einstein in fact was awarded the Nobel Prize in physics in 1921 for his research that showed that the energy of the electrons ejected from a photoelectric plate were dependent not on amplitude (i.e., light intensity) as wave theory predicted, but on frequency, which is the inverse of wavelength. The shorter the wavelength of incident light, the higher the frequency of the light and the more energy possessed by ejected electrons. This knowledge is employed today in the design and manufacturing of solar cells which are sensitive to wavelength and respond better to sunlight in some parts of the spectrum than others [16].

Wavelengths in the infrared spectrum have too little of the energy to produce an electric current in a PV. Ultraviolet wavelengths have too much energy and create wasteful heat, which reduces cell efficiency. A silicon PV cell (preferred designs) absorbs large segments of incident sunlight. It will start to respond with output at approximately 300 nanometers, achieves maximum response at about 700 nanometers, and abruptly falls at 1,100 nanometers (i.e., it works best with photons in the red and near-infrared portion of the spectrum). That is why solar cells have efficiency ranges of 20–30 percent [17, 18]. Since 2000, the United States has seen significant growth in solar electricity generation, as presented in Figure 8.4. In part, this growth can be attributed to two important dynamics. The first is that the costs of PV costs have dramatically fallen by over 90 percent in the last four decades [19]. However, part of the driver for the reduced costs is the increased demand, which in part is the result of states across the country requiring utilities to implement Renewable Portfolio Standards (RPS). As utility companies go before their regulator such as an energy or corporation commission with a formal request to raise how much they charge customers and consumer, these commissions have been requiring the utilities to increase the share of their generated electricity from renewable sources as well as invest in homeowner programs that reduce the demand for electricity, such as new windows, insulation, and lighting.

As an example, in North Carolina, home to Duke Energy, the nation's largest utility company, the state required investor-owned utility companies to supply 12.5 percent of retail electricity sales from eligible renewable energy sources[6]

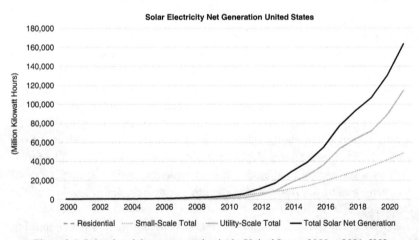

Figure 8.4 Solar electricity net generation in the United States, 2000 to 2021 [22].

---

[6] Eligible energy resources include solar-electric, solar thermal, wind, hydropower up to 10 megawatts (MW), ocean current or wave energy, biomass that uses Best Available Control Technology (BACT) for air emissions, landfill gas, combined heat and power (CHP) using waste heat from renewables, hydrogen derived from renewables, and electricity demand reduction. Up to 25 percent of the requirement may be met through energy efficiency technologies, including CHP systems powered by non-renewable fuels. After 2021, up to 40 percent of the standard may be met through energy efficiency.

by 2021 [20]. Roughly half of the growth in US renewable energy generation since the beginning of the 2000s can be attributed to state renewable energy requirements [21].

There are two primary types of photovoltaic solar panels:

1. Silicon modules and cells
2. Thin-film modules and cells

Crystalline silicon cells and modules, which include both monocrystalline and polycrystalline, are expected to dominate the market. These products are popular due to their high efficiency. In 2022, silicon modules and cells are estimated to account for 66.6 percent of total revenue for the solar panel manufacturing industry. Thin-film modules and cells are manufactured by laying different types of semiconducting material on top of one another in a series of thin layers. Producing large quantities of thin-film modules and cells is much easier than producing silicon products; therefore, their cost is significantly lower, which makes them popular with price-conscious customers. However, their efficiency is also lower than silicon and other types of modules and cells.

8.4.1 Solar Marketplace

In the United States, the domestic solar panel manufacturing industry was significantly impacted by the flood of low-cost imports primarily from China. In response the US Department of Commerce under both the Obama Administration (December 2014) and the Trump Administration (2018) implemented antidumping regulations on China for imports of solar panels and solar cells. This resulted in significant reduction of Chinese imports and expansion of domestic manufacturing [23]. The Biden Administration further ordered the Department of Commerce to investigate if solar manufacturers in Malaysia, Vietnam, Thailand, and Cambodia are trying to circumvent antidumping and countervailing tariffs from China [23, 24]. The domestic industry is expected to be further enhanced because the US Department of Energy announced in July 2022 that $56 million in new funding to expand domestic manufacturing and recycling will be made available [25]. The industry is expected to increase at an annualized rate of 5.6 percent to $5 billion over the five-year period 2022–7, with the major domestic player being First Solar, Inc., which accounts for approximately 21.3 percent; the western United States has the most manufacturing facilities at 41.9 percent of all establishments, followed by the southwest at 16.4 percent [26].

8.5 Wind

Today in the United States, wind is the largest source of renewable electricity generation, providing 9.8 percent of the country's electricity [27]. The origins of wind energy likely started with the harnessing of wind for sailing, but in 200 BC the Chinese began to use windmills to pump water in China, and in Persia and the Middle East they were used for milling grain. Moving forward to the first quarter of the twentieth century, Europe, primarily via Denmark, began to create a decentralized model for electrification. In 1908 there were seventy-two wind generators with a power of between 5 kW and 25 kW [27]. This was all on land but in 1991 the world's first offshore wind farm of eleven turbines (450 kW each) was built off the coast of Vindeby on the Danish island of Lolland [28, 29].

Modern wind turbines, both land-based and ocean-based, generally generate electricity when wind speeds reach 6 to 9 miles per hour (mph); this is known as the cut-in speed. Similarly, these wind turbines will shut down when the wind is blowing too hard, which the industry places at 55 mph or above. This is done to prevent equipment damage. Obviously, the stronger the wind, the more electricity produced by a turbine [27].

In the United States almost all of the installed wind capacity is land-based. The only offshore wind farm in the United States is Block Island Wind Farm with 30 MW installed capacity and 125 GWh annual output. It was developed by Deepwater Wind 3 miles (4.8 km) southeast of Block Island, Rhode Island. It became operational in December 2016 and provides electricity to just 17,000 households [29]. By comparison, the total installed wind capacity in the United States in 2021 was 135,886 MW, which accounted for more than 9 percent of electricity nationwide and over 50 percent in Iowa and South Dakota, and over 30 percent in Kansas, Oklahoma, and North Dakota [30].

In fact, in both 2019 and 2020, project developers in the United States installed more wind-power capacity than any other generating technology. Annual wind turbine capacity additions in the United States set a record in 2020, totaling 14.2 GW and surpassing the previous record of 13.2 GW added in 2012. Much of the investment was as a result of the risk of the expiration of the US production tax credit (PTC) at the end of 2020[7] [31].

---

[7] In December 2020, Congress extended the PTC.

8.5.1 Offshore Wind Primer

While land-based wind is an established and well-known renewable energy source, the dynamic transition will come from the rapid development of offshore wind in the United States as well as globally. Hence, the remaining discussion on wind energy will focus on this dynamic. In his first few months in office, President Biden established a target of 30 GW (30,000 MW) of offshore wind by 2030, enough to meet the demand of 10 million households for a year and avoid 78 million metric tons of CO_2 emissions. The White House estimated that this will bring more than \$12 billion per year in capital investment in projects on both US coasts, with more than 44,000 workers employed in offshore wind by 2030 and nearly 33,000 additional jobs in communities supported by offshore wind activity [32].

The costs for offshore wind varies by the location of the wind farm as well as the type of installation, but the generalized distribution of costs is presented in Figure 8.5, which indicates that four categories account for 80 percent of the

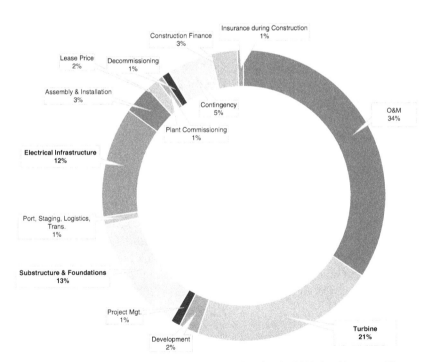

Figure 8.5 Component-level LCOE contribution for the 2019 fixed-bottom off-shore wind reference project operating for twenty-five years [33].

costs, which come from (1) operation and maintenance (O&M) at 34 percent, (2) the turbine at 21 percent, (3) the sub-structure and foundation at 13 percent, and (4) electrical infrastructure at 12 percent [34].

8.5.2 Offshore Wind Expansion

While today there is only 30 MW installed offshore wind in the United States and 35 GW installed offshore wind primarily in Europe and China, the World Bank has identified more than 71,000 GW of technical resource potential available worldwide – nearly ten times the world's current installed electricity capacity [34]. Federal law under the Submerged Lands Act (SLA) of 1953 allows individual states the rights to natural resources of submerged lands from the coastline to no more than 3 nautical miles (5.6 km)[8] into the Atlantic, Pacific, Arctic Oceans, and Gulf of Mexico. Federal water extends out to 200 nautical miles based on President Ronald Reagan's 1983 Presidential Proclamation.[9] The SLA led to the passage of the Outer Continental Shelf Lands Act in 1953 (OCSLA), which authorizes the Secretary of the Interior to lease those lands for mineral development [35].

The first commercial offshore wind project[10] started construction in November 2021, 15 miles from Martha's Vineyard near Cape Cod in Massachusetts. It is designed as an 800 MW wind farm using sixty-two GE Haliade-X turbines to provide electricity to over 400,000 homes and businesses by 2023 [36]. According to the developers, the project will reduce carbon emissions by over 1.6 MMT annually[11] [37, 38].

Yet, this is just the beginning of a rapid transition to the development and operation of offshore wind in the United States. According to the National Renewable Energy Laboratory (NREL) [39], the US offshore wind energy project development and operational pipeline grew to a potential generating capacity of 40,083 MW as of a 13.5 percent growth from 2021, primarily from the addition of eight new lease areas that were auctioned in the Atlantic and two Call Areas that were converted into wind energy areas (WEAs) in California [40]. The market is largely driven by states and policies that aim to procure at least 39,322 MW of offshore wind energy capacity by 2040. In October 2021, the Bureau of Ocean Energy Management (BOEM)[12] announced in its

---

[8] The only exceptions are Texas and the west coast of Florida, where state jurisdiction extends from the coastline to no more than 3 marine leagues (16.2 km) into the Gulf of Mexico.
[9] Presidential Proclamation 5030 signed on March 10, 1983.
[10] Block Island is too small to be considered a commercial wind farm.
[11] Equivalent to approximately 325,000 gasoline cars removed every year.
[12] The BOEM is a unit of the Department of the Interior and is the lead agency in the US to manage the development of US outer continental shelf energy and mineral resources.

"Offshore Wind Leasing Path Forward 2021–2025 plan" [41] that the agency will hold up to seven new offshore WEA lease auctions, including the New York Bight, Carolina Long Bay, Central Atlantic, Gulf of Maine, California, Oregon, and the Gulf of Mexico by 2025 [42].

The BOEM held auctions for six new lease areas in the New York Bight and two lease areas in Carolina Long Bay. In February 2022, BOEM auctioned six lease areas in the New York Bight, which sold for $4.37 billion. The lease area selling prices ranged from a winning bid of $285 million for OCS-A 0544 ($1,637,931 per square kilometer [km^2]) to a winning bid of $1.1 billion for OCS-A 0539 ($2,380,952/$km^2$) [42].

The auction set records for total revenue generated from an offshore energy lease auction in the United States. In May 2022, the two lease areas in the Carolina Long Bay auction sold for a combined total of $315 million, with an average sale price of $707,894/$km^2$. As of May 31, 2022, twenty-four power purchase agreements for offshore wind energy procurement have been signed in the United States [40].

8.5.3 Offshore Wind Offtake Agreements

While lease agreements are important, of equal importance are power offtake commitments. An Offtake Agreement (OTA) is the same as a Power Purchase Agreement (PPA). Globally, both utilities (i.e., power companies) and some large companies seek to source renewable energy directly from project developers. This helps to meet their net-zero-carbon commitments but also provides the opportunity to negotiate a lower long-term cost for their electricity. These types of agreements are referred to as corporate PPAs (CPPAs). A developer to utility agreement is a two-way PPA, while when entered into with a company it is usually a three-way CPPA.

For the project developers, these agreements are critical. With these agreements in place, they can finance the development of the projects and ensure the long-term viability of the projects [42]. Eight states in the US have varied targets with varying power offtake mechanisms to procure electrical generation from specific offshore wind projects. These state policies have resulted in twenty-four power purchase (offtake) agreements, adding up to 17,597 MW in offshore wind energy contracts. From the beginning of 2021 through May 31, 2022, ten new power purchase agreements, totaling 11,874 MW, were signed [43].

In New York state, for instance, the state has issued calls for proposals from offshore wind developers to deliver offshore wind energy to New York state. The selected developers must enter into contracts to sell Offshore Wind

Renewable Energy Certificates (ORECs)[13] to the New York State Energy Research and Development Authority (NYSERDA) on behalf of New York's electricity ratepayers statewide [44].

8.5.4 Types of Offshore Wind Structures

Offshore wind technologies are evolving with larger and larger turbines being constructed to improve the economics of the developments. However, geology also plays a significant role. For example, some of the strongest winds with good wind energy production potential are located in northern California. However, the continental shelf in the region drops off quickly, which prohibits traditional monopile directly on the seafloor. Hence, for developers, floating turbines will need to be used [45].

8.5.4.1 Monopiles

Monopiles go to depths up to 40 m and are commonly used in shallow water (less than 35 m). Their advantages are that they work well in sand and gravel soils and have a simple design that installs quickly. They are adaptable for shallow and deeper installations of various sizes and are cost-effective for installations up to 40 m. Because the monopiles are driven into the seabed, there are disadvantages including installation and transportation costs, which increase as the size of the units increases due to hydrodynamic loads. Additionally, seismic studies and installation have been known to disorient, injure, or kill marine life sensitive to pressure waves. This includes humpback whales, loggerhead turtles, and manatees. Finally, wind, wave, and seismic loading can negatively affect monopile foundations. This can cause early fatigue damage to the structure if it is not accounted for during installation [46, 47].

8.5.4.2 Jacket Foundations

Jacket foundations are lattice-truss structures that look similar to offshore oil and gas platforms. They have four tubular legs that are connected by diagonal struts. This design was used for the Block Island Wind Farm in Rhode Island and can go to depths of 60 m. Rhode Island's Block Island Wind Farm used 400 tons of steel jacket foundations when it was installed in 2016 [48, 49].

Jacket foundations can be installed using piles or suction caissons in stiff clays or medium-to-dense sands. Soft-soil installations are possible with longer

---

[13] ORECs represent the positive environmental attributes associated with 1 megawatt hour (MWh) of electricity generated from offshore wind resources and consumed by retail customers in New York state.

pile lengths that significantly increase friction resistance. The larger surface area of the lattice configuration may provide an artificial reef location, providing a new habitat for local species. They are an economical choice using straightforward manufacturing methods and can be moved by barge.

The disadvantages of jacket foundations include the risk that invasive species will establish and spread. North Sea installations of jacket foundations have reported ongoing grout joint issues, causing long periods of maintenance downtime to sustain structural integrity. Changes to local water patterns may be detrimental to native marine ecosystems, and installations using pile drivers can create underwater noise that may injure or kill some marine life.

8.5.4.3 Floating Foundations

Floating foundations offer opportunities where traditional foundations cannot cost-effectively or safely be installed in deep waters. They increase the reach of wind farms, allowing installations to over 200 m. In fact, 58 percent of offshore wind resources are located in deep water where traditional foundations cannot reach. The turbines and bases can be assembled in port, then towed to site for installation. Longer maintenance can also be done in port, if desired, by towing the turbine back to port. Some of the disadvantages include trying to affix the required cabling and the requisite inspections and maintenance [50]. The three types of floating turbine designs are as follows [45].

- A spar buoy platform is a long, hollow cylinder that extends downward from the turbine tower. It floats vertically in deep water, weighted with ballast in the bottom of the cylinder to lower its center of gravity. It is then anchored in place, but with slack lines that allow it to move with the water to avoid damage.
- Semi-submersible platforms have large floating hulls that spread out from the tower, also anchored to prevent drifting.
- Tension leg platforms have smaller platforms with taut lines running straight to the floor below. These are lighter but more vulnerable to earthquakes or tsunamis because they rely more on the mooring lines and anchors for stability.

8.6 Hydrogen

Imagine driving your car and the only emission being water vapor. That is the promise of hydrogen fuel cell cars. However, going from promise to reality has not proven to be economically feasible. Hydrogen does not exist freely in nature and is only produced from other sources of energy, primarily found in methane (natural gas), which is a potent greenhouse gas, so the carbon dioxide released in the reformation process adds to the greenhouse gas emissions. Hydrogen can be produced in a process known as electrolysis. Electrolysis is the process of using electricity to split water into hydrogen and oxygen in a unit called an electrolyser. The issue again is that most of our current electricity supply is from fossil fuels such as coal and natural gas. So hydrogen is only as clean as the energy source being used to produce the hydrogen. It has very high energy for its weight, but very low energy for its volume, so new technology is needed to store and transport it. The carbon emissions resulting from the type of process used to produce the hydrogen are reflected within the industry by a color code of hydrogen (Table 8.3) [51, 52].

While there is ongoing research including by the US Department of Energy and their Hydrogen Shot to bring to market clean hydrogen at a cost target of $1/kg H_2$ by 2030, it is unlikely that we will see major further investments by automobile manufacturers in the near term as the world is focused on EVs.

8.6.1 Energy Storage

The future of the renewable energy transition is highly dependent on advances and deployment in energy storage. Utility companies work in two realms. The first is "base load." This is the known average demand for electricity. These loads were historically met by very large thermoelectric power stations, primarily coal and nuclear. They are very expensive to build and operate and require days to start up and turn off during maintenance. The second realm is "peak power demand." This is when areas experience extreme temperatures

Table 8.3 *Color types of hydrogen [53]*

Green	Produced using renewable energy
Blue	Produced using natural gas in steam reforming and using carbon capture and sequestration
Grey	Created from natural gas or steam methane reformation without capturing the greenhouse gas emissions
Black and brown	Uses coal (black or brown)
Pink, purple, red	Generated through electrolysis powered by nuclear energy
Turquoise	In R&D phase using methane pyrolysis to produce hydrogen and solid carbon
Yellow	Produced using solar energy

such as the summer when air conditioners are operated. Utilities generally meet peak demand by the use of natural gas plants, which can be started in 1–2 hours [54]. I once interviewed a former chief executive officer of Pinnacle West Energy when he was in office and when Pinnacle West Energy was the largest utility in the United States. I asked him what it was like running the utility and he responded that it was like running a hospital. It took me a moment to realize what he meant. No one ever thinks of the hospital until the day that you or a loved one has a medical emergency and no one ever thinks of the utility until the moment that the power goes out. And you are not likely to be thinking of the utility kindly.

The transition to a renewable and low-carbon economy gives pause to utilities. First, there is the issue of connection to the grid,[14] and second, solar is dependent on the sun, which sets at night or is covered by clouds, and wind is dependent on an adequate flow of wind.

The World Economic Forum has identified four primary technologies [55]:

1. Pumped hydro: This is where water is pumped from a basin up a hill where energy demand is low. The water then is stored and when there is high demand for energy the water is released, thus spinning turbines to create lower-cost renewable electricity. Pumped hydro will account for the majority of new hydro power projects in Europe and China.
2. Batteries: The world is becoming more and more dependent on batteries, especially lithium-ion batteries. For example, Moss Landing Energy Storage Facility at the Moss Landing Power Plant in Monterrey, California has 400 MW/1,600 MWh capacity, making it the world's biggest battery storage facility. It connected and began operating in December 2020, comprising 4,500 stacked battery racks each containing twenty-two individual battery modules. PG&E contracted for the power offtake [56]. Before leaving office, President Trump signed into law the Energy Act of 2020, which included the bipartisan Better Energy Storage Technology (BEST) Act, authorizing a billion dollars to be spent over five years on the "research, development, and demonstration" of new energy storage technology. Many states are now setting storage-capacity targets, and in 2018 the Federal Energy Regulatory Commission issued Order 841, which integrates stored energy into the wholesale electricity market [57]. More recently, the US Department of Energy issued two notices of intent in February 2022 to provide $2.91 billion to boost production of the advanced batteries for EVs and energy storage, as directed by the Bipartisan Infrastructure Law [58].

[14] See Chapter 13, which discusses transmission.

3. Thermal energy storage: This is primarily used in buildings and industrial processes by storing in solid form in water, sand, or rocks surplus energy such as waste heat and using it later for cooling or heating.
4. Mechanical energy storage: This includes flywheel technology, which is not new. A flywheel stores rotational energy and can be called upon to release it. Think of winding an old-fashioned clock really tight, then being able to release all that energy. Other processes include storing pressurized air or gas and then heating and expanding it in a turbine to generate power when needed.

While we are early in the rapid deployment of energy storage technologies, it is clear that for now, battery energy storage will be the industry leader. In 2020, the US had less than 1 GW of large battery installations. But by the end of 2021, the US was on pace to add roughly 5.3 GW of large battery energy storage installations in addition to an estimated 9 GW in 2022 [59, 60].

References

1. CNBC (2022). Bill Gates Climate Fund Plans to Mobilize $15 Billion into Clean Tech. January 10. www.cnbc.com/2022/01/10/bill-gates-bec-climate-fund-plans-to-invest-15-billion-in-clean-tech.html.
2. International Energy Agency (2021). Renewable Electricity Growth Is Accelerating Faster Than Ever Worldwide, Supporting the Emergence of the New Global Energy Economy. International Energy Agency Press Release. December 1. www.iea.org/news/renewable-electricity-growth-is-accelerating-faster-than-ever-worldwide-supporting-the-emergence-of-the-new-global-energy-economy.
3. Energy Information Agency (2022). Monthly Energy Review Data Resources. Release, July 26. www.eia.gov/totalenergy/data/monthly/previous.php.
4. Energy Information Agency (2022). Renewable Energy Explained. www.eia.gov/energyexplained/renewable-sources.
5. National Renewable Energy Laboratory (2021). Life Cycle Greenhouse Gas Emissions from Electricity Generation: Update. NREL/FS-6A50-80580. September 2021. www.nrel.gov/docs/fy21osti/80580.pdf.
6. International Energy Agency (2021). Net Zero by 2050. www.iea.org/reports/net-zero-by-2050.
7. Elements (2022). Ranked: The Top 10 Countries by Energy Transition Investment. www.visualcapitalist.com/ranked-the-top-10-countries-by-energy-transition-investment.
8. New York Greenbank (n.d.). About. https://greenbank.ny.gov.
9. Governing.com (2022). What Does the Inflation Reduction Act Do for State and Local Government? April 17. www.governing.com/now/what-does-the-inflation-reduction-act-do-for-state-and-local-government.

10. PBS (2022). What the Inflation Reduction Act Does for Green Energy. www.pbs
    .org/newshour/science/what-the-inflation-reduction-act-does-for-green-energy.
11. National Law Review (2021). Key Energy Provisions in Biden Administration
    $1.2 Trillion Infrastructure Investment and Jobs Act. November 17. www.natla
    wreview.com/article/key-energy-provisions-biden-administration-12-trillion-
    infrastructure-investment-and.
12. Our World in Data (2020). Why Did Renewable Become Cheap So Fast? https://
    ourworldindata.org/cheap-renewables-growth#:~:text=Fossil%20fuels%20dom
    inate%20the%20global,cheaper%20than%20new%20fossil%20fuels.
13. Energy Information Agency (2022). Glossary. www.eia.gov/tools/glossary/index
    .php?id=Capacity_factor.
14. Global Wind Energy Council (2021). Global Offshore Wind Report 2021. https://
    gwec.net/wp-content/uploads/2021/09/GWEC-offshore-wind-2021-updated-
    1.pdf.
15. W. Palz (2010). *Power for the World: The Emergence of Electricity from the Sun*.
    Louvain-la-Neuve: Pan Stanford Publishing, p. 6.
16. Sciencing (2020). The Effect of Wavelength on Photovoltaic Cells. https://scien
    cing.com/effect-wavelength-photovoltaic-cells-6957.html.
17. Seattle PI (n.d.). The Effect of Wavelength on Photovoltaic Cells. https://educa
    tion.seattlepi.com/effect-wavelength-photovoltaic-cells-3353.html.
18. *Nature* (2021). Solar Cells That Make Use of Wasted Light. Outlook. June 24.
    www.nature.com/articles/d41586-021-01673-w.
19. Massachusetts Institute of Technology (2018). Explaining the Plummeting Cost
    of Solar Power. https://news.mit.edu/2018/explaining-dropping-solar-cost-1120.
20. DSIRE (2022). Renewable Energy and Energy Efficiency Portfolio Standard.
    https://programs.dsireusa.org/system/program/detail/2660.
21. Portfolio Standards and Goals. www.ncsl.org/research/energy/renewable-port
    folio-standards.aspx.
22. Energy Information Agency (2022). Total Energy. www.eia.gov/totalenergy/data/
    browser/index.php?tbl=T10.06#/?f=A&start=1949&end=2021&charted=0-4-
    9–10.
23. S&P Global Market Intelligence (2022). A Decade into Tariffs, US Solar
    Manufacturing Is Still Deep in Asia's Shadow. May 23. www.spglobal.com/
    marketintelligence/en/news-insights/latest-news-headlines/a-decade-into-tariffs-
    us-solar-manufacturing-is-still-deep-in-asia-s-shadow-70236202.
24. Politico (2018). Trump Imposes Tariffs on Solar Imports. January 22. www
    .politico.com/story/2018/01/22/trump-solar-tariffs-china-357612.
25. Electrek (2022). Biden Administration Announces $56 Million for US Solar
    Manufacturing. July 15. https://electrek.co/2022/07/15/us-solar-manufacturing.
26. IBIS World (2022). Solar Panel Manufacturing in the United States. Industry
    report. 33441C.
27. Cleanpower.org (2022). Wind Power Facts. https://cleanpower.org/facts/wind-
    power.
28. BBVA (2021). History of Windpower: From Origins to World War 2. March 11.
    www.bbvaopenmind.com/en/technology/innovation/history-of-windpower-
    from-origins-to-world-war-ii.

29. Orsted (2019). Making Green Energy Affordable: How the Offshore Wind Energy Industry Matured – And What We Can Learn from It. https://orsted.com/-/media/www/docs/corp/com/explore/making-green-energy-affordable-june-2019.pdf.
30. Orsted (2022). Our Offshore Wind Projects in the U.S. https://us.orsted.com/wind-projects.
31. US Department of Energy (2022). Wind Market Reports: 2022 Edition. www.energy.gov/eere/wind/wind-market-reports-2022-edition.
32. Energy Information Agency (2021). Today in Energy: The United States Installed More Wind Turbine Capacity in 2020 Than in Any Other Year. March 3. www.eia.gov/todayinenergy/detail.php?id=46976.
33. White House (2021). Fact Sheet: Biden Administration Jumpstarts Offshore Wind Energy Projects to Create Jobs. March 29. Briefing Room Fact Sheet.
34. National Renewable Energy Laboratory (2020). 2019 Cost of Wind Energy Review. Technical Report NREL/TP-5000–78471 December 2020. www.nrel.gov/docs/fy21osti/78471.pdf.
35. World Bank (2022). Global Offshore Wind Technical Potential. https://datacatalog.worldbank.org/search/dataset/0037787.
36. Bureau of Ocean Energy Management (2022). Federal Offshore Lands. www.boem.gov/oil-gas-energy/leasing/federal-offshore-lands.
37. CNBC (2021). Construction Starts at America's First Major Offshore Wind Farm. November 19. www.cnbc.com/2021/11/19/construction-starts-at-americas-first-major-offshore-wind-farm.html.
38. Vineyard Wind (2021). Vineyard Wind Breaks Ground on First-in-the-Nation Commercial Scale Offshore Windfarm. www.vineyardwind.com/press-releases/2021/11/19/vineyard-wind-breaks-ground-on-first-in-the-nation-commercial-scale-offshore-windfarm.
39. National Renewable Energy Laboratory (2022). Offshore Wind Market Report: 2022 Edition. US Department of Energy. Office of Energy Efficiency and Renewable Energy. www.nrel.gov/wind/offshore-market-assessment.html.
40. US Department of the Interior (2021). Secretary Haaland Outlines Ambitious Offshore Wind Leasing Strategy. Press Release. October 13. www.doi.gov/pressreleases/secretary-haaland-outlines-ambitious-offshore-wind-leasingstrategy.
41. Bureau of Ocean Energy Management (2022). Offshore Wind Leasing Path Forward 2021–2025. www.boem.gov/sites/default/files/documents/renewable-energy/state-activities/OSW-Proposed-Leasing-Schedule.pdf.
42. Peak Wind (2022). Revenue and Energy Offtake Management in Offshore Wind – Part I. What Are the Key Levers in a PPA Negotiation? https://peak-wind.com/insights/revenue-and-energy-offtake-management-in-offshore-wind-part-i-what-are-the-key-levers-in-a-ppa-negotiation.
43. Department of Energy (2022). Offshore Wind Market Report. 2021 Report. www.energy.gov/sites/default/files/2021-08/Offshore%20Wind%20Market%20Report%202021%20Edition_Final.pdf.
44. New York State Energy Research and Development Authority (NYSERDA) (2022). Offshore Wind Solicitations: How NYSERDA Competitively Selects Offshore Wind Projects. www.nyserda.ny.gov/All-Programs/Offshore-Wind/Focus-Areas/Offshore-Wind-Solicitations.

45. *The Conversation* (2021). California Is Planning Floating Wind Farms Offshore to Boost Its Power Supply – Here's How They Work. July 14. https://theconversa tion.com/california-is-planning-floating-wind-farms-offshore-to-boost-its-power-supply-heres-how-they-work-163419.

46. W. Schaffer (2017). Monopile Foundation Offshore Wind Turbine Simulation and Retrofitting. Open PRAIRIE. South Dakota State University.

47. Windpower Engineering and Development (2021). Comparing Offshore Wind Turbine Foundations. January 4. www.windpowerengineering.com/comparing-offshore-wind-turbine-foundations.

48. Power Technology (2016). Block Island Wind Farm. December 30. www.power-technology.com/projects/block-island-wind-farm.

49. Orsted (2022). Our Offshore Wind Projects in the U.S. https://us.orsted.com/wind-projects.

50. S. Walcott and J. S. Golden (2022). Offshore Wind Technical Bulletin: A Report by the Dynamic Sustainability Lab. www.dynamicslab.org.

51. Department of Energy (2022). Hydrogen Production: Electrolysis. Hydrogen and Fuel Cell Technologies Office. www.energy.gov/eere/fuelcells/hydrogen-produc tion-electrolysis.

52. National Renewable Energy Laboratory (2022). Hydrogen Basics. www.nrel.gov/research/eds-hydrogen.html.

53. National Grid (n.d.). Energy Explained. www.nationalgrid.com/stories/energy-explained/hydrogen-colour-spectrum.

54. Energy Information Agency (2020). Today in Energy: About 25% of U.S. Power Plants Can Start Up within an Hour. November 19. www.eia.gov/todayinenergy/detail.php?id=45956#:~:text=Natural%20gas%20combined%2Dcycle%20sys tems,start%20up%20within%20an%20hour.

55. World Economic Forum (2021). How Can We Store Renewable Energy? 4 Technologies That Can Help. April 23. www.weforum.org/agenda/2021/04/renewable-energy-storage-pumped-batteries-thermal-mechanical.

56. NS Energy (n.d.). Moss Landing Battery Storage Project. www.nsenergybusiness .com/projects/moss-landing.

57. M. Hutson (2022). The Renewable Energy Revolution Will Need Renewable Storage. *The New Yorker*. April 18. www.newyorker.com/magazine/2022/04/25/the-renewable-energy-revolution-will-need-renewable-storage.

58. Energy.gov (2022). Biden Administration, DOE to Invest $3 Billion to Strengthen U.S. Supply Chain for Advanced Batteries for Vehicles and Energy Storage. February 11. www.energy.gov/articles/biden-administration-doe-invest-3-bil lion-strengthen-us-supply-chain-advanced-batteries.

59. *Wall Street Journal* (2021). Battery Storage Soars on the U.S. Electric Grid. December 21. www.wsj.com/articles/battery-storage-soars-on-u-s-electric-grid-11640082783.

60. International Energy Agency (2021). Renewables 2021 Data Explorer. www.iea .org/articles/renewables-2021-data-explorer.

9

Biobased and Agricultural Transitions

Let us build a 21st-century rural economy of cutting-edge companies and technologies that lead us to energy and food security . . .. Such an investment will revitalize rural America, re-establish our moral leadership on climate security and eliminate our addiction to foreign oil.

Tom Vilsack, secretary of the United States Department of Agriculture under Presidents Obama and Biden, 2008 [1]

9.1 Overview

It is amazing to me that all of us heavily depend on agriculture for our daily lives, yet the majority of us know so little about where our food comes from, let alone the broader uses of modern-day agriculture. We have to start with this important fact. Agriculture is the world's largest industry! It generates over $1.3 trillion dollars' worth of food annually. Pasture and cropland occupy around 50 percent of the earth's habitable land and provide habitat and food for a multitude of species [2].

What we now know of as human agriculture dates back around 12,000 years to the "Neolithic Revolution"[1] that transformed humans from traveling hunter-gatherers to forming settlements based on reliable food supply [3]. Today there are an estimated 570 million farms[2] around the world [4] and the average size of farms spans from 178.4 hectares (ha) (441 acres) and 45 ha (111 acres) in

---

[1] Gordon Childe coined the term "Neolithic Revolution" in 1935 to describe the radical and important period of change in which humans began cultivating plants, breeding animals for food, and forming permanent settlements. The advent of agriculture separated Neolithic people from their Paleolithic ancestors (www.history.com/topics/pre-history/neolithic-revolution).

[2] Likely this number is a lower-bound estimate as not all countries in this study had estimates and were not included.

France to 1.3 ha in India and 0.7 ha in Vietnam (3.2 acres and 1.7 acres, respectively) [4, 5].

Agriculture is also crucial to economic growth: In 2018, it accounted for 4 percent of global gross domestic product (GDP) and in some least-developing countries it can account for more than 25 percent of GDP [6].

9.2 Global Agriculture

Globally, as reported by the Food and Agriculture Organization of the United Nations [7], the share of GDP from agriculture in 2020 was 4 percent, which has been consistent since 2000 and employed 884 million people in 2019, which was 27 percent of the global workforce. In 2018, the global agricultural land area was 4.8 billion ha and between 2000 and 2018 roughly two-thirds of agricultural land were used for permanent meadows and pastures[3] (3.2 billion ha). One-third of the total agricultural land was cropland (1.6 billion ha), which increased by 5 percent (0.07 billion ha). One-third of the global permanent meadows and pasture land comes from just three countries in order (China 12 percent, Australia 10 percent, and the United States 8 percent). Similarly, three countries contain one-third of the global cropland in order (India 11 percent, United States 10 percent, and China 9 percent).

In 2018 the top crops grown around the world for four individual crops accounted for half the global production of primary crops: sugar cane (21 percent of the total with 1.9 billion toes), maize (13 percent with 1.1 billion tons), rice (9 percent with 0.8 billion tons), and wheat (8 percent with 0.7 billion tons), as presented in Figure 9.1 [7].

Certain countries dominate the global production of major crops, as presented in Figure 9.2.

Cotton is the most widespread profitable non-food crop in the world. Its production provides income for more than 250 million people worldwide and employs almost 7 percent of all labor in developing countries. Approximately half of all textiles are made of cotton. The top two cotton producers, India and China, contribute approximately 45–50 percent of the world's production, while the top four producers (India, China, the United States, and Brazil) comprise 70–75 percent of global cotton production. Although yields in India are well below the global average, the cotton area in India dwarfs that of any other country, accounting for approximately 40 percent of the world total.

---

[3] Permanent meadows and pastures is defined by the FAO as: "the land used permanently (five years or more) to grow herbaceous forage crops, either cultivated or growing wild (wild prairie or grazing land)."

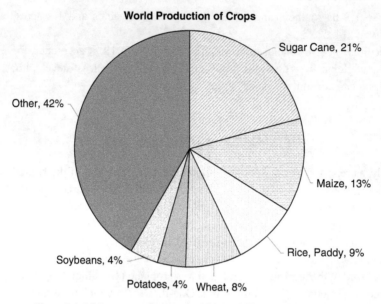

Figure 9.1 Major crops grown around the world in 2018 [7].

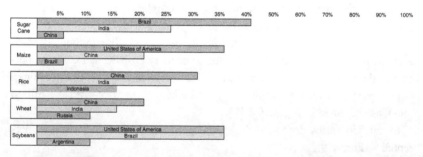

Figure 9.2 Top three countries of specified global crops in 2018 (rounded percentages) [7].

In 2019 the United States, which is the world's leading cotton exporter, produced nearly 20 million bales of cotton, representing about $7 billion in total (lint plus seed) value and approximately 35 percent of global cotton exports. One bale of cotton – approximately 480 pounds of cleaned cotton lint – can make more than 200 pairs of jeans or 1,200 t-shirts. In the United States and around the world, there are two main species of cotton cultivated for commercial use: upland cotton and Pima (extra-long staple) cotton. Upland cotton comprises the vast majority of production. The primary difference between species is fiber length, with other small differences in growing conditions and end uses [8, 9].

9.3 Agriculture in the United States

Agriculture plays a significant role in the United States. Not only do American farmers feed the country and a good portion of the world but the value chain also plays an important role in the American economy.

1. Agriculture is the major land use, accounting for 52 percent of the US land base ranked by (1) grassland pasture and range, (2) forest use, and (3) cropland [10].
2. In 2020, nearly 20 million full- and part-time jobs were related to agriculture. This is over 10 percent of total US employment. Direct on-farm jobs accounted for over 2.6 million jobs, which is almost 1.5 percent of the total jobs in the country [11].
3. Food accounted for over 10 percent of US household expenditure in 2020. This is third in total household spending behind housing and transportation [12].
4. The United States is the world's second largest agricultural trader after the European Union [13].
5. In 2021 exports of US farm and food products to the world totaled $177 billion, topping the 2020 total by 18 percent and eclipsing the previous record, set in 2014, by 14.6 percent [14].
6. China has been the largest market for US agriculture exports and from 2000 to 2017 US agriculture exports to China increased by 700 percent [15].

American agriculture has continued to increase productivity, but the number of Americans farming has dramatically declined. It reached a peak of 6.8 million farms in 1935, but by 2021 there were only 2.01 million US farms, down from 2.20 million in 2007. With 895 million acres of land in farms in 2021, the average farm size was 445 acres, only slightly greater than the 440 acres recorded in the early 1970s [16].

9.4 IPAT and Agriculture

As discussed at the start of Chapter 2[4], population, affluence, and technology drive many of our sustainability impacts. This is true with agriculture as well. Since 1961, global meat consumption has quadrupled in both absolute and per-capita terms, requiring the expansion of livestock and 80 billion animals slaughtered annually to produce 340 million tons of meat for human consumption. World meat consumption per capita increased between 2000 and 2019 (29.5 kg vs. 34.0 kg) by 0.34 kg/capita/year [17, 18]. As presented in Table 9.1, in 1990 pork was the most consumed meat followed by beef and veal.

---

[4] $I = P \times A \times T$ (impact = population $\times$ affluence $\times$ technology).

Table 9.1 *Global meat consumption worldwide from 1990 to 2021 by meat type (in million tons) [19]*

	1990	2000	2010	2021
Beef and veal	48	58.8	65	71.5
Pork	63.5	89.2	108.7	108.8
Sheep and goat	7.8	11.4	13.2	15.7
Poultry	34.6	67.7	100.2	132.4
Total	2,143.9	2,227.11	2,297.1	2,349.4

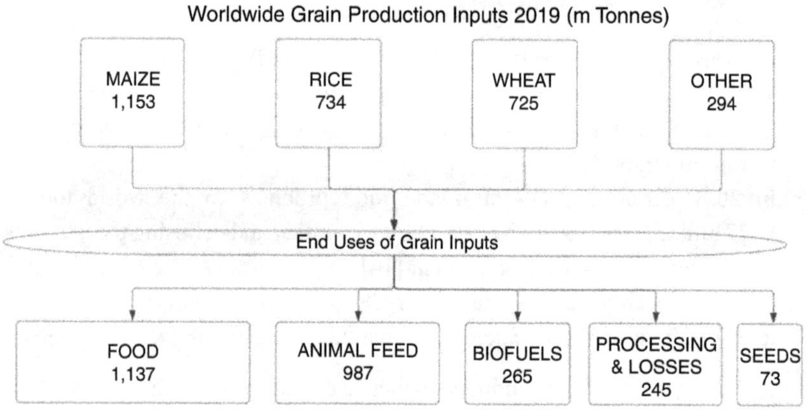

Worldwide Grain Production Inputs 2019 (m Tonnes)

| MAIZE 1,153 | RICE 734 | WHEAT 725 | OTHER 294 |

End Uses of Grain Inputs

| FOOD 1,137 | ANIMAL FEED 987 | BIOFUELS 265 | PROCESSING & LOSSES 245 | SEEDS 73 |

Figure 9.3 Worldwide grain production inputs in 2019 [23].

By 2021, poultry had become the dominant meat consumed [19]. However, all categories increased and thus the land use required to feed livestock also increased. As presented in Figure 9.3, less than half of the world's grains produced are consumed by humans. Globally, of the produced almost 80 percent is used for pastures or crops used in animal feed rather than for direct human consumption. Recent studies show that if we switched to a plant-based diet, we would require just a quarter of the land agriculture uses today from 4 billion ha to 1 billion ha. A diet avoiding only meat from cattle and sheep would cut land use in half. This restored farmland could play an important role in carbon sequestration [20, 21, 22].

9.5 Forestry

Today, globally, there are over 3 trillion trees. Forests cover 31 percent of the earth's land, equivalent to 4 billion ha. Forests are home to 80 percent of all land-based species and three-quarters of the world's accessible freshwater comes from forested watersheds. Alarmingly, we are losing 10 million ha of forests every year. Between 2010 and 2020, global forest area fell by 1.2 percent, with declines concentrated in Africa and South America. The most alarming decline was in the Amazon in Brazil where in the first six months of 2022, 3,988 square kilometers (1,540 square miles) of land were cleared [24] and where many around the world blame the anti-environmental policies and actions[5] of Brazil's controversial President Jair Bolsonaro.

This is critical as our forests are also our largest land (terrestrial) carbon sink, absorbing roughly 2 billion tons of CO_2 each year. An estimated 1.6 billion people, or 25 percent of the global population, rely on forests for their subsistence needs, livelihoods, employment, and income. Of the extreme poor in rural areas, 40 percent live in forest and savannah areas [25, 26, 27, 28].

Of all the forest land, about 1.15 billion ha is managed primarily for the production of wood and non-wood forest products and about one-third of the world's population use wood as an energy source for boiling water, cooking food, and providing heat [27]. Over 60 percent of the world's roundwood production originates from just eight regions: Brazil, Canada, China, the European Union, India, Indonesia, Russia, and the US [29]. Until the mid-1800s, wood was the primary energy source for the United States and the rest of the world, yet by 2021 only 2.1 percent of the annual energy consumption in the US was from wood feedstocks [30]. Today, the largest industrial uses of wood are for wood products such as in construction, as well as paper products such as napkins, packaging, and toilet paper [30].

Globally, 73 percent of forests are publicly owned and 22 percent are privately owned. In the United States, the numbers are different as corporations own 137 million acres or 19.5 percent of total forestland (excluding interior Alaska), and are the third largest ownership group after family and federal ownership categories [31].

Many of the purchases were made by timber investment management organizations (TIMOs), which are entities that manage and often purchase timberland for investors but that do not usually own the land themselves. In addition to TIMOs, the other major financial transaction was through real estate investment trusts (REITs) by corporations that invest at least 75 percent of their total assets in real estate and who are required to distribute 90 percent of their taxable income to their investors; the investors pay income tax on those dividends, and the REITs avoid corporate income tax for that income [32].

As reported by both Wang [33] and Gunnoe et al. [34], there were forest industry companies that divested most of their wood-processing facilities, set

---

[5] See www.nytimes.com/2019/08/27/world/americas/bolsonaro-brazil-environment.html.

up the rest of their processing facilities in a "taxable REIT subsidiary," and chose to focus on land investment using the REIT structure. Examples of major corporate ownership in the United States includes Weyerhaeuser (public REIT), Rayonier (public REIT), and Sierra Pacific Industries [35].

9.6 Agriculture and Climate Change

Globally, agriculture contributes between 19 and 29 percent of greenhouse gas emissions [36]. In the United States, the Environmental Protection Agency estimates that agriculture accounted for 11.2 percent of US greenhouse gas emissions in 2020 [37]. Agriculture plays a very unique and important role. Not only is it a significant contributor to climate change, it is also critically important as a potential sink to sequester carbon and is highly vulnerable to climate change impacts, including warming temperatures, increased droughts, and forest fires, as well as stronger, more frequent, and more damaging weather events [38].

Agriculture includes raising livestock, managing forests, and growing crops.[6] Agriculture is primarily responsible for:

1. Non-CO_2 emissions: agriculture is the largest source of non-CO_2 emissions, primarily methane (CH_4) and nitrous oxide (N_2O) emissions generated within the farm gate by crops and livestock activities [39]
2. CO_2 emissions: such as the conversion of natural ecosystems, mostly forest land and natural peatlands to agriculture land use [40].

As presented in Figure 9.4, different agriculture commodities have a wide range of CO_2 impacts ranging from cattle meat (26 kg CO_2eq/kg) to cereals excluding rice, which have the lowest emissions intensity of all major commodities at 0.2 kg CO_2eq/kg [41].

Interestingly, 30 percent of global agriculture emissions were attributable to just three countries in 2018 [42]:

1. Brazil, almost equally distributed between both crops and livestock and agricultural land use
2. Indonesia, predominantly from agricultural land use
3. India, predominantly from crops and livestock.

---

[6] In this chapter I focus on terrestrial (i.e., land-based) agriculture. There exist very important books in regard to the unique role of aquatic-based agriculture.

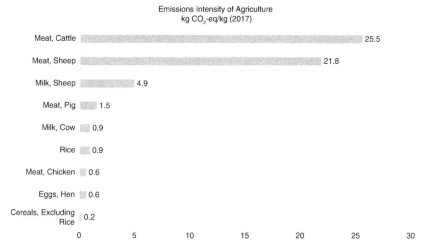

Figure 9.4 Intensities of different types of agriculture [42].

The remaining countries in the top ten included:

4. Democratic Republic of Congo (agricultural land use)
5. China (almost exclusively crops and livestock)
6. United States (crops and livestock predominantly)
7. Myanmar (equally divided)
8. Argentina (predominantly crops and livestock)
9. Pakistan (almost exclusively crops and livestock)
10. Canada (heavier in agricultural land use).

9.6.1 Livestock Management

Cattle are the number one agriculture source of greenhouse gases worldwide. Each year, a single cow will belch about 220 pounds of methane. Humans by comparison produce a paltry 1 L of flatus per day, only 7 percent of which is methane, and we do not burp methane; if you are a vegetarian, you will produce more flatus per day. But back to cattle. Methane from cattle is shorter lived than carbon dioxide but twenty-eight times more potent in warming the atmosphere. And again, all of this varies by geography. India has the world's largest cattle population but the lowest beef consumption of any country, which results in cows living longer and emitting more methane over their lifetimes [43, 44]. Further, beef requires twenty times more land and emits twenty times more greenhouse gas emissions per gram of edible protein than common plant proteins, such as beans [45].

9.6.2 Nitrogen Fertilizers

Feeding the almost 8 billion persons on earth today and the growing numbers in the near future will require the continued use of large amounts of nitrogen (N) input, which, as Cassman and Dobermann [46] state, "represents an inherent weakness in our global food production system." The global annual input of fertilizer N to cropland is double the N input from the natural processes of biological N fixation (BNF) [47]. The impacts of nitrogen occur in a few ways. First, manufacturing of synthetic nitrogen fertilizer via ammonia[7] is very energy intensive, using legacy non-renewable energy-releasing carbon dioxide (CO_2) and nitrous oxide (N_2O).

Once applied to the land, microbes in the soil convert nitrogen fertilizer into nitrous oxide (N_2O), which, as we know, is a potent greenhouse gas. In addition to climate change impacts, watersheds can also be impacted by runoff from the fertilizer [48, 49, 50]. China is the world's largest consumer of nitrogen fertilizer (24,109 k metric tons), using more than double the amount of the United States (11,729 k metric tons), which is the third largest consumer.

9.6.3 Cover Crops

A cover crop is generally a non-cash crop grown in addition to the cash crop. Cover crops add organic matter to the soil and add nitrogen in a slow-release way that plants can handle, leading to less nitrogen volatilization. In recent years the increased focus on soil quality and reducing chemical inputs such as nitrogen fertilizers and pesticides has led to a renewed interest in the potential benefits of including cover crops in an agricultural production system. Some reasons to implement cover crops in a crop management regime include to slow erosion, improve soil health, enhance water infiltration, smother weeds, control pests and diseases, and increase biodiversity. These crops are often planted after the harvest of a cash crop and before planting the next crop, when fields would otherwise lie fallow.[8] Cover crops can also absorb carbon dioxide through photosynthesis and store the carbon in the soil.

It is estimated that 20 million acres of cover crops can sequester over 66 million tons of carbon dioxide equivalent per year, equal to the emissions of about 13 million vehicles. However, it is uncertain how long sequestered carbon stays in the soil. While cover crop usage has increased over the last decade in the United States, only 5 percent of cropland in the United States – equal to about 15.4 million acres – used cover crops in 2017 [52, 53, 54].

[7] The second most commonly produced chemical in the world.
[8] A fallow phase is a stage of crop rotation whereby the land is deliberately not used to grow a crop.

9.7 Biobased Transition

While agriculture does contribute to climate change, it is now also being utilized as a strategy to mitigate climate change. I call this the *biobased transition*, where companies seek to replace fossil fuel feedstocks with agriculture feedstocks to provide energy, electricity, chemicals, and products. It is also part of both federal and state efforts to achieve a net-zero-carbon economy.

In the United States, in an unprecedented move both Republicans and Democrats in Congress back in January 2021 overrode a veto by then President Trump to enact the bipartisan Sustainable Chemistry Research and Development Act as part of a larger piece of legislation. The Act directs the White House Office of Science and Technology Policy to convene an interagency entity with the responsibility of coordinating and strengthening federal programs and activities in support of sustainable chemistry, which is heavily reliant on biobased solutions as we move away from fossil fuel-based chemicals [55]. In 2022, the United States Department of Agriculture (USDA) put out a $1 billion request for proposals for climate-smart commodities finance pilot projects that can create market opportunities for US agricultural and forestry products that use climate-smart practices and include innovative, cost-effective ways to measure and verify greenhouse gas benefits [56]. This is in addition to the existing USDA Biopreferred program.[9]

The USDA each year reports on the domestic biobased products sector, excluding biobased energy and fuels. The most recent report [57] released in 2021 examined data from 2017 and found that the biobased products industry supports 4.6 million American jobs in both rural and urban parts of our country and generates 2.8 additional jobs in the US economy for every biobased products job.

The sector contributes more than $470 billion to the US economy despite competing with a deeply entrenched fossil sector. Moreover, the biobased products sector is growing, and the report's findings show notable growth in jobs and economic contributions since 2013 despite the presence of low fossil product prices during most of the last decade. There have also been numerous presidential Executive Orders issued requiring agencies of the federal government to purchase biobased fuels and products since the Clinton Administration, though some of those were revoked by subsequent presidential administrations.[10]

---

[9] www.biopreferred.gov/BioPreferred.

[10] See https://clintonwhitehouse4.archives.gov/Initiatives/Climate/biobased.html and https://obamawhitehouse.archives.gov/the-press-office/2015/03/19/executive-order-planning-federal-sustainability-next-decade.

At the state level, in 2019 New York state passed the Climate Leadership and Community Protection Act[11] (CLCPA), immediately making it one of the nation's most ambitious pieces of deep decarbonization legislation. In 2022, the state released the law's expansive implementation plan that, among other things, proposes the rapid scale-up and commercialization of a "Climate-Focused Bioeconomy."

New York's proposal calls for the bioeconomy to be deployed across multiple economic sectors in order to spur a shift away from both fuel and non-fuel fossil products while simultaneously achieving the net sequestration of atmospheric carbon dioxide that the United Nations' Intergovernmental Panel on Climate Change has deemed essential if catastrophic climate change is to be avoided. New York's proposal would make it a national leader in the utilization of the bioeconomy in pursuit of climate objectives [58].

Finally, industry is perhaps the largest driver of the biobased transition. One only needs to look at recent announcements to start to understand the breadth. In March 2021 US-based airlines through their collective industry association Airlines for America (A4A) announced that all of the members had committed to achieve net-zero-carbon emissions by 2050 [59]. This will be achieved through the adoption and utilization of biobased Sustainable Aviation Fuels (SAF) with the hope that 2 billion gallons of SAF will be available to US aircraft by 2030. Aviation is the most carbon-impactful means of transportation, with a flight between London and San Francisco having a carbon footprint per economy ticket of nearly 1 ton of CO_2e.

With the aviation industry expected to double to over 8 billion passengers by 2050, the global impacts are only set to rise. SAF provides up to 80 percent reduction in CO_2 emissions as compared to traditional kerosene-based jet fuels – depending on the feedstock used [60]. Current SAF is blended 50 percent with traditional jet fuel and uses feedstocks ranging from cooking oil to plant oils, municipal waste, waste gases, and agricultural residues [61].

Also in 2021, Coca-Cola announced after almost a decade of scaling up, it has finally achieved a 100 percent plant-based plastic bottle.[12] In the past, Coca-Cola's PlantBottle, which was introduced in 2009, consisted of recyclable polyethylene terephthalate (PET) plastic made from up to 30 percent plant-based material, with the other 70 percent made from terephthalic acid (PTA), which is derived from non-renewable oil-based fossil fuels [62, 63].

In the consumer goods sector, Unilever, which owns brands including Ben & Jerry's, Dove, Persil, Hellmann's, Magnum, Degree, and many more,

---

[11] https://climate.ny.gov. [12] Excluding the cap and label.

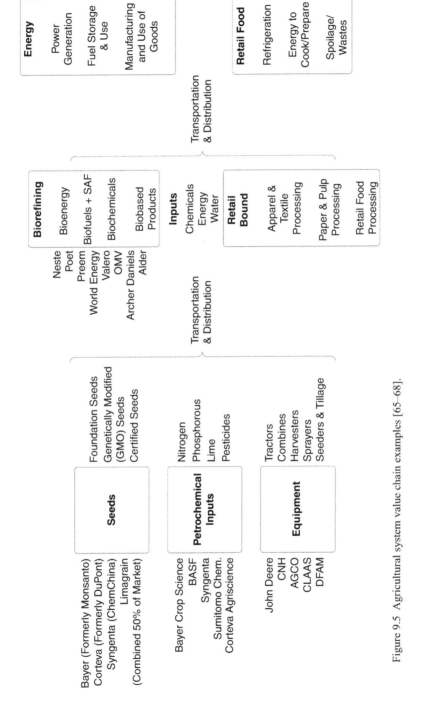

Figure 9.5 Agricultural system value chain examples [65–68].

announced an investment of $120 million to scale biobased fossil fuel and palm oil alternatives in cleaning products through a partnership with San Diego-based Genomatica [64].

These are just some of the examples of how land-based agriculture will play a vital role in the transition to a net-zero-carbon economy. And this does not include the emergence of ocean-based solutions, including the use of kelp and algae. Yet the question remains: Can all of this be done in a way that protects the environment and the economy?

As presented, the modern-day agriculture system is complex and impacts various industrial sectors of our economy, as presented in Figure 9.5. Each of these key players has an interest in ensuring the sustained growth of agriculture as a feedstock beyond feeding the world.

References

1. *New York Times* (2008). Iowa Ex-Governor Picked for Agriculture Secretary. December 16.
2. World Wildlife Fund (n.d.). Sustainable Agriculture Overview. www.worldwildlife.org/industries/sustainable-agriculture#:~:text=Agriculture%20is%20the%20world's%20largest,for%20a%20multitude%20of%20species.
3. National Geographic (2022). The Development of Agriculture. https://education.nationalgeographic.org/resource/development-agriculture.
4. S. K. Lowder, J. Skoet, and Raney, T. (2016). The Number, Size, and Distribution of Farms, Smallholder Farms, and Family Farms Worldwide. *World Development*, 87: 16–29.
5. Our World in Data (2021). Farm Size. https://ourworldindata.org/farm-size.
6. World Bank (n.d.). Agriculture and Food. worldbank.org/en/topic/agriculture/overview.
7. Food and Agriculture Organization (2020). *World Food and Agriculture – Statistical Yearbook 2020*. Rome. https://doi.org/10.4060/cb1329en.
8. World Wildlife Fund (2022). Industries – Cotton. www.worldwildlife.org/industries/cotton#:~:text=Cotton%20is%20the%20most%20widespread,all%20labor%20in%20developing%20countries.
9. United States Department of Agriculture Economic Research Service (2022). Cotton Sector at a Glance. www.ers.usda.gov/topics/crops/cotton-wool/cotton-sector-at-a-glance.
10. United States Department of Agriculture Economic Research Service (2022). Land Use, Land Value and Tenure. www.ers.usda.gov/topics/farm-economy/land-use-land-value-tenure/#:~:text=Agricultural%20production%20is%20a%20major,data%20on%20Major%20Land%20Uses.
11. United States Department of Agriculture (2022). Ag and Food Sectors and the Economy. www.ers.usda.gov/data-products/ag-and-food-statistics-charting-the-essentials/ag-and-food-sectors-and-the-economy.

12. Bureau of Labor Statistics (2021). Consumer Expenditures in 2020. www.bls.gov/opub/reports/consumer-expenditures/2020/home.htm.

13. United States Department of Agriculture (2022). U.S. Agricultural Trade at a Glance. www.ers.usda.gov/topics/international-markets-u-s-trade/u-s-agricultural-trade/u-s-agricultural-trade-at-a-glance.

14. United States Department of Agriculture (2022). American Agricultural Exports Shattered Records in 2021. www.usda.gov/media/press-releases/2022/02/08/american-agricultural-exports-shattered-records-2021#:~:text=The%20final%202021%20trade%20data,in%202014%2C%20by%2014.6%20percent.

15. Minnesota Department of Agriculture (2018). China Top Market for U.S. Ag Exports. www.mda.state.mn.us/sites/default/files/inline-files/profilechina.pdf.

16. United States Department of Agriculture Economic Research Service (2022). Farm and Farming Income. www.ers.usda.gov/data-products/ag-and-food-statistics-charting-the-essentials/farming-and-farm-income/.

17. H. Ritchie and M. Roser (2019). Meat and Dairy Production. Our World in Data. https://ourworldindata.org/meat-production.

18. C. Whitton, D. Bogueva, D. Marinova, and C. J. C. Phillips (2021). Are We Approaching Peak Meat Consumption? Analysis of Meat Consumption from 2000 to 2019 in 35 Countries and Its Relationship to Gross Domestic Product. *Animals*, 11(12): 3466. https://doi.org/10.3390/ani11123466.

19. Statista (2022). Meat Consumption Worldwide from 1990 to 2021, by Meat Type. www.statista.com/statistics/274522/global-per-capita-consumption-of-meat.

20. *Economist* (2022). If Everyone Were Vegan, Only a Quarter of Current Farmland Would Be Needed. January 28. www.economist.com/graphic-detail/2022/01/28/if-everyone-were-vegan-only-a-quarter-of-current-farmland-would-be-needed.

21. J. Poore and T. Nemecek (2018). Reducing Food's Environmental Impacts through Producers and Consumers. *Science*, 360: 987–992.

22. Our World in Data (2021). If the World Adopted a Plant-Based Diet We Would Reduce Global Agricultural Land Use from 4 to 1 billion Hectares. https://ourworldindata.org/land-use-diets.

23. United Nations Food and Agriculture Organization (2022). FAOSTAT Data. www.fao.org/faostat/en/#data.

24. BBC News (2022). Amazon Rainforest: Highest Deforestation Rate in Six Years. July 9. www.bbc.com/news/world-latin-america-62103336.

25. United Nations Department of Economic and Social Affairs (2021). World Economic Situation and Prospects 2021. www.un.org/development/desa/dpad/publication/world-economic-situation-and-prospects–2021.

26. United Nations General Assembly, United Nations Strategic Plan for Forests 2017–2030. A/RES/71/285. https://undocs.org/pdf?symbol=E/RES/2017/4.

27. United Nations (2021). The Global Forest Goals Report 2021. www.un.org/esa/forests/wp-content/uploads/2021/04/Global-Forest-Goals-Report-2021.pdf.

28. Science (2015). Earth Home to 3 Trillion Trees, Half As Many As When Human Civilization Arose. September 2, 2015. www.science.org/content/article/earth-home-3-trillion-trees-half-many-when-human-civilization-arose#:~:text=Earth%20today%20supports%20more%20than,we%20thought%20a%20decade%20ago.

29. United Nations Forum on Forests (2018). Background Analytical Study 4 Sustainable Consumption and Production of Forest Products. www.un.org/esa/forests/wp-content/uploads/2018/04/UNFF13_BkgdStudy_ForestsSCP.pdf.
30. Energy Information Agency (2022). Biomass Explained. Wood and Wood Wastes. www.eia.gov/energyexplained/biomass/wood-and-wood-waste.php.
31. B. J. Butler, S. M. Butler, J. Caputo, J. Dias, A. Robillard, and E. M. Sass. 2020. Family Forest Ownerships of the United States, 2018: Results from the USDA Forest Service, National Woodland Owner Survey. USDA Forest Service Gen. Tech. Rep. GTR-NRS-199, Northern Research Station, Madison, WI. 56 pp.
32. E. M. Sass, M. Markowski-Lindsay, B. J. Butler et al. (2021). Dynamics of Large Corporate Forestland Ownerships in the United States. *Journal of Forestry*, 119(4): 363–375. https://doi.org/10.1093/jofore/fvab013.
33. L. Wang (2011). Timber REITs and Taxation. USDA Forest Service Tech. Rep. 3 pp. www.fs.fed.us/spf/coop/library/timber_reits_report.pdf.
34. A. Gunnoe, C. Bailey, and L. Ameyaw (2018). Millions of Acres, Billions of Trees: Socioecological Impacts of Shifting Timberland Ownership. *Rural Sociology*, 83(4): 799–822.
35. Forisk (2020). North America's Top Timberland Owners and Managers, 2020 update. https://forisk.com/blog/2020/05/21/north-americas-top-timberland-owners-and-managers-2020-update/#:~:text=Weyerhaeuser%20continues%20to%20lead%20with,12.3%20million%20acres%20last%20year.
36. World Bank (2021). Climate Smart Agriculture. www.worldbank.org/en/topic/climate-smart-agriculture.
37. US Environmental Protection Agency (2022). Sources of Greenhouse Gas Emissions. www.epa.gov/ghgemissions/sources-greenhouse-gas-emissions.
38. T. Sulser, K. D. Wiebe, S. Dunston et al. (2021). *Climate Change and Hunger: Estimating Costs of Adaptation in the Agrifood System.* Food policy report, June. Washington, DC: International Food Policy Research Institute (IFPRI). https://doi.org/10.2499/9780896294165.
39. S. Frank, P. Havlík, E. Stehfest et al. (2019) Agricultural Non-CO_2 Emission Reduction Potential in the Context of the 1.5°C Target. *Nature Climate Change*, 9: 66–72. https://doi.org/10.1038/s41558-018-0358-8.
40. H. Sieverding, E. Kebreab, J. Johnson et al. (2020). A Life Cycle Analysis (LCA) Primer for the Agriculture Community. *Agronomy Journal*, 112: 3788–3807.
41. Food and Agriculture Organization. 2020. *World Food and Agriculture – Statistical Yearbook 2020*. Rome. https://doi.org/10.4060/cb1329en.
42. Food and Agriculture Organization. (2020). Emissions Due to Agriculture. Global, Regional and Country Trends 2000–2018. FAOSTAT Analytical Brief Series No. 18. Rome.
43. UC Davis (2019). Cows and Climate Change. Making Cattle More Sustainable. June 27. www.ucdavis.edu/food/news/making-cattle-more-sustainable#:~:text=The%20global%20problem&text=Livestock%20are%20responsible%20for%2014.5,more%20methane%20over%20their%20lifetime.
44. Climate Conscious (2021). Do Humans Fart More Methane Than Cows? Ronan Cray. November 5. https://medium.com/climate-conscious/do-humans-fart-more-methane-than-cows-a0f48c590fb0.

45. World Resources Institute (2022). 6 Pressing Questions about Beef and Climate Change Answered. March 7. www.wri.org/insights/6-pressing-questions-about-beef-and-climate-change-answered.

46. K. G. Cassman and A. Dobermann (2022). Nitrogen and the Future of Agriculture: 20 Years On. *Ambio*, 51: 17–24. https://doi.org/10.1007/s13280-021-01526-w.

47. D. Fowler, M. Coyle, U. Skiba et al. (2013). The Global Nitrogen Cycle in the Twenty-First Century. *Philosophical Transactions of the Royal Society of London. Series B, Biological Sciences*, 368: 20130164. https://doi.org/10.1098/rstb.2013.0164.

48. Inside Climate News (2018). Infographic: Why Farmers Are Ideally Positioned to Fight Climate Change. October 24.

49. H. Tian, R. Xu, J. G. Canadell et al. (2020). A Comprehensive Quantification of Global Nitrous Oxide Sources and Sinks. *Nature*, 586: 248–256. https://doi.org/10.1038/s41586-020-2780-0.

50. United Nations (2019). Why Nitrogen Management Is Key for Climate Change Mitigation. October 22. www.unep.org/news-and-stories/story/why-nitrogen-management-key-climate-change-mitigation.

51. UC Sustainable Agriculture Research and Education Program. (2017). Cover Crops. What Is Sustainable Agriculture? UC Division of Agriculture and Natural Resources. https://sarep.ucdavis.edu/sustainable-ag/cover-crops.

52. Sustainable Agriculture Research and Education (2015). Cover Crops and Carbon Sequestration. www.sare.org/publications/cover-crops/ecosystem-services/cover-crops-and-carbon-sequestration.

53. Environmental and Energy Study Institute (2022). Cover Crops for Climate and Mitigation. February 25. www.eesi.org/articles/view/cover-crops-for-climate-change-adaptation-and-mitigation#:~:text=Cover%20crops%20absorb%20carbon%20dioxide,of%20about%2013%20million%20vehicles.

54. S. Wallander, D. Smith, M. Bowman, and R. Claassen (2021). Cover Crop Trends, Programs, and Practices in the United States, EIB 222, US Department of Agriculture, Economic Research Service, February.

55. JD SUPRA (2021). Sustainable Chemistry Research and Development Act Passed As Part of National Defense Authorization Act. www.jdsupra.com/legalnews/sustainable-chemistry-research-and-6705080.

56. United States Department of Agriculture (2022). USDA to Invest $1 Billion in Climate Smart Commodities, Expanding Markets, Strengthening Rural America. www.usda.gov/media/press-releases/2022/02/07/usda-invest-1-billion-climate-smart-commodities-expanding-markets.

57. United States Department of Agriculture (2021). USDA Releases Economic Impact Analysis of the U.S. Biobased Products Industry. www.usda.gov/media/press-releases/2021/07/29/usda-releases-economic-impact-analysis-us-biobased-products.

58. New York (2022). Climate Action Council Draft Scoping Plan. https://climate.ny.gov/Our-Climate-Act/Draft-Scoping-Plan.

59. Airlines.org (2021). Major U.S. Airlines Commit to Net-Zero Carbon Emissions by 2050. March 30. www.airlines.org/news/major-u-s-airlines-commit-to-net-zero-carbon-emissions-by-2050.

60. BP (2022). What Is Sustainable Aviation Fuel? www.bp.com/en/global/air-bp/news-and-views/views/what-is-sustainable-aviation-fuel-saf-and-why-is-it-important.html.

61. International Air Transport Association (n.d.). What Is SAF? www.iata.org/contentassets/d13875e9ed784f75bac90f000760e998/saf-what-is-saf.pdf.

62. Newatlas (2021). Coca Cola Launches a Bottle Made from 100% Plant-Based Plastics. https://newatlas.com/environment/coca-cola-plantbottle-plant-based-plastic.

63. Packaging Europe (2021). The Inside Story of Coca-Cola's 100% Plant-Based Bottle. https://packagingeurope.com/features/the-inside-story-of-coca-colas-100-plant-based-bottle/7626.article.

64. Edie.net (2022). Unilever Spearheads $120 m Programme to Scale Bio-based Fossil Fuel and Palm Oil Alternatives. www.edie.net/unilever-spearheads-120m-programme-to-scale-bio-based-fossil-fuel-and-palm-oil-alternatives.

65. IBIS World (2022). Biotechnology in the US. August. Industry Report NN001.

66. IBIS World (2022). Tractors & Agriculture Machinery Manufacturing in the US. August. Industry Report 33311.

67. Fortune Business Insights (2021). 10 Leading Bioenergy Producers in the World by 2021. August. www.fortunebusinessinsights.com/blog/10-leading-bioenergy-producers-in-the-world–10598.

68. Thomas (2022). Biochemicals Suppliers. www.thomasnet.com/products/biochemicals-5280250-1.html.

PART III

Dynamics of the Transition

In Part II we explored the current trends in both the United States and around the world as governments and companies rapidly transition to a net-zero-carbon economy. In this necessary haste, there will no doubt be risks and unintended consequences resulting from a new generation of both organizational and technological strategies.

In this part we explore some of the dynamics of the transition. The following chapters offer just a glimpse of what our policymakers in both government and industry need to consider and evaluate in their leadership roles.

10

National Security and Critical Resources

Since 1990, at least 18 violent conflicts have been fueled by the exploitation of natural resources, whether high-value resources like timber, diamonds, gold, minerals and oil, or scarce ones like fertile land and water.

The United Nations Environment Programme (UNEP) suggests that in the last 60 years, at least 40 per cent of all intrastate conflicts have a link to natural resources, and that this link doubles the risk of a conflict relapse in the first five years.

The United Nations Peacekeeping [1]

10.1 Overview

As the title holds, this chapter is focused on the nexus of national security and critical resources. National security might immediately invoke images of the military, but while defense and the military are certainly important parts of national security, the term is more expansive in the context of this book. It also includes issues focused on jobs, our economy, and civil unrest, as well as policies that can ultimately lead to elevated tensions among countries.

Throughout our history there have been numerous conflicts due to perceived rights or determined needs for various natural resources. Prior to World War I, especially during the period of colonialism and colonial wars, the world witnessed conflict resulting from ambitions to control valuable resources, such as gold, silver, spices, timber, and slaves [2]. Leading up to the United States' entry into World War II, Japan undertook a preemptive attack on the United States in large measure to secure natural resources, namely petroleum,

141

oil, and metal; there was also a growing demand for food commodities located throughout South Asia [3, 4].

After World War II, we have witnessed a number of transboundary energy-related and natural resource conflicts such as the Iran–Iraq War (1980–1988) and the Gulf War (1990–1991), as well as numerous intrastate civil wars that not only include disputes over energy-related resources but also fights over water rights and minerals, as well as illicit drug crops such as in Colombia [5–8]. In fact, water scarcity affects approximately 40 percent of the world's population and both the World Bank and the United Nations predict further drought could place 700 million people at risk of displacement [9, 10]. As my political science and sociology academic colleagues will no doubt want to emphasize, correctly, none of these conflicts are simply a result of the desire to acquire a given resource; rather, there are a number of other determinant factors that influence conflict. These include poverty, corruption, rules of governance, and lacking institutions for law [11].

While the adverse impacts from global climate change may give rise to greater risks of conflicts over such things as transboundary rights to water resources [12, 13], so too I believe we will witness increased risks resulting from our efforts to mitigate the impacts of climate change through green technologies. To better understand this, we need to look at the trends. The annual demand around the world for rare-earth minerals, which are a subset of the broader grouping of critical minerals, is anticipated to increase from 208,250 metric tons in 2019 to 304,678 metric tons in 2025 [14]. This demand increase, as presented in Figure 10.1, is being driven by the accelerated need of minerals for electric vehicles (EVs), charging stations, batteries, and battery storage, as well as renewable energy technologies.

10.2 Critical Minerals and Clean Energy

First, many people interchange the terms rare-earth minerals and critical minerals. In fact, rare-earth minerals are a subset of critical minerals. Additionally, it is important to understand that rare-earth elements – defined as the fifteen lanthanides plus scandium (Sc) and yttrium (Y) – are actually not rare. The US Geological Survey finds the more abundant rare-earth elements are as common in concentration as other industrial metals, such as chromium, nickel, tungsten, and lead. Even the two least abundant rare-earth elements (thulium and lutetium) are nearly 200 times more common than gold.

However, because of the difficulties in extracting the metal from the ore, "rare" is a fitting term. These elements rarely exist in pure form; they are

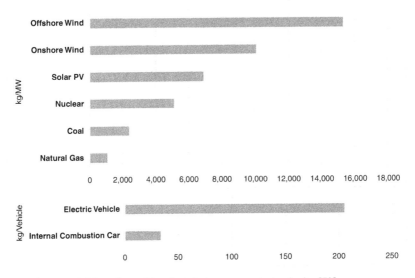

Figure 10.1 Minerals used in selected clean energy technologies [73].

usually found within other minerals, making them costly to mine. Consequently, most rare earths come from a small number of sources [15].

In the United States, the government established the definition of "critical minerals" under the Energy Act 2020 as minerals, elements, substances, or materials:

- that are essential to the economic or national security of the United States
- whose supply chain is vulnerable to disruptions, including restrictions associated with foreign political risk, abrupt demand growth, military conflict, violent unrest, anti-competitive or protectionist behaviors, and other risks
- that serve an essential function in the manufacturing of a product (including energy technology-, defense-, currency-, agriculture-, consumer electronics-, and health-care-related applications), the absence of which would have significant consequences for the economic or national security of the United States.[1]

In February 2022, the US Geological Survey issued the most recent listing of critical minerals, which increased from thirty-five listed in 2018 to now contain fifty minerals. The fifty listed critical minerals are [16]:

---

[1] Public Law 116–260, section 7002 (c) (4) (A).

1. Aluminum, used in almost all sectors of the economy
2. Antimony, used in lead-acid batteries and flame retardants
3. Arsenic, used in semiconductors
4. Barite, used in hydrocarbon production
5. Beryllium, used as an alloying agent in aerospace and defense industries
6. Bismuth, used in medical and atomic research
7. Cerium, used in catalytic converters, ceramics, glass, metallurgy, and polishing compounds
8. Cesium, used in research and development
9. Chromium, used primarily in stainless steel and other alloys
10. Cobalt, used in rechargeable batteries and superalloys
11. Dysprosium, used in permanent magnets, data storage devices, and lasers
12. Erbium, used in fiber optics, optical amplifiers, lasers, and glass colorants
13. Europium, used in phosphors and nuclear control rods
14. Fluorspar, used in the manufacture of aluminum, cement, steel, gasoline, and fluorine chemicals
15. Gadolinium, used in medical imaging, permanent magnets, and steelmaking
16. Gallium, used for integrated circuits and optical devices such as light-emitting diodes (LEDs)
17. Germanium, used for fiber optics and night-vision applications
18. Graphite, used for lubricants, batteries, and fuel cells
19. Hafnium, used for nuclear control rods, alloys, and high-temperature ceramics
20. Holmium, used in permanent magnets, nuclear control rods, and lasers
21. Indium, used in liquid-crystal display screens
22. Iridium, used as coating of anodes for electrochemical processes and as a chemical catalyst
23. Lanthanum, used to produce catalysts, ceramics, glass, polishing compounds, metallurgy, and batteries
24. Lithium, used for rechargeable batteries
25. Lutetium, used in scintillators for medical imaging, electronics, and some cancer therapies
26. Magnesium, used as an alloy and for reducing metals
27. Manganese, used in steelmaking and batteries
28. Neodymium, used in permanent magnets, rubber catalysts, and medical and industrial lasers
29. Nickel, used to make stainless steel, superalloys, and rechargeable batteries
30. Niobium, used mostly in steel and superalloys

31. Palladium, used in catalytic converters and as a catalyst agent
32. Platinum, used in catalytic converters
33. Praseodymium, used in permanent magnets, batteries, aerospace alloys, ceramics, and colorants
34. Rhodium, used in catalytic converters, electrical components, and as a catalyst
35. Rubidium, used for research and development in electronics
36. Ruthenium, used as catalysts, as well as electrical contacts and chip resistors in computers
37. Samarium, used in permanent magnets, as an absorber in nuclear reactors, and in cancer treatments
38. Scandium, used for alloys, ceramics, and fuel cells
39. Tantalum, used in electronic components, mostly capacitors, and in superalloys
40. Tellurium, used in solar cells, thermoelectric devices, and as an alloying additive
41. Terbium, used in permanent magnets, fiber optics, lasers, and solid-state devices
42. Thulium, used in various metal alloys and lasers
43. Tin, used as protective coatings and alloys for steel
44. Titanium, used as a white pigment or metal alloys
45. Tungsten, primarily used to make wear-resistant metals
46. Vanadium, primarily used as an alloying agent for iron and steel
47. Ytterbium, used for catalysts, scintillometers, lasers, and metallurgy
48. Yttrium, used for ceramic, catalysts, lasers, metallurgy, and phosphors
49. Zinc, primarily used in metallurgy to produce galvanized steel
50. Zirconium, used in high-temperature ceramics and corrosion-resistant alloys.

Up to 2010, minerals required for the energy sector represented a very small portion of total mineral demand. However, since the mid-2010s the clean energy sector is becoming the fastest-growing segment of demand. By implementing the Paris Climate Agreement goals, the clean energy technologies sectors' share of total demand will rise significantly over the next twenty years. This includes 40 percent for copper and rare-earth elements, 60–70 percent for nickel and cobalt, and almost 90 percent for lithium [17].

In fact, EVs and the required battery storage have already become greater users of lithium than consumer electronics and are set to take over from stainless steel as the largest end user of nickel by 2040 [17]. A typical EV battery cell with a 60 kilowatt-hour (kWh) capacity, just below the industry

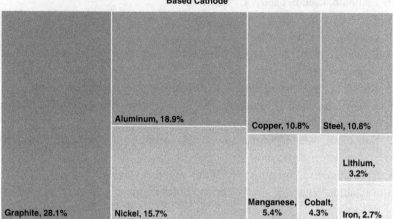

Figure 10.2 Minerals in a battery pack [18].

average of 64.2 kWh [18], contains approximately 185 kg (407.8 lbs) of minerals, not including the electrolyte, binder, separator, and battery pack casing, as presented in Figure 10.2.

Further, the projections of increased demand for minerals just for EV batteries are fairly staggering. Between 2019 and 2030, the global demand for lithium-ion batteries in EVs alone, not counting commercial and utility-scale battery storage, will grow from 120 gigawatt-hours (GWh) in 2019 to 1.525 terawatt-hours (TWh) [19], and this number is conservative as the estimates were conducted in 2019, well before the additional EV transition commitments by automotive manufacturers, states, and federal governments. In addition to the role of critical minerals in EV manufacturing, there are many other uses, as presented in Table 10.1.

10.3 Critical Minerals and National Defense

While critical minerals play such an important role in our clean energy and EV buildup, they also play a vital role in the defense of the United States. No other nation on the planet invests as much on military spending and national defense as the United States. In 2021, US military spending reached $801 billion, which is more than the next nine countries combined, including China, with the second largest military budget spending an estimated $293 billion,

Table 10.1 *Critical mineral needs for clean energy technologies [74]*

	Copper	Cobalt	Nickel	Lithium	Rare Earths	Chromium	Zinc	PGMs	Aluminum
Solar photovoltaics (PV)	**High**	Medium	Medium	Medium	Medium	Medium	Medium	Medium	**High**
Wind	**High**	Medium	Low	Medium	**High**	Low	**High**	Medium	Low
Hydro	Low	Medium	Medium	Medium	Medium	Low	Low	Medium	Low
Concentrating solar power	Low	Medium	Low	Medium	Medium	**High**	Low	Medium	**High**
Bioenergy	**High**	Medium	Medium	Medium	Medium	Low	Low	Medium	Low
Geothermal	Medium	Medium	**High**	Medium	Medium	**High**	Medium	Medium	Medium
Nuclear	Low	Medium	Low	Medium	Medium	Low	Medium	Medium	Medium
Electricity networks	**High**	Medium	Medium	Medium	**High**	Medium	Medium	Medium	**High**
Electric vehicles	**High**	**High**	**High**	**High**	**High**	Medium	Medium	Medium	**High**
Battery storage	**High**	**High**	**High**	**High**	**High**	Medium	Medium	Medium	**High**
Hydrogen	Medium	Medium	**High**	Medium	Low	Medium	Medium	**High**	Low

Note: Platinum group metals (PGMs) are among the rarest mineral commodities in the earth's crust. They include iridium, osmium, palladium, platinum, rhodium, and ruthenium. The PGMs occur together in nature, closely associated with nickel and copper, primarily in two major types of ore deposits.

Table 10.2 *Examples of military uses of critical minerals [75]*

Name	Properties	Aerospace Uses
Gallium	Superconductivity	Computer chips, light-emitting diodes
Neodymium	Extremely powerful, durable magnets	Missile guidance systems
Samarium	High-temperature magnetism, absorbs neutrons	Nuclear reactor control rods, lasers
Praseodymium	Makes stronger, more heat-tolerant alloys, permanent magnets	Aircraft engines, satellite components
Yttrium	Allow strengthener, glass clarifier	Microwave emitters, optical coatings, light-emitting diodes
Promethium	Low radioactivity	Long-lived batteries for missiles
Lanthanum	Class clarifier, reacts with hydrogen	Optics and lenses, night-vision goggles, fuel cells
Europium	Phosphorescence	Light-emitting diodes, plasma displays

a 4.7 percent increase year over year and an increase for the twenty-seventh consecutive year [20, 21]. Obviously, these numbers also do not reflect all of the additional expenditures by either country for national security such as spy satellites. Why is this important? Because the technologies of today and the next-generation technologies that serve our military and national defense are based on a readily accessible and growing supply of critical minerals.

For example, according to a 2017 document by the National Mining Association [22], the US Department of Defense uses up to 750,000 tons of minerals each year for military gear, weapon systems, and other defense systems. According to a report from the Congressional Research Service, each F-35 Lightning II aircraft requires 920 pounds of rare-earth materials. Lanthanum is used for night-vision goggles and up to 21 percent of the substance that is processed is used in defense applications including surveillance. Copper and silver are extensively used for naval vessels and rare earths are used in manufacturing jet engines; yttrium and terbium are used for laser targeting and weapons in combat vehicles [23] (Table 10.2).

10.4 The "So What" Question

You might be saying to yourself, okay, I get it, the world is going to be requiring a lot of minerals and there are fifty minerals that are critical to the national security of the United States. The "so what" moment is that many of these critical minerals are controlled by just a few countries, which does not include the United States and does include China. In fact, three-quarters (75 percent) of lithium, cobalt, and rare-earth elements are controlled by just the top three producing countries.

A Congressional Research Service[2] report [24] indicated that

> The United States is 100 percent import reliant on 14 minerals on the critical minerals list (aside from a small amount of recycling). These minerals are difficult to substitute inputs into the US economy and national security applications; they include graphite, manganese, niobium, rare earths, and tantalum, among others. The United States is more than 75 percent import reliant on an additional 10 critical minerals: antimony, barite, bauxite, bismuth, potash, rhenium, tellurium, tin, titanium concentrate, and uranium.

And the current big geopolitical risk for the United States and other countries is the dependence on and domination of, China. As stated by President Trump's Executive Order 13953 issued on October 5, 2020[3] [25]:

> Our dependence on one country, the People's Republic of China (China), for multiple critical minerals is particularly concerning. *The United States now imports 80 percent of its rare earth elements directly from China*, with portions of the remainder indirectly sourced from China through other countries. In the 1980s, the United States produced more of these elements than any other country in the world, but China used aggressive economic practices to strategically flood the global market for rare earth elements and displace its competitors. Since gaining this advantage, *China has exploited its position in the rare earth elements market by coercing industries that rely on these elements to locate their facilities, intellectual property, and technology in China.* For instance, multiple companies were forced to add factory capacity in China after it suspended exports of processed rare earth elements to Japan in 2010, threatening that country's industrial and defense sectors and disrupting rare earth elements prices worldwide.

Before we further explore China's global control of the processing of various critical minerals, let us explore just one – copper. Prior to my entering into academia, I was president of a multi-state environmental services company that supported both hard rock (copper, gold, molybdenum, etc.) and soft rock (coal) mining operations throughout the United States.

When I started with the mining sector in 1995, the United States was the world's second largest mine producer of cooper, accounting for about 19 percent of world production, and the world's largest producer and consumer of

---

[2] The Congressional Research Service is a public policy research institute of the United States Congress. Operating within the Library of Congress, it works primarily and directly for members of Congress and their committees and staff on a nonpartisan basis.
[3] Emphasis added by the author.

refined copper. There were thirty-eight mines operating in eleven states, mainly in the southwest as well as Wisconsin and Michigan. Mine capacity in the United States was estimated to be 2.08 million tons.

China's production back in 1995 was barely a footnote at 370,000 metric tons [26]. And even prior to 1995, historically, US companies accounted for most of the output of the copper mines in South America, chiefly Chile and Peru, thus representing effective US control of about 45 percent of free world production. However, US-owned mines in Chile began to be nationalized in the late 1960s, and the government of Chile has greatly expanded their output [27]. Today the US share of world mine production is about 18 percent. Chile has over a 23 percent share, nearly all of which is exported, and has the largest copper reserves in the world. Other important producers are, in order of mine production, Russia, Canada, China, Australia, and Zambia.

Fast forward to today. China consumes nearly 14 million tons of copper each year – more than the rest of the world combined – and Chile and Peru combined now produce close to 40 percent of global copper production. Both of these countries have newly elected leftist presidents who have proposed or endorsed bills to raise taxes on copper mining or to reduce mining to mitigate environmental and social impacts [28].

And while China consumes nearly 14 million tons, their domestic supply in 2020 was only around 2 million tons, ranking third in the world, including scrap, and mined output has been stagnant for years and further impacted due to lockdowns from COVID-19 [28]. The United States in 2020 ranked fifth with 1.2 million tons of copper mined [29].

Let's put the copper issue in context. S&P Global reports that by 2050, demand for copper driven by the net-zero-carbon transition will reach more than 53 million metric tons, which is "more than all the copper consumed in the world between 1900 and 2021" [30]. And it's not just a matter of access and quantity; it is also a matter of quality. As an example, the average ore quality in Chile has declined over 30 percent in just fifteen years [30].

So how are the United States and China planning for this and taking a leadership position to manufacture the world's green technologies? Let us explore.

10.5 The Battle between China and the US

The United States has only very poor ores of uranium in moderate quantities. There is some good ore in Canada and the former

Czechoslovakia, while the most important source of uranium is *Belgian Congo*.

In view of this situation you may think it desirable to have some permanent contact maintained between the Administration and the group of physicists working on chain reactions in America. One possible way of achieving this might be for you to entrust with this task a person who has your confidence and who could perhaps serve in an inofficial capacity. His task might comprise the following:

a) to approach Government Departments, keep them informed of the further development, and put forward recommendations for Government action, *giving particular attention to the problem of securing a supply of uranium ore for the United States*.

This is an excerpt from a letter[4] from Albert Einstein to President F. D. Roosevelt delivered in person by an Einstein associate, Alexander Sachs, on October 11, 1939 [31, 32]. We can go further back in time to document national interests in critical minerals. However, this letter from Einstein does provide an important platform for modern-day efforts led by China and with the United States now trying to play catch-up to secure the critical minerals required for the green-tech transition, as well as for advancements in civilian and military technologies.

The United States did not always play the laggard. In fact, the country after World War II was well ahead of China. However, the long-term lack of foresight and planning and poor governance have placed the economic and national security of the country in a precarious position – but one that certainly can be addressed.

The Democratic Republic of the Congo (DRC)[5] provides an illustrative example of how the US allowed China to supplant the country in the race to secure critical minerals. A *New York Times* in-depth report [33] does a nice job of capturing some of the policy failures of the US rather well and in a non-partisan manner. Historically, the US government, including the Central Intelligence Agency, was very concerned during the Cold War about the Soviet Union gaining access to the vast and important mineral resources in the DRC, including copper, cobalt, and uranium.

However, after the collapse of the Soviet Union,[6] the United States quickly reduced its attention and supportive actions and this was further exasperated post-9/11 with the War on Terror. Fast forward to 2022. Today the DRC is the

---

[4] Emphasis added by the author.
[5] Formerly called Zaire and the second largest country in Africa. It achieved independence from Belgium on June 30, 1960.
[6] December 26, 1991.

world's largest supplier of cobalt at up to 70 percent of the global supply as a by-product of their expansive copper mines. Of this vast supply of cobalt, approximately 80 percent of its industrial cobalt mines are either owned or financed by China/Chinese companies [34].

The United States did have access to this very important critical mineral in the DRC until Phoenix, Arizona-based Freeport-McMoRan Copper and Gold (NYSE:FCX) sold the Tenke Fungurume mine in May 2016 to China Molybdenum (CMOC) for $2.65 billion. CMOC in 2021 announced a further investment of $2.5 billion to expand the mine. And just a few years later, Freeport-McMoRan sold its other asset in the DRC, the Kisanfu mining project, to the same China Molybdenum for $550 million. The Kisanfu project is a large cobalt and copper resource with an estimated 6.3 Mt of copper and 3.1 Mt of cbalt and CMOC is now planning to invest $1.82 billion for the initial development [35, 36].

So why did Freeport-McMoRan sell to the Chinese? As reported by the *New York Times* [33], the company had made a "catastrophically bad bet on the oil and gas industry, just before oil prices tanked and the world began to shift to renewables." The company's stock went from a high of $60 per share in 2010 to $4 per share in January 2016 and the company sought to cut $20 billion in debt [37]. And while mismanagement of Freeport was the driver for the sell, both the Obama and Trump Administrations allowed the sales to happen without attempts to intervene in a serious manner [33] to ensure America's national security.

And while China has gained accension to be the global controller of raw critical minerals through investments and ownership in the "mines and mining companies," it has also been strategic in controlling the global supply of the "processed minerals." It refines 68 percent of nickel globally, 40 percent of copper, 59 percent of lithium, and 73 percent of cobalt [38, 39]. China also plays a critical role in the manufacturing of clean energy technologies, including manufacturing battery cell components.

China accounts for most of the global production of mineral-rich components for battery cells, including 70 percent of cathodes, which are the most important component and can account for half the cost of a manufactured cell, 85 percent of anodes, 66 percent of separators, and 62 percent of electrolytes. Importantly, China holds 78 percent of the world's cell manufacturing capacity for EV batteries, which are then assembled into modules that are used to form a battery pack. The country also hosts three-quarters of the world's lithium-ion battery mega-factories. This makes China the largest consumer of the minerals it refines [40, 41, 42, 43].

And what has the United States done? Well, quite simply, not a lot! And this has significant implications for its national security. The lack of a proactive strategy has been the fault of both Republican and Democratic leaders that has existed for a very long time and countered by a very deliberate strategy by the Chinese Communist Party.

10.6 Belt and Road Initiative

Since 1953, the Chinese Communist Party has developed a series of five-year plans to be implemented by the People's Republic of China (PRC) to shape the country's economic development and strategies. The first five-year plan sent a strong signal with its focus on industrial development [44]. In 2012 Xi Jinping became general secretary of the Chinese Communist Party and in 2013 was elected chairman of the PRC Central Military Commission and president of the People's Republic of China [45]. During this power transition, the PRC undertook the development of two important five-year plans. The twelfth plan (2011–2015) laid out a plan to grow GDP by 8 percent[7] (7 percent growth/year/capita). The plan also laid out a vision foreign investment in modern agriculture, high-tech, and importantly environment protection industries. The plan outlined seven strategic new industries including new energy, new materials, and new-energy-powered automobiles [46, 47].

It was during the implementation of the twelfth five-year plan that President Xi made a historic and in many ways his centerpiece policy announcement. On September 7, 2013, Xi gave a speech at Nazarbayev University, an autonomous research university in Nur-Sultan, the capital of Kazakhstan [48]. It was this speech that introduced the world to China's Belt and Road Initiative (BRI). More specifically, he laid out the structure of the "Silk Road Economic Belt" and a counterpart "21st Century Maritime Silk Road" – "One Belt, One Road." These words put together formed what is now known as the BRI. In 2014 this was followed at the November 2014 Asia-Pacific Economic Cooperation meeting by Xi announcing that China would establish a $40 billion fund to finance the BRI and credit of at least $120 billion more over the next few years [49].

There is no question that the BRI has been a success for China, mostly in filling a gap created by the lack of active investments by the United States and multilateral development banks [50, 51]. While there are no hard statistical facts regarding the program as there is no central governing institution and, in

---

[7] In 2011 the United States had 1.6 percent growth; China had 9.6 percent growth.

most views, the government has intentionally kept the details in some secrecy, it is believed that China has invested between $1 trillion and $8 trillion in infrastructure, transport, and energy and linking to more than 100 countries throughout the world [51]. Prior to the BRI between 2000 and 2012, China and the United States were basically on a par with one another in overseas spending, with the annual average development finance commitments at $32 billion for China and $34 billion for the US.

However, with the inception of the BRI and its implementation during 2013–2017, China outspent the United States by an almost two-to-one margin. China invested $85.4 billion a year on average and the United States spent $37 billion per year on average [52]. During the same period, roughly 47 percent or 5,152 finance projects (the largest number) made by China were in Africa – a resource-rich continent. Further, during 2000–2017, the two sectors with the greatest amount of Chinese development finance around the globe were [52]:

1. Mining, industry, and construction with 302 projects and accounting for 29.7 percent of the 2017 USD billions ($123.3 billion)
2. Energy, with 431 projects and accounting for 21.5 percent and $89.5 billion (USD 2017).

As presented in Figure 10.3, China's share of processing of critical minerals has grown into a national monopoly and national security threat to other countries, as was experienced by Japan in 2010 when China cut off the supply of rare-earth minerals to the country as a result of a fishing incident and Japan detaining a Chinese fishing trawler captain [53].

Beyond the investments by China in mining and energy sectors, the BRI also helped foreign government leaders to construct large infrastructure projects, such as airports, ports, and roads. The results of this provided direct engagement and contracts by Chinese design/building firms and suppliers, but it also advanced the positive political images of various foreign leaders – bringing favor to China. In fact, by 2016, China was the largest exporter to Africa accounting for 17.5 percent of Africa's imports and a year later it was reported that more than 10,000 Chinese-owned companies operated in Africa [55].

To combat this, the G7[8] on June 26, 2022 presented their plan to take China head-on with a plan to provide $600 billion of private and public investment over the next five years called the Partnership for Global Infrastructure and Investment. The plan is not intended to take on BRI infrastructure-type projects of China but rather to focus on climate and energy security, digital, health, and

---

[8] The G7 is an informal grouping of seven of the world's advanced economies: Canada, France, Germany, Italy, Japan, the United Kingdom, and the United States, as well as the European Union.

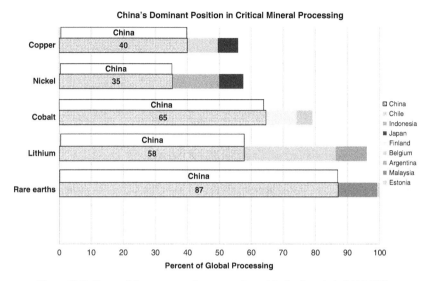

Figure 10.3 Share of the top countries processing critical minerals in 2019 [54].

women's equality. The US committed up to $200 billion. The plan is to use limited government resources to leverage larger private investments [56]. The West will wait to see how much progress it will make in countering China's in securing a pathway for leading in acquiring critical minerals and developing the capacity to meet global demand for green-tech manufacturing.

10.7 The Next Frontiers

If Africa has been the at the crosshairs of foreign policy and critical minerals for the first two decades of the twenty-first century, then both South America and the Arctic are likely to be the next areas.

10.7.1 Lithium Triangle

While Africa remains an area of focus, much of the world's attention has moved recently to South America. Here lies the "Lithium Triangle" which holds up to 75 percent of the world's supply under its salt flats [57]. Including Argentina, Bolivia, and Chile, the Lithium Triangle is just as the name sounds: a lithium-rich region in the Andean southwest corner of the continent.

Of the world's 86 million tons of identified lithium resources, Bolivia possesses 21 million tons, followed by Argentina with 19.3 million tons and

Chile with 9.6 million tons. Chile has been the most successful in turning its vast reserves into economically viable reserves available for commercial production. In fact, Chile possesses the largest quantity of "commercially viable" lithium reserves in the world – despite having far fewer potential resources than both Bolivia and Argentina – and is the world's second largest commercial producer after Australia. Two main companies control Chile's lithium extraction industry: Albemarle, a US-based company that also controls the largest lithium operations in Australia, and Sociedad Química y Minera de Chile (SQM), Chile's largest lithium mining company.

Because of both challenging geography and equally important challenging investment climates, both Argentina and Bolivia are lagging behind Chile in commercial production. Beneath the ancestral land of the Indigenous Atacamas, Bolivia is home to Salar de Uyuni, the world's largest salt flat that spans 4,000 square miles with massive lithium deposits, composing about 50 percent of the earth's total.

However, just as we have witnessed in Africa, Chinese companies are now increasing their focus and investments in the Lithium Triangle. China's Ganfeng Lithium is the majority stakeholder in Argentina's Cauchari-Olaroz operation, which observed its initial production in July 2023 and will further ramp up production into 2025.

In Chile, China's Tianqi Lithium became the second largest shareholder in SQM, Chile's largest lithium mining company, holding 23.8 percent of shares. Chinese companies Ganfeng Lithium and Tianqi Lithium now represent two of the top three lithium mining companies in the world.

As reported by CSIS, not only has China increased its investment in the Lithium Triangle countries but it has also strengthened its bilateral relationships through its vaccine diplomacy in which both Chile and Argentina deployed the Chinese vaccines Sinovac and Sinopharm to fight off COVID-19. It will be worth seeing if US national security policy in fact ramps up diplomatic and investment in these important South American countries [58, 59].

10.7.2 The Arctic

The Arctic as an area is essentially an ocean surrounded by the land north of the Arctic circle (66032′ N) that covers a region of 33 million km^2, larger than Africa or Asia [60].

Title 15 U.S.C. § 4111 defines the Arctic as "all U.S. and foreign territory north of the Arctic Circle and all U.S. territory north and west of the boundary formed by the Porcupine, Yukon, and Kuskokwim Rivers; all contiguous seas, including the Arctic Ocean and the Beaufort, Bering, and Chukchi Seas; and the Aleutian islands chain" [61].

Why has this geography become so important? First, you have to understand that the Arctic sea ice has diminished from 6.1 million sq km in 1999 to 4.3 million sq km in 2019 and continues this pace, meaning that greater access to the region is made available as the ice continues to melt. In 2008, the United States Geological Survey published the results of their appraisal of oil and gas reserves from new field discoveries in the Arctic. Their results indicated that 84 percent of the reserves were offshore and were estimated to be 90 billion barrels of oil, 1,699 trillion cubic feet of natural gas, and 44 billion barrels of natural gas liquids [62].

Important for the net-zero-carbon transition predicated on critical minerals for deployment in green technologies is the potential for vast critical mineral resources in the Arctic. Tiny balls of oxides are thought to be scattered on the ocean floor. These nodules hold special promise because of the fact that they contain the critical minerals we need for our transition.

Part of the intrigue of what lies in the non-nation Arctic is that Article 7 of the Protocol on Environmental Protection to the Antarctic Treaty of 1991 bans all mineral resource activities on the continent except those related to scientific research. "The Arctic Region is thus, on a global scale, one of the few remaining land regions with extensive areas of 'prospective' geology in which knowledge of the mineral potential is limited" [63].

However, what is known is that the surrounding land-based resources of Arctic countries do contain extensive critical resources including [63]:

• copper
• nickel
• zinc
• lead
• titanium
• vanadium
• molybdenum
• cobalt
• platinum
• palladium
• tantalum
• uranium and other rare-earth elements.

In fact, in Greenland the Kvanefjeld proposed mining operation is home to the second largest rare-earth oxides deposit and the sixth largest for uranium. The mine is being developed by Australia-based Greenland Minerals, which is part-owned by Chinese Shenghe Resources [64]. The project will provide China unique insights into mineral resource opportunities in the Arctic.

The governance of the Arctic is unique. There are in fact eight Arctic sovereign states – Canada, Denmark, Finland, Iceland, Norway, Russia, Sweden, and the United States, who in 1996 formed the Arctic Council along with six organizations representing Indigenous people. The PRC was an Arctic Council Observer in 2013 [65, 66].

China's role is interesting as it has described the Arctic as one of the world's "new strategic frontiers," ripe for rivalry and extraction. It has followed this up building its first produced icebreaker, which now total two, but work has been started to construct a nuclear-powered icebreaker fleet. Meanwhile, the United States has only recently invested in an icebreaker, the Polar Sentinel, which at best will be delivered in 2025 and currently has no icebreakers patrolling the Arctic. The two ships the US Coast Guard does have are the Polar Star, which has outlived its thirty-year life, and the Healy, which caught fire in 2020. Meanwhile, Russia has over forty icebreakers [67, 68, 69, 70].

Finally, satellite imagery shows that Russia is on a fast track to expanding its military presence in the Arctic [71]. As NATO Secretary General Jens Stoltenberg recently stated, "Russia has set up a new Arctic Command. It has opened hundreds of new and former Soviet-era Arctic military sites, including airfields and deep water ports. Russia is also using the region as a testbed for many of its new and novel weapons systems" [72]. All of this is concerning as the world looks to the Arctic as a potential resource for needed critical minerals.

References

1. United Nations Peacekeeping (n.d.). Conflict and Natural Resources. https:// peacekeeping.un.org/en/conflict-and-natural-resources#:~:text=Since% 201990%2C%20at%20least%2018,like%20fertile%20land%20and%20water.
2. M. T. Klare, B. S. Levy, and V. W. Sidel (2011). The Public Health Implications of Resource Wars. *American Journal of Public Health*, 101(9): 1615–1619. doi: 10.2105/AJPH.2011.300267.
3. M. Badkar (2012). 9 Wars That Were Really about Commodities. *Insider*. August 15. www.businessinsider.com/nine-wars-that-were-fought-over-commod ities–2012-8.
4. The National Interest (2019). The 1 Reason Imperial Japan Attacked Pearl Harbor: Oil. October 16. https://nationalinterest.org/blog/buzz/1-reason-imper ial-japan-attacked-pearl-harbor-oil–88771.
5. M. Klare (2015). Fighting for Oil: 21st Century Energy Wars. *Middle East Eye*. February 12. www.middleeasteye.net/big-story/fighting-oil-21st-century-energy- wars.

6. M. Ross (2002). Natural Resources and Civil War: An Overview with Some Policy Options. Conference on the Governance of Natural Resources. The World Bank and the Agence Francaise de Developpement, Paris, December 9–10.

7. F. Diaz (2014). Drug Trafficking and the Columbian Conflict. *Peace Insight*. www.peaceinsight.org/en/articles/drug-trafficking-colombian-conflict/?location=colombia&theme=.

8. W. M. LeoGrande and K. E. Sharpe (2000). Two Wars or One? Drugs, Guerrillas, and Colombia's New "Violencia." *World Policy Journal*, 17(3): 1–11. www.jstor.org/stable/40209699.

9. BBC (2021). How Water Shortages Are Brewing Wars. August 16. www.bbc.com/future/article/20210816-how-water-shortages-are-brewing-wars.

10. United Nations (n.d.). The Drought Initiative. www.unccd.int/land-and-life/drought/drought-initiative.

11. O. Akpan and U. E. Umoh (2021). "Resource Curse" and "Resource Wars" and the Proliferation of Small Arms in Africa. In U. A. Tar and C. P. Onwurah (eds.), *The Palgrave Handbook of Small Arms and Conflicts in Africa*. Cham: Palgrave Macmillan. https://doi.org/10.1007/978-3-030-62183-4_12.

12. World Economic Forum (2020). Water Wars: How Conflicts over Resources Are Set to Rise Amid Climate Change. www.weforum.org/agenda/2020/09/climate-change-impact-water-security-risk.

13. S. Sengupta (2022). Climate Change Is Making Armed Conflict Worse. Here's How. New York Times. March 18.

14. Forbes (2022). China and Russia Make Critical Mineral Grabs in Africa while the U.S. Snoozes. January 13. www.forbes.com/sites/arielcohen/2022/01/13/china-and-russia-make-critical-mineral-grabs-in-africa-while-the-us-snoozes/?sh=51be68d86dc4.

15. ThermoFisher Scientific (2013). What's So Rare about Rare Earth Elements? July 8. www.thermofisher.com/blog/mining/whats-so-rare-about-rare-earth-elements/#:~:text=Nothing.,common%20in%20the%20Earth's%20crust.

16. US Geological Survey (2022). U.S. Geological Survey Releases 2022 List of Critical Minerals. www.usgs.gov/news/national-news-release/us-geological-survey-releases-2022-list-critical-minerals.

17. International Energy Agency (2021). The Role of Critical Minerals in Clean Energy Transitions. Paris. www.iea.org/reports/the-role-of-critical-minerals-in-clean-energy-transitions.

18. Electric Vehicle Database (2022). Useable Battery Capacity of Full Electric Vehicles. https://ev-database.org/cheatsheet/useable-battery-capacity-electric-car.

19. Statista (2022). Estimated Global Lithium-Ion Battery Demand in Electric Vehicles (EVs) in 2019 with a Forecast for 2020 through 2030 by Region. www.statista.com/statistics/1103229/global-battery-demand-by-region-forecast.

20. Peterson Foundation (2022). The United States Spends More on Defense Than the Next 9 Countries combined. June 1. www.pgpf.org/blog/2022/06/the-united-states-spends-more-on-defense-than-the-next-9-countries-combined.

21. Stockholm International Peace Research Institute (2022). World Military Expenditures Passes $2 Trillion for First Time. www.sipri.org/media/press-release/2022/world-military-expenditure-passes-2-trillion-first-time.

22. National Mining Association (2017). U.S. National Defense: Stronger with Minerals. https://nma.org/wp-content/uploads/2017/10/infographic_defense-01 .pdf1.

23. US Army (2019). An Elemental Issue. September 26. www.army.mil/article/ 227715/an_elemental_issue.

24. Congressional Research Service (2019). Critical Minerals and U.S. Public Policy. R45810. June 28. https://crsreports.congress.gov/product/details?prodcode=R45810.

25. Federal Register (n.d.). Addressing the Threat to the Domestic Supply Chain From Reliance on Critical Minerals From Foreign Adversaries and Supporting the Domestic Mining and Processing Industries. www.federalregister.gov/docu ments/2020/10/05/2020-22064/addressing-the-threat-to-the-domestic-supply- chain-from-reliance-on-critical-minerals-from-foreign.

26. Bureau of Mines (1995). Minerals Yearbook Volume 1. Copper. D. Edelstein. https://d9-wret.s3.us-west-2.amazonaws.com/assets/palladium/production/min eral-pubs/copper/240495.pdf.

27. Copper Development Association (2022). Copper in the USA: Bright Future Glorious Past. www.copper.org/education/history/us-history/g_fact_indus try.php.

28. Mining.com (2022). Copper Supply in 2022 – Eyes on Chile, Peru, DRC. December 24. www.mining.com/top-copper-stories-of-2021-and-what-to- expect-in–2022.

29. NS Energy (2021). Profiling the World's Top Five Copper Mining Countries in 2020. www.nsenergybusiness.com/news/top-five-copper-mining-countries.

30. S&P Global (2022). Looming Copper Supply Shortfalls Present a Challenge to Achieving Net-Zero 2050 Goals, S&P Global Study Finds. https://press.spglobal .com/2022-07-14-Looming-Copper-Supply-Shortfalls-Present-a-Challenge-to- Achieving-Net-Zero-2050-Goals,-S-P-Global-Study-Finds.

31. Atomic Heritage Foundation (2019). Einstein-Szilar Letter. www.atomicheritage .org/key-documents/einstein-szilard-letter.

32. Library of Congress (2020). Einstein's Fateful Letter. August 13. https://blogs .loc.gov/law/2020/08/einsteins-fateful-letter.

33. E. Lipton and D. Searcy (2021). How the U.S. Lost Ground to China in the Contest for Clean Energy. *New York Times*. November 21. www.nytimes.com/ 2021/11/21/world/us-china-energy.html.

34. Michigan State University (2022). Congo's Cobalt Controversy. Published as Global Business Knowledge. April 20. https://globaledge.msu.edu/blog/post/ 57136/congos-cobalt-controversy#:~:text=The%20DRC%20supplies%20about %2070and%20its%20domestic%20mining%20companies.

35. Mining Technology (2020). Freeport Sells Interests in DRC's Kisanfu Project to CMOC for $550 M. December 15. www.mining-technology.com/news/freeport- sells-interests-in-drcs-kisanfu-project-to-cmoc-for-550m/#:~:text=Gwyndafh %20from%20Pixabay.-American%20copper%20major%20Freeport %2DMcMoRan%20has%20sold%20its%20interests%20in,proceeds%20 stood%20at%20%24415m.

36. Mining Technology (2022). China's CMOC Plans $1.8bn Investment in Congo Copper-Cobalt Mine. July 1. www.mining-technology.com/news/

cmoc-congo-copper/#:~:text=Located%2033km%20south%2Dwest%20of,cop
per%20and%203.1Mt%20cobalt.

37. Bloomberg (2016). Freeport Said Offering Packages of Assets to Cut $20 Billion
    Debt. April 22. www.bloomberg.com/news/articles/2016-04-22/freeport-said-
    offering-package-of-assets-to-cut-20-billion-debt.

38. J. Yeomans and F. Harter (2022). Who Owns the Earth? The Scramble Turns
    Critical. *The Times*. www.thetimes.co.uk/article/who-ownsthe-earth-the-scram
    ble-for-minerals-turnscritical-jbglsgm02.

39. International Energy Agency (2021). The Role of Critical Minerals in Clean
    Energy Transitions. www.iea.org/reports/the-role-of-criticalminerals-in-clean-
    energy-transitions.

40. International Energy Agency (2022). Shares for Cathodes and Anodes
    Correspond to IEA Estimates. Global Supply Chains of EV Batteries. www.iea
    .org/reports/global-supply-chains-of-evbatteries.

41. S. Ladislaw, E. Zindler, J. Nakano et al. (2021). Industrial Policy, Trade, and
    Clean Energy Supply Chains. Center for Strategic and International Studies.
    www.csis.org/analysis/industrial-policy-trade-and-cleanenergy-supply-chains.

42. J. Pettitt (2022). How the U.S. Fell Behind in Lithium, the "White Gold" of
    Electric Vehicles. CNBC. January 15. www.cnbc.com/2022/01/15/how-the-us-
    fell-way-behindin-lithium-white-gold-for-evs.html.

43. R. Castillo and C. Purdy (2022). China's Role in Supplying Critical Minerals for
    the Global Energy Transition. What Could the Future Hold? LTRC and Brookings
    Institute. www.brookings.edu/wp-content/uploads/2022/08/LTRC_China
    SupplyChain.pdf.

44. Britannica (2022). First Five-Year Plan. Chinese Economics. www.britannica
    .com/topic/First-Five-Year-Plan-Chinese-economics.

45. China Vitae (2022). Xi Jinping. www.chinavitae.com/biography/xi_jinping/full.

46. KraneShares (2013). China's 12th Five Year Plan. F. Gang. https://kraneshares
    .com/resources/2013_10_kfyp_fan_gang_white_paper.pdf.

47. Europe China Research and Advice Network (2012). *China, the EU and China's
    Twelfth Five-Year Programme. Funded by the European Union*. London.

48. *China Daily* (2013). President Xi Proposes Silk Road Economic Belt. www
    .chinadaily.com.cn/china/2013xivisitcenterasia/2013-09/07/content_16951811.htm.

49. CSIS (2016). President Xi Jinping's Belt and Road Initiative: A Practical
    Assessment of the Chinese Communist Party's Roadmap for China's Global
    Resurgence. C. Johnson for the Center for Strategic and International Studies.
    Washington, DC, March. www.csis.org/analysis/president-xi-jinpings-belt-and-
    road-initiative.

50. Insider (2019). The US Is Scrambling to Invest More in Asia to Counter China's
    Belt and Road Mega-Project. Here's What China's Plan to Connect the World
    through Infrastructure Is Like. November 11. www.businessinsider.com/what-is-
    belt-and-road-china-infrastructure-project–2018–1.

51. Council on Foreign Relations (2021). *China's Belt and Road. Implications for the
    United States. Independent Task Force Report* No. 79. Lew, J., G. Roughead
    chairs.

162Dynamics of the Transition

52. A. Malik, B. Parks, B. Russell et al. (2021). Banking on the Belt and Road: Insights from a New Global Dataset of 13,247 Chinese Development Projects. AIDDATA-A research lab at William and Mary College. September.

53. *New York Times* (2010). Amid Tension, China Blocks Vital Exports to Japan. September 22. www.nytimes.com/2010/09/23/business/global/23rare.html.

54. International Energy Agency (2019). Share of Processing Volume by Country for Selected Minerals. Paris. www.iea.org/data-and-statistics/charts/share-of-processing-volume-by-country-for-selected-minerals–2019.

55. GIS (2022). How China's Belt and Road Initiative Is Faring. April 8. www.gisreportsonline.com/r/belt-road-initiative.

56. *The Economist* (2022). The G7 at Last Presents an Alternative to China's Belt and Road Initiative. July 7. www.economist.com/china/2022/07/07/the-g7-at-last-presents-an-alternative-to-chinas-belt-and-road-initiative.

57. *Harvard International Review* (2020). The Lithium Triangle: Where Chile, Argentina, and Bolivia Meet. https://hir.harvard.edu/lithium-triangle.

58. CSIS (2021). South America's Lithium Triangle: Opportunities for the Biden Administration. August 17. Ryan Berg. www.csis.org/analysis/south-americas-lithium-triangle-opportunities-biden-administration.

59. *Economist* (2017). A Battle for Supremacy in the Lithium Triangle. June 15. www.economist.com/the-americas/2017/06/15/a-battle-for-supremacy-in-the-lithium-triangle.

60. United Nations Environment Programme (2022). Arctic Region. www.unep.org/explore-topics/oceans-seas/what-we-do/working-regional-seas/regional-seas-programmes/arctic-region.

61. US Army (2021). Regaining Arctic Dominance. Headquarters U.S. Army. January 19. Chief of Staff Paper #3. www.army.mil/e2/downloads/rv7/about/2021_army_arctic_strategy.pdf.

62. United States Geological Survey (2008). Circum-Arctic Resource Appraisal: Estimates of Undiscovered Oil and Gas North of the Arctic Circle. Fact Sheet 2008–3049.

63. Geological Survey of Norway (2016). Mineral Resources in the Arctic. www.ngu.no/upload/Aktuelt/CircumArtic/Mineral_Resources_Arctic_Shortver_Eng.pdf.

64. High North News (2021). Chinese Company into Greenlandic Mining Project. February 9. www.highnorthnews.com/en/chinese-company-greenlandic-mining-project.

65. Arctic Council (2022). Arctic Council. The leading Intergovernmental Forum Promoting Cooperation in the Arctic. www.arctic-council.org/about.

66. *New York Times* (2013). Arctic Council Adds 6 Nations As Observer States, Including China. May 15.

67. 合作才能避免失序 (Cooperation to Avoid Disaster), 中工网 (Zhonggongwang), May 12. http://world.workercn.cn/63/201405/12/140512054028106.shtml. (This piece was written by Tang Yongsheng, the executive deputy director of the National Defense University's Strategic Research Institute.)

68. Brookings (2021). Northern Expedition: China's Arctic Activities and Ambitions. April. www.brookings.edu/articles/northern-expedition-chinas-arctic-activities-and-ambitions.

69. Heritage Foundation (2021). U.S. Needs Icebreakers to Keep Up with China and Russia in Arctic. June 18. www.heritage.org/global-politics/commentary/us-needs-icebreakers-keep-china-and-russia-arctic.

70. Arctic Today (2022). The Newest US Icebreaker Now Has a Name but Construction Is Still Delayed. February 28. www.arctictoday.com/the-newest-us-icebreaker-now-has-a-name-but-construction-is-still-delayed.

71. CNN (2021). Satellite Images Show Huge Russian Military Buildup in the Arctic. April 5. www.cnn.com/2021/04/05/europe/russia-arctic-nato-military-intl-cmd/index.html.

72. Euronews (2022). NATO Chief Warns about Russia's Arctic Military Build-Up on Canadian Visit. www.euronews.com/2022/08/27/nato-chief-warns-about-rus sias-arctic-military-build-up-on-canada-visit#:~:text=%22Russia%20has%20set %20up%20a,weapons%20systems%2C%E2%80%9D%20Stoltenberg%20said.

73. International Energy Agency (2021). Minerals Used in Clean Energy Technologies Compared to Other Power Generation. Paris. www.iea.org/data-and-statistics/charts/minerals-used-in-clean-energy-technologies-compared-to-other-power-generation-sources.

74. International Energy Agency (2021). The Role of Critical World Energy Outlook Special Report Minerals in Clean Energy Transitions. Paris. https://iea.blob.core .windows.net/assets/24d5dfbb-a77a-4647-abcc-667867207f74/TheRoleofCritical MineralsinCleanEnergyTransitions.pdf.

75. *Air Force Magazine* (2020). Rare Elements of Security. November 1.

11

Rural versus Urban

Geographic polarization, or the urban-rural divide, is arguably the most defining feature of American politics.
Kal Munis and Robert Saldin, "The Democrats' Rural Problem" [1]

Over the past 20 years, the Democratic Party has hemorrhaged support in the countryside. They've got a five-alarm fire in rural America, but much of the party's elite doesn't even see the smoke.
T. B. Edsall, "Red and Blue America Will Never Be the Same" [2]

11.1 Rural–Urban Divide

Let's begin with one immediate observation about the unintended consequences of the net-zero-carbon transition and its affiliated reliance on electric vehicles (EVs). And that observation quite simply is this: in the near term EVs will make winners in urban America and losers in rural America. That is not to say that the US cannot achieve equilibrium, but it will not in the near term and this is a risky proposition.

Rural America is home to approximately 60 million people or 20 percent of its population. In fact, urban areas make up only 3 percent of the entire land area of the United States but are home to more than 80 percent of the population, whereas 97 percent of the country's land mass is rural but only 19.3 percent of the population lives there [3].

Additionally, 70 percent of US road miles are in rural regions [4], and in many states throughout the southwest and west there are vast distances of roads without infrastructure, including electricity, that go well beyond current EV battery capacity, unlike in the country's cities and densely populated coasts [5]. Even though the Biden Administration wants to construct EV charging stations every 50 miles, the policies are mired with constraints that would allow the states the flexibility to meet deployment in the best way to meet state needs [5].

A study by the bipartisan Environmental and Energy Study Institute reinforced the notion that rural areas are EV and charging station deserts. They indicate that major metro areas have 500 to over 1,000 public outlets per 25 square miles, while the majority of rural areas and small towns have none [6]. Nationally, the states with the greatest number of EV sales in the United States with advanced technology vehicles[1] are [7]:

1. California: 12.98 percent
2. Washington: 10.60 percent
3. Oregon: 9.69 percent
4. District of Columbia: 8.87 percent
5. Hawaii: 6.25 percent
6. Vermont: 6.09 percent
7. Colorado: 6.0 percent
8. Maryland: 5.83 percent
9. Massachusetts: 5.69 percent
10. Virginia: 5.53 percent

States carrying the bottom of the market share include Wyoming, South and North Dakota, West Virginia, Alabama, Arkansas, Mississippi, and Louisiana, with Oklahoma coming in at the very bottom.

Meanwhile, the federal government through the National Electric Vehicle Infrastructure (NEVI) Formula Program, established as part of the Bipartisan Infrastructure Law, has set aside $900 million in NEVI formula funding from FY22 and FY23 to help build EV charging networks [8]. Overall, the federal infrastructure package Congress passed in 2021 includes $7.5 billion for EV charging stations, with $5 billion given directly to the states. Households can also obtain up to $7,500 in federal tax credits for purchasing a new EV in addition to state incentives [9]. Additionally, the Inflation Reduction Act (IRA) of 2022 includes over $60 billion in incentives for US clean energy and transportation technology manufacturing, $10 billion in investment tax credits for building domestic clean technology manufacturing facilities, and $2 billion in grants for retooling existing auto manufacturing facilities to produce clean vehicles. Additionally, the IRA provides up to $20 billion in loans to build new clean vehicle manufacturing facilities [10].

---

[1] Fuel cell electric vehicles (FCEVs), battery electric vehicles (BEVs), plug-in hybrid electric vehicles (PHEVs), and hybrid electric vehicles (HEVs).

And all of this is essential as one important pathway for the US and states to meet net-zero-carbon commitments. However, at the same time that the federal government is making these investments, which in the near term benefit mostly those living in urban areas, those living in rural regions are facing a very different scenario.

First, we must remember the main premise of the EV; that is, to escape our dependence on fossil fuels used for transportation – the largest contributor to greenhouse gas emissions in the United States, as presented in earlier chapters. The issue is twofold. Remember earlier that I mentioned Oklahoma had the lowest market penetration of EVs. Well, Washington County, Oklahoma has the highest concentration of employment in the oil and gas extraction industry of any county in the United States[2] and the vast majority of those employed in the sector are in rural counties of the United States. In fact, for 2022, the top six oil-producing states were Texas, North Dakota, New Mexico, Oklahoma, Colorado, and Alaska [11, 12].

And what crop is the largest crop grown in the United States in terms of total production? Yes, you were right: it is corn. In 2019, American farmers planted 91.7 million acres of corn or about 69 million football fields, which is far more acres than the next largest crop, soybeans [13]. And of the 13.7 billion bushels of corn produced [26], 40 percent was refined into the gasoline additive ethanol. That is because nearly every gallon of gas sold in the US contains at least 10 percent ethanol as mandated by the federal Renewable Fuel Standard (RFS), enacted in 2005 as part of the Energy Policy Act and later updated through the Energy Independence and Security Act of 2007 [14]. And to the farmer, dry mill ethanol plants add $2 of additional value to a bushel of corn. An Iowa State University study indicates that the RFS returned $14.1 billion in profits to the domestic agriculture sector [15, 16, 17]. And where is corn grown in America? The answer is obvious: rural America.

American views on EVs reflect this divide and are representative of the US's current geopolitical situation. The Pew Research Center conducted a poll in 2022. Their findings [18] are as follows:

1. Democrats are much more likely than Republicans and GOP leaners to say they favor incentives to increase the use of EVs (84 to 46 percent).
2. Those living in urban areas (53 percent) are more likely than those in suburban (44 percent) and rural areas (27 percent) to report interest in purchasing an EV.

---

[2] The latest numbers the author was able to obtain were for 2014.

3. Fifty-eight percent of Democrats are likely to consider an EV the next time they purchase a new car versus just 23 percent of Republicans.
4. Democrats and Republicans (including those who lean to each party) continue to be deeply divided over whether to end the production of cars and trucks with internal combustion engines. About two-thirds of Democrats (65 percent) favor phasing out gasoline-powered cars and trucks by 2035. In contrast, just 17 percent of Republicans support the idea, while 82 percent oppose it.

11.2 Possible Pathways

One emerging pathway to address the divide is to find possible solutions that provide hope and a real plan to those American industries and families in rural regions that are dependent on the current gasoline-based automotive industrial structure.

11.2.1 A Biobased Economy

The first pathway is something that the Biden Administration initiated in 2022. This is the development of funding and policy initiatives to advance the biobased economy, where American agriculture is used to develop a new generation of low- or net-negative-carbon energy sources, aviation fuels, chemicals, and products. In 2022 the administration issued a $1 billion request for proposals to advance "climate-SMART commodities" but ended up funding seventy projects across the country for $2.8 billion [19].

This program in association with other federal programs such as the Biorefinery, Renewable Chemical, and Biobased Product Manufacturing Assistance Program (aka 9003 Program), which provides up to $250 million in loan guarantees to develop, build, or retrofit facilities to support new and emerging technologies, and produce advanced biofuels, renewable chemicals, and biobased products [20], are important means to offset the eventual losses of the ethanol and bio-diesel industry. The programs provide pathways not just for corn and soybean growers but also for many other crops, as well as processors and manufactures to develop new uses of agriculture to meet the needs of industry and governments transitioning to net-zero carbon.[3]

---

[3] See Chapters 15 and 16 to obtain insights into some of the real-world barriers.

The second effort is a bit more complicated. It entails identifying pathways to re-purpose the country's extensive oil and natural gas infrastructure. Certainly, there are theoretical opportunities to utilize some of the infrastructure for bio-based chemicals and energy. In the United States alone there are over 1.8 million miles of pipelines [21] – enough to circle the earth[4] almost seventy-six times! However, the pathways many in the industry are banking on are either:

1. Carbon capture and sequestration (CCS)
2. Co-produced carbon materials hydrogen from fossil fuels.

11.3 Carbon Capture and Sequestration (CCS)

CCS is focused on stationary sources of carbon releases such as fossil fuel power plants. As described by the US Environmental Protection Agency (EPA) [22]: "after capture, carbon dioxide (CO_2) is compressed and then transported to a site where it is injected underground for permanent storage (also known as 'sequestration')."

The most common way that CO_2 would be transported is in fact by the country's extensive network of pipelines, though in certain circumstances it could also be transported by train, truck, or ship. The EPA points out that geologic formations suitable for sequestration include depleted oil and gas fields, deep coal seams, and saline formations [22]. The US Department of Energy estimates that anywhere from 1,800 to 20,000 billion metric tons of CO_2 could be stored underground in the United States. That is equivalent to 600 to 6,700 years of current-level emissions from large stationary sources in the United States [23]. The technology is very nascent in implementation. As of 2019, there were only ten CCS facilities in the US with a combined capacity to capture more than 25 million tons per annum. In total, there are nineteen operating facilities globally; however, many more have been put forward in the United States due in part to tax benefits, which are detailed in Chapter 17 [24].

11.4 Co-produced Products

This is an effort funded by the petroleum industry and best known to be researched at Rice University in Houston at the university's Carbon Hub research center. The Carbon Hub is supported in part by Shell, Saudi

---

[4] Earth's distance at the equator is 24,902 miles.

Aramco, Huntsman, and so on. Their efforts are exploring how to effectively create renewable hydrogen from fossil fuels and capturing the carbon for beneficial reuse rather than capturing and injecting. The research focuses on the ability to split hydrocarbons into solid carbon and cleaner-burning hydrogen fuel. Then the leftover carbon theoretically could form the basis for replacing already high-carbon feedstocks used in cement, aluminum, building materials, and even synthetics for clothing. It is a very difficult problem to overcome but if achieved would give promise to the existing oil and natural gas industries.

References

1. K. Munis and R. Saldin (2022). The Democrats' Rural Problem. *Washington Monthly*. July 28. https://washingtonmonthly.com/2022/07/28/the-democrats-rural-problem.
2. T. B. Edsall (2022). Red and Blue America Will Never Be the Same. *The New York Times*. July 27. www.nytimes.com/2022/07/27/opinion/trump-red-blue-america.html.
3. Census (2017). One of Five Americans Live in Rural Areas. August 9. www.census.gov/library/stories/2017/08/rural-america.html.
4. US Department of Transportation (n.d.). Electric Vehicles and Rural Transportation. www.transportation.gov/rural/ev.
5. *Wall Street Journal* (2022). Biden Plan for EV Chargers on Highways Meets Skepticism in Rural West. June 13. www.wsj.com/articles/biden-plan-for-ev-chargers-on-highways-meets-skepticism-in-rural-west–11655112780.
6. Environmental and Energy Study Institute (2022). Rural Electric Cooperatives Take the Charge in Boosting Electric Vehicle Infrastructure. April 13. www.eesi.org/articles/view/rural-electric-cooperatives-take-the-lead-on-boosting-electric-vehicle-charging-infrastructure.
7. Alliance for Automotive Innovation (2022). Electric Vehicle Sales Dashboard. www.autosinnovate.org/resources/electric-vehicle-sales-dashboard.
8. US Department of Transportation (2022). President Biden's Bipartisan Infrastructure Law Provides $5B in NEVI Formula Funding to Help States Install EV Chargers Along Interstate Highways Additional EV Charging Funding to Come. https://highways.dot.gov/newsroom/biden-harris-administration-announces-approval-first-35-state-plans-build-out-ev-charging.
9. New York State Energy Research and Development Authority (2022). Drive Clean Rebate for Plug-In Electric Vehicles. www.nyserda.ny.gov/Drive-Clean-Rebate.
10. Congress.gov (2022). H.R.5376 – Inflation Reduction Act of 2022. www.congress.gov/bill/117th-congress/house-bill/5376.
11. Bureau of Economic Statistics (2015). Counties with the Highest Employment in the Oil and Gas Extraction. TED. *Economics Daily*. January 9. www.bls.gov/

opub/ted/2015/counties-with-highest-concentration-of-employment-in-oil-and-gas-extraction-june-2014.htm.

12. Investopia (2022). Top 6 Oil-Producing States. August 1. www.investopedia.com/financial-edge/0511/top-6-oil-producing-states.aspx.

13. United States Department of Agriculture (2021). Corn Is America's Largest Crop in 2019. July 29. www.usda.gov/media/blog/2019/07/29/corn-americas-largest-crop–2019.

14. United States Department of Agriculture (2020). Crop Production 2019 Summary. www.nass.usda.gov/Publications/Todays_Reports/reports/cropan20.pdf.

15. Agamerica (2020). Ethanol Market Is Disturbing to American Farmers. And Now There's Covid-19. March 30. www.agriculture.com/news/business/ethanol-market-is-disturbing-as-hell-to-american-farmers-and-now-there-s-covid-19.

16. G. Moschini, H. Lapan, and H. Kim (2017). The Renewable Fuel Standard in Competitive Equilibrium: Market and Welfare Effects. *American Journal of Agricultural Economics*, 99: 1117–1142. https://doi.org/10.1093/ajae/aax041.

17. Renewable Fuels Association (2020). Why Is Ethanol Important? Renewable Fuels Association (blog). https://ethanolrfa.org/consumers/why-is-ethanol-important.

18. International Council on Clean Transportation (2021). The Impact of the U.S. Renewable Fuel Standard on Food and Feed Prices. https://theicct.org/sites/default/files/publications/RFS-and-feed-prices-jan2021.pdf.

19. Pew Center (2022). Americans Support Incentives for Electric Vehicles but Are Divided over Buying One Themselves. www.pewresearch.org/fact-tank/2022/08/01/americans-support-incentives-for-electric-vehicles-but-are-divided-over-buying-one-themselves.

20. United States Department of Agriculture (2022). Partnership for Climate-Smart Commodities. www.usda.gov/climate-solutions/climate-smart-commodities.

21. Federal Register (2020). Biorefinery, Renewable Chemical, and Biobased Product Manufacturing Assistance Program. www.federalregister.gov/documents/2020/05/18/2020-08078/biorefinery-renewable-chemical-and-biobased-product-manufacturing-assistance-program.

22. US Department of Transportation (2022). U.S. Oil and Gas Pipeline Mileage. www.bts.gov/content/us-oil-and-gas-pipeline-mileage.

23. US Environmental Protection Agency (2017). Carbon Dioxide Capture and Sequestration: Overview. https://19january2017snapshot.epa.gov/climatechange/carbon-dioxide-capture-and-sequestration-overview_.html.

24. Greenhouse Gas Reporting Program (2012). EPA Greenhouse Gas Reporting Data-Subpart PP-Suppliers of Carbon Dioxide. Based on 2011 data. www.epa.gov/ghgreporting/subpart-pp-suppliers-carbon-dioxide.

25. L. Beck (2020). Carbon Capture and Storage in the USA: The Role of US Innovation Leadership in Climate-Technology Commercialization. *Clean Energy*, 4(1): 2–11. https://doi.org/10.1093/ce/zkz031.

26. United States Department of Agriculture (2020). Crop Production 2019 Summary. www.nass.usda.gov/Publications/Todays_Reports/reports/cropan20.pdf.

12

The Vanishing Industries

Neither RedBox nor Netflix are even on the radar screen in terms of competition.

Blockbuster chief executive officer Jim Keyes in an interview with Motley Fool in 2008 (his video-rental chain filed for bankruptcy in 2010 and as of September 26, 2022 Netflix had a market cap of $100.69 billion [1, 2])

12.1 Loss of an Industry

In its heyday, the video-rental powerhouse Blockbuster had over 9,000 stores; as of today, there exists only one store in the world located in Bend, Oregon [3]. There was great hubris by both the leadership and the industry with a lack of appreciating the disruptive nature of a new technology and consumer preference. In many ways, I see the same happening today by our legacy fossil fuel industry in taking immediate action to adopt or die. While automotive manufacturers have made the pivot to their production and supply chains and are focusing on the electric vehicle (EV) transition, the rest of the value chain is lagging.

If I were either an investor in those industry segments or a state/local official, I would be very concerned. Unfortunately, as I have learned from first-hand experience, neither is very focused on the issues as of the writing of this book. In part, this is because the transition will not be overnight; however, there will certainly be first-mover advantages.

12.2 Your Local Convenience Store

The first purpose-built, drive-up gas station in the United States opened in 1913 when there were just 500,000 vehicles driving mostly on dirt or gravel roads. When I was growing up, the local gas station was a full-service experience with equal parts gas and mechanic services. It was where you took your car for repairs and maintenance. There were gas attendants who cleaned your windshield and checked your tire pressure. Technology and economics changed the fueling experience. A transformation started on June 10, 1964 when John Roscoe started to offer self-service gasoline in conjunction with his Big Top convenience store in Westminster, Colorado, which sold groceries, milk, sodas, and so on [4]. The rapid expansion of convenience stores selling gasoline took place in the 1980s as pay-at-the-pump technologies took off and the economics of selling gas flipped.

As I write this chapter, gas prices are starting to come down from near-term highs. When I go to the convenience store or Costco to fill up for gas, the price at the pump is $4.33 a gallon. It is important to understand the breakdown of the costs:

1. $2.60 – crude oil exploration and extraction (where the greatest profit is located)
2. $0.62 – refining
3. $0.62 – federal and state taxes
4. $0.35 – transportation of the fuel throughout the process
5. $0.14 – markup

The average profit is actually between $0.05 and $0.07 per gallon. At $0.05/gallon with a store selling 4,000 gallons per day, the average income is $200 per day. Compare that with the margins inside the stores such as soda from dispensers (200 percent), ATM machine fees (100 percent), lottery tickets (100 percent), prepared foods (50 percent), and bottled water and candies (50 percent). In fact, while gasoline accounts for approximately 70 percent of the revenue, it is what is sold inside the stores that provides convenience store owners around 70 percent of their profit [5, 6].

Today, there are over 150,000 convenience and fuel-only stations in the United States, with almost 80 percent being convenience stores. This includes [7]:

1. 6,494 hypermarkets such as big box stores Walmart, Costs, and other wholesalers that sell gasoline
2. 121,538 convenience stores
3. 3,000 to 8,000 service stations
4. 15,638 fueling kiosks similar to convenience stores but with smaller and limited in-store selections

Included in this grouping are over 960,300 persons employed by the industry from food preparation workers to cashiers, technicians/mechanics, supervisors, and so on.

12.3 The Economic Fallout

As I contemplated the EV transition and the future of convenience stores, the obvious question is: What happens to those 150,000 properties? You generally don't find a convenience store in a residential or industrial neighborhood. Rather, the stores are located in prime real estate with high-traffic patterns. Most developers seek prime corner or strip mall locations. These are high-traffic and high-property-tax locations. And it was the latter question that captured my attention. What are the tax and revenue implications and how are states preparing for them?

So, in 2022, I reached out to multiple states on the east coast who I won't name. I spoke with elected representatives who chair transportation committees as well as budget committees. I spoke with staff who lead budget offices and tax offices. I had just three simple questions for each:

Question 1: Given the EV transition, have you calculated the tax and revenue impacts to your state?

Question 2: Given the EV transition, have you calculated any changes in state expenditures to support the transition?

Question 3: What policies are you developing for questions 1 and 2?

I thought these were questions that no doubt our leaders have considered and were working on. I was wrong!

The general responses were along the lines of, "Wow, those are great questions, but we have not worked on them in any detail. It's on our radar. But if you and your students want to work on them, that would be great."

So, in spring 2022 a small group of my students and I undertook this challenge. And the findings were interesting.

12.3.1 State Expenditure Implications

States are highly dependent on both fuel taxes and sales taxes that are derived from our current fossil fuel vehicle industry. Generally, the largest per-capita revenue source for states comes from federal transfers. Based on the tax structure of the state, individual income tax might be the second largest, as it is in Delaware, or general sales tax, as it is in Arizona. In Texas, property taxes are the second largest stream right behind federal transfers, while in California "charges" are the second largest revenue stream [8]. However, for all states, "selective sales taxes," which include fuel taxes that we all pay at the pump, are usually in the top five state per-capita revenues.

Before we get into the lost revenues, we need to consider the other side of the ledger – expenses. In most states, the greatest per-capita expenditure is for K-12 education but not for all states, some of whom have health and hospitals or public welfare. These are followed generally by higher education and highways and roads, which round out the top five [8].

State motor vehicle fuel taxes are the major sources of revenues that a state generates to maintain, repair, replace, and construct new highways, roads, and associated facilities. In most cases, a significant portion of these revenues is allocated to county and local jurisdictions. Take the state of California as an example of the implications of the EV transition. For 2021–2022 the state projected motor vehicle fuel tax revenue to reach $8,638,712,000 [9].

We need to consider how expenditures may change during the transition. First, EVs generally weigh more than internal combustion vehicles because of the batteries. For instance, a Ford F-150 Lightning will weigh about 1,600 pounds more than a similar gas-powered F-150 truck and the electric Volvo XC40 Recharge weighs about 1,000 pounds more than a gas-powered Volvo XC40 [10]. This will likely result in higher road maintenance requirements.

Second, we need to consider how climate change will impact road and highway costs. While there is no recent study on the economic impact on maintaining our roads as a result of the increased frequency and intensity of storms, as well as increased temperatures such as urban heat islands, a 2013 study indicated that unchecked, climate change could increase the costs of roads by $2.8 billion in 2050 in the United States [11].

Third, unless the convenience stores find a way to effectively repurpose their property, there will be property management and environmental consider-ations. Let us consider the environmental implications. In the United States as of 2021, there were 542,000 underground storage tanks (USTs). These USTs range in size from 10,000 to 20,000 gallons and on average the neighborhood gas station/convenience store will have three tanks [7, 12]. The US Environmental Protection Agency (EPA) reports that over 566,000 UST releases had been confirmed as of March 2022 and there remain about 61,000 UST sites to be cleaned up [13]. UST releases have a significant impact to groundwater and drinking water supplies.

As reported by the US EPA [14]:

1. Thirty-six states have state financial assurance funds, which help UST owners comply with the federal financial responsibility regulation. These funds pay to clean up newly reported releases as well as ongoing cleanups.

2. Five states have funds that no longer provide financial responsibility for UST owners but continue to pay for those ongoing cleanups where they assumed financial responsibility in the past.
3. Nine states, the District of Columbia, and five territories rely entirely on EPA-approved, privately funded financial responsibility mechanisms to finance all UST cleanups and comply with the federal financial responsibility regulation.

The federal governments obtain $0.01/gallon from a federal fuel tax for UST remediation. States vary on the amount of fuel tax. A study conducted by the Dynamic Sustainability Lab [14] indicated that many states have negative Leaking Underground Storage Tank trust fund balances, which will become even greater if not addressed, with decreasing fuel tax revenues.

12.3.2 State Revenue Implications

Beyond the implications of fuel tax reductions, the transition to EVs will also impact state revenues in a number of ways, including the necessity to build out infrastructure for charging networks.

Sales tax revenue will be impacted as fewer people are likely to make a quick stop at a convenience store while filling up the car with gas. How about that lottery ticket we buy at the gas station? I highlight the state of Rhode Island. The lottery is the largest voluntary source of income for the state [15]. The lottery paid $301.8 million to the state of Rhode Island's general fund, which ended on June 30, 2021 after payouts and operating expenses [16].

And just as convenience stores make most of their profit from sales inside the building, car dealers make most of their profits from repairs and maintenance. New car sales account for about 58 percent of sales but less than 26 percent of gross profit. Used cars represent about 31 percent of sales, accounting for about 25 percent of gross profit. The remaining profit is derived by the service and parts department, accounting for the other 49.6 percent of the dealership's gross profits, according to the National Automobile Dealers Association [17].

For most states and local jurisdictions, sales tax is also collected from when we pay for maintenance on our current internal combustion vehicles. However, as reported by a number of research organizations, including Consumer Reports, pure EVs – which have fewer moving parts – need less maintenance and generally cost less to repair than the average gas-powered vehicle [18]. Less maintenance and less purchasing of new parts and supplies equate to sales tax revenue reductions.

Then we also need to consider sales tax from electricity sales. How will that work in the EV future? Some states tax electricity at the commercial and industrial rates and not at the residential level. New York state, for instance, has a 4 percent sales tax on electricity while excluding residentials [19]. This is relevant when we work through the deployment of charging stations. Will EV charging stations be standard in home construction, negating having to run to a commercial store to charge up? We just do not know as of now how this will play out.

Finally, policymakers need to get their arms around the future of automotive sales. With lower maintenance requirements and continued direct-to-consumer purchasing options, will we need dealerships, and how do states and local jurisdictions manage tax policies for vehicles ordered directly from locations outside their jurisdiction and delivered directly to the owner?

12.4 The Privacy Equation

So just how will states adapt to the loss of revenues? One option is to adopt technologies that can track an individual car owner's driving habits; more specifically, that can track how many miles are driven in each state per year and allocate taxes proportionally. This has two significant drawbacks. First, it would be complicated for states to work together, let alone manage the administration of the program. Second, and likely more impactful, how would Americans react to the government tracking them and the locations of their movements?

Other alternatives are being piloted in Oregon and Utah. In Oregon, the OReGO program requires a \$115/year EV fee or a \$0.019/mile fee. Users select from one of three options [20]:

1. Plug-in device with GPS
2. Plug-in device without GPS
3. Manual entry reporting

The state of Utah has a road usage charge program of \$123/year or a fee of \$0.0152/mile. They use an onboard GPS device (OBD). As part of this program, they offer year-to-year driving statistics such as braking, emissions, and so on [21]. Users can choose between the options. If you drive a lot, you would likely select the flat fee. However, if you drive infrequently, the OBD would be a better economic option, if you are comfortable with the government (or in the case of Utah, a third party) tracking. For the states, vehicle miles traveled taxes have higher collection costs versus fuel taxes.

The next few years will be important for states and local jurisdictions to calculate the implications for revenue shortfalls and expenditure increases and, importantly, to develop strategies to meet these transition challenges.

References

1. Motley Fool (2008). Blockbuster CEO Has Answers. Updated 2017. www.fool .com/investing/general/2008/12/10/blockbuster-ceo-has-answers.aspx? awc=12195_1664191902_845d0d61b2b25282efc020cbefcbf1d9&campaig n=78888&pc_source=TheMotleyFool_Awin&utm_source=aw&utm_campaig n=78888.
2. Y Charts (2022). Netflix Inc. https://ycharts.com/companies/NFLX/market_cap.
3. ABC News (2021). World's Last Blockbuster More Popular after Netflix Show. March 30. https://abcnews.go.com/Business/wireStory/bends-blockbuster-popu lar-netflix-show-76774655#:~:text=In%20its%20heyday%2C%20Blockbuster% 20Video,now%20offering%20the%20Blockbuster%20documentary.
4. CBS News (2014). The Modern American Convenience Store Turns 50. Jonathan Berr. June 10. www.cbsnews.com/news/the-american-convenience-store-turns–50.
5. The Hustle (2021). The Economics of Gas Stations. https://thehustle.co/the-eco nomics-of-gas-stations.
6. National Association of Convenience Stores (2022). The History for Fuel Retailing. www.convenience.org/Topics/Fuels/The-History-of-Fuels-Retailing.
7. A. Greenberg and J. S. Golden (2022). The EV Transition: Implications for the US Gas Station and Convenience Store Industry. The Dynamic Sustainability Lab. Bulletin No. 20220303. www.dynamicslab.org.
8. Urban Institute (2022). State Fiscal Briefs. www.urban.org/policy-centers/cross-center-initiatives/state-and-local-finance-initiative/projects/state-fiscal-briefs.
9. State of California (2021). Budget Summary – Revenue Estimates. www.ebudget .ca.gov/2021–22/pdf/BudgetSummary/RevenueEstimates.pdf.
10. CNN (2021). Why Electric Cars Are So Much Heavier Than Regular Cars. June 7. www.cnn.com/2021/06/07/business/electric-vehicles-weight/index.html.
11. P. Chinowsky, J. Price, and J. Neumann (2013). Assessment of Climate Change Adaptation Costs for the U.S. Road Network. *Global Environmental Change*, 23(4): 0959–3780.
12. GeoForward (2022). Underground Storage Tank Sizes and Volumes. May 16. www.geoforward.com/underground-storage-tank-sizes-volumes/#:~:text=For% 20instance%2C%20some%20underground%20dieseland%20hold%20just% 2055%20gallons.
13. US Environmental Protection Agency (2022). Cleaning Up Underground Storage Tank (UST) Releases. www.epa.gov/ust/cleaning-underground-storage-tank-ust-releases.
14. US Environmental Protection Agency (2022). State Financial Assurance Funds. www.epa.gov/ust/state-financial-assurance-funds.

15. The Lot (2022). Financial Information. www.rilot.com/en-us/financials.html.
16. The Lot (2022). The Rhode Island Lottery Made $301.8 Million for Fiscal Year 2021. www.rilot.com/en-us/about-us/lottery-description.html.
17. Edmunds (2019). Where Does the Car Dealer Make Money? Mostly From Service, Not from Car Sales. www.edmunds.com/car-buying/where-does-the-car-dealer-make-money.html.
18. Consumer Reports (2020). Pay Less for Vehicle Maintenance with an EV. www .consumerreports.org/car-repair-maintenance/pay-less-for-vehicle-maintenance-with-an-ev.
19. Salesandusetax.com (2018). New York Utility Tax Exemption Opportunities. www.consumerreports.org/car-repair-maintenance/pay-less-for-vehicle-mainten ance-with-an-ev.
20. OreGO (2022). Sign Up for OreGO. www.myorego.org/get-started.
21. Utah Department of Transportation (2022). Welcome to Utah's Road Usage Charge Program. https://roadusagecharge.utah.gov/#:~:text=How%20does% 20Utah's%20Road%20Usage,of%20the%20set%20flat%20fee.

13

Tailwinds and Headwinds for Offshore Wind

Offshore wind could generate 11 times more electricity than the world needs and could attract $1 trillion in investment by 2040.

International Energy Agency, 2019 [1, 2]

13.1 Offshore Wind in the United States

On March 29, 2021, the White House announced a target of deploying 30 gigawatts (30,000 megawatts) of offshore wind by 2030 with the hope of realizing more than $12 billion per year in capital investment in projects, more than 44,000 workers employed in the industry, and nearly 33,000 additional jobs in communities that are supported by the offshore wind activity [3].

If the United States were able to generate 30 GW, that would provide enough power to meet the demand of more than 10 million American homes for a year and avoid 78 million metric tons of CO_2 emissions [3]. To give some context to this build-up, the United States averaged 11.0 GW a year of retirements of US coal-fired electric generating capacity from 2015 to 2020 and that increased to 12.6 GW of coal capacity retirements scheduled in 2022 [4]. The greenhouse gas benefits of wind are obviously great. Wind energy produces around 11 grams of CO_2 per kilowatt-hour (g CO_2/kWh) of electricity generated, compared with about 980 g CO_2/kWh for coal and roughly 465 g CO_2/kWh for natural gas [5].

But for all of its potential, there are headwinds that impede its quick adoption. Accessing offshore wind and harnessing its potential is not the problem. The largest risk in meeting US offshore renewable energy targets is not the country's manufacturing capacity or a lack of a trained workforce, and actually not even financing capacity. Rather, it is the federalist government regulatory structure and regulations and policies that have lacked vision and

179

forethought to have envisioned the rapid demand for renewable energy and transitioning away from legacy large-scale thermoelectric power plants. Yes, in fact the overly burdened and strained permitting process, especially as compared to China and the European Union, is what presents the greatest risks and frustration to developers, financers, utilities, and climate advocates. This issue may in fact be one of the rare instances that will bring the more liberal portions of the political spectrum together with the more conservative American politicians in developing policy solutions to reduce many of the regulatory burdens that block progress on both addressing climate change and the development of a robust and competitive domestic green-tech manufacturing base.

Remember, it is projected that by 2050 in the United States the combined sales per year of electric vehicles (battery electric vehicles [BEVs] and plug-in hybrid electric vehicles [PHEVs]) will increase from 0.5 million in 2021 to 2.0 million per year in 2050. If half of all cars sold by 2030 were electric vehicles (EVs), EVs could make up between 60 and 70 percent of cars on the road by 2050 in the United States. Globally, the Energy Information Agency (EIA) predicts there will be up to 672 million EVs on the road, reflecting growth from 0.7 percent to 31 percent [6, 7, 8].

In fact, the EV transition makes no sense if the electricity powering them is not based on renewable electricity. It has been projected that global demand for electricity from cars will grow from 21,655 GW in 2020 to 486,088 GW in 2030 and grow even further through 2050 [9].

While much of the west coast of the United States will focus on floating offshore wind because the continental shelf on the west coast drops off steeply to depths of 13,000 feet (4,000 meters), in the east coast the depths are much shallower and so it is easier to install fixed-bottom turbines. This has resulted in all of the attention and initial offshore wind development projects taking place along the east coast in the Atlantic, which is presented in Figure 13.1. The data in this figure, obtained from the US Department of Energy, are structured so that the location of the project is defined by where the project's power is intended to be sold. If the project does not have an offtake agreement, the location is the project's physical location. This clarification is needed where projects are located in a certain location but sell their power to a neighboring state market [10].

13.2 The Permitting Headwinds

The aspiration for 30 GW of offshore renewable wind electricity in the United States is a welcomed vision. However, turning that vision into reality is not going to be easy. The headwinds the industry is facing are daunting. And most

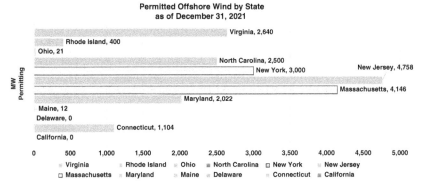

Figure 13.1 Offshore wind permitting in place by state in United States as of December 31, 2021 in MW.
Adapted from [10].

of these hurdles are government induced. While there are supply chain issues, I believe that the US's free market can overcome most of these deficiencies, perhaps not as quickly and efficiently as China, but in the longer term it can be more effective and robust than its Chinese counterparts. However, the larger near-term issues that risk the US's ability to realize not only the renewable energy goals but as importantly jobs and regional/national economic development revolve around government policies. Specifically:

1. Permitting requirements and timelines needed to develop and construct offshore wind
2. Permitting, uncertainty, and timelines to connect to the electrical transmission network; that is, the grid
3. Outdated US policies that limit the supporting infrastructure to deploy
4. A lack of coordination between public–private organizations primarily at the state level in regard to permitting, workforce development, and manufacturing development.

13.2.1 The Permitting Conundrum

The United States is woefully slow and obstructive in the permitting process, which is a legacy of its federalist system. This is not a problem isolated to offshore wind but spans across its industrial sectors and is only exasperated when those run parallel with the plethora of relevant environmental regulations. That is not just frustrating to those focused on developing offshore renewable energy but also inhibits the US's national security from an economic and jobs perspective, which fairly needs to be balanced with long-term environmental protection. However, the US's political divide has only worsened. Just two weeks after Russia illegally invaded Ukraine, the European Union (EU) Commission mapped out a new EU energy policy called "REPowerEU," which would create renewable "go-to" areas that member countries would set up and be permitted within one year. This is in addition to the existing permitting deadlines of two years for new projects and one year for repowered projects [11].

The EU recommendations for "go-to" areas would have a low environmental impact, therefore allowing for a single environmental assessment requirement for the areas as a whole, removing the need for individual projects to go through the full process [12].

While not facing the complexities of a much larger country, Denmark[1] offers some potential innovations and streamlining in permitting design. It has a single government agency that manages the permitting process – the Danish Energy Agency. As stated in a reference document, "The Energy Agency acting as a one-stop-shop for the operators is ensuring a smooth licensing procedure, where the interests of other authorities are managed internally, thus minimizing the administrative work of the operators" [13].

Additionally, the Danish RE Act[2] provides for the ability of local municipalities to object to the issuance of a pre-investigation license for a wind farm that will be located within 8 km of the coastline. However, the complaint is handled in a manner that is more expedient, with the objection being forwarded to the Energy, Utilities and Climate Committee of the Danish Parliament for review. Ultimately, the Minister for Energy, Utilities, and Climate makes the final decision on whether to issue the license. An objection from a municipality will therefore not automatically result in the application being rejected [14].

In the United States, however, the federalist government structure more frequently than not lacks flexibility and adaptability, and the permitting process is overwhelmed by constituent groups as well as a multitude of overlapping government agencies who do not want to cede their own authority to another agency of the government. In the US, an offshore wind project must navigate the agencies set out in Table 13.1 for approval [15].

In America, a federal agency not known outside of the offshore wind and energy industry rules the administrative process. This is the Bureau of Ocean

---

[1] Denmark has a population of 5.8 million, roughly equivalent to the US state of Minnesota, which is only the twenty-second most populated state in the United States.

[2] See https://ens.dk/sites/ens.dk/files/Vindenergi/promotion_of_renewable_energy_act_-_extract.pdf.

Table 13.1 *Offshore wind permitting process in the United States, adapted from [15]*

Permitting/Consultation Requirement	Federal Regulatory Agency
Obtain a commercial lease of submerged lands for renewable energy development	BOEM
Receive approval for a Site Assessment Plan (SAP)	BOEM
Receive approval for a Construction and Operations Plan (COP)	BOEM
Receive approval for a Facility and Design Report (FDR)	BOEM
Receive approval for a Fabrication and Installation Report (FIR)	BOEM
Consultations pertaining to: • Magnuson-Stevens Fishery Conservation and Management Act • Marine Mammal Protection Act • National Historic Preservation Act • Endangered Species Act	NOAA Fisheries NOAA Fisheries, USFWS Advisory Council on Historic Preservation NOAA Fisheries, USFWS
Receive permit for subsea cables under the Clean Water Act	USACE
Receive permit for navigational lighting	US Coast Guard
Consultations pertaining to siting	DoD, FAA
Receive permits for air quality and pollution prevention	EPA, USACE
Receive authorization for incidental take or harassment under the Marine Mammal Protection Act, Endangered Species Act, Migratory Bird Treaty Act, the Bald and Golden Eagle Protection Act, and the Magnuson-Stevens Fishery Conservation and Management Act	NOAA Fisheries, USFWS
State agencies and state-assembled working groups	New York example: NYSERDA, DEC, 4 Technical Working Groups (Fisheries, Environmental, Maritime, Job and Supply Chain)
Local jurisdiction permits and industry/ non-governmental organizations	Numerous. Responsible Offshore Development Alliance, Responsible Offshore Science Alliance, Regional Wildlife Science Entity

Note: BOEM = Bureau of Ocean Energy Management; DEC = Department of Environmental Conservation; DoD = Department of Defense; EPA = Environmental Protection Agency; FAA = Federal Aviation Administration; NYSERDA = New York State Energy Research and Development Authority; USACE = US Army Corps of Engineers; USFWS = US Fish and Wildlife Service.

Energy Management (BOEM),[3] which is not part of the US Department of Energy but rather a part of the US Department of Interior. Formed in 2011 by the Secretary of the Interior, and with fewer than 600 employees, BOEM is the agency responsible for the development of America's offshore energy and mineral resources on the US Outer Continental Shelf and has primacy for the development of offshore wind in the United States [16].

Yet, as shown in Table 13.1, the permitting process in the US is much more of a complicated soup with many different agencies at play at the federal level, let alone at the state and local level. The process to date has been slow. In fact, a recent market report by the National Renewable Energy Lab (NREL) of the US Department of Energy [14] stated that as of May 31, 2022 the US offshore wind energy pipeline has 40,083 MW of capacity, yet with all of that capacity, the US has been very slow to permit and realize the potential:

- Permitting: The developer has site control of a lease area and has submitted a Construction and Operation Plan (COP) to BOEM, and BOEM has published a Notice of Intent to prepare an Environmental Impact Statement on the project's COP. This equals 18,581 MW.
- Site Control: The developer has acquired the right to develop a lease area and has begun surveying the lease area. This equals 15,996 MW.
- Unleased Wind Energy Area: The rights to a lease area have yet to be auctioned to offshore wind energy developers. Capacity is estimated using a 3MW/km^2 wind turbine density assumption. This equals 4,532 MW.

While the permitting process is arduous, there has been some progress. In 2021 the offshore wind pipeline increased by 24 percent to 35 GW with eight, and state-level offshore wind procurement commitments have grown to 39 GW by 2040. BOEM has stated it will review sixteen COPs by 2025 and published seven Notices of Intent from March through September 2021 to begin the Environmental Impact Scoping process for projects on the path to meeting that target. In May 2021, Vineyard Wind 1 in Massachusetts was the first large-scale project (~800 MW) to receive federal approval for construction and operation. The project reached financial close in September 2021 [17].

And while far from an ideal or an expedient process, BOEM has recently undertaken in partnership with some of its sister agencies to identify bottlenecks and to address them. In fact, in June 2022, BOEM issued a guidance document[4] for the "Process for Identifying Alternatives for Environmental Reviews of Offshore Wind Construction and Operations Plans pursuant to

---

[3] See www.boem.gov.
[4] See www.boem.gov/sites/default/files/documents/renewable-energy/BOEM%20COP%20EIS %20Alternatives-2022–06–22.pdf.

the National Environmental Policy Act (NEPA)." This approach by the bureau should result in more expedient agency review processes for offshore wind. As suggested by Josh Kaplowitz, Vice President for Offshore Wind at the non-governmental organization CleanPower.org,

> limiting the amount of time that agencies spend suggesting – and that BOEM subsequently spends analyzing – inappropriate and ineffective alternatives whose consideration will not improve the environmental review process or projects themselves. This, in turn, will allow reviewing agencies to devote more resources to the most important part of the review process: analyzing project effects and benefits and working with developers to develop workable mitigation measures [18].

13.3 Deployment Headwinds

As a developer, while you patiently wait out the permitting process, you must also secure all of the incredibly complex supply chain and operational issues required. For the sake of brevity and to give a flavor of the dynamics, I take a look at just three supply chain topics: (1) underwater transmission cables, (2) securing a ship, and (3) connecting to the grid.

13.3.1 Underwater Transmission Cables

The arguments of direct current (DC) versus alternating current (AC) have long been in the USA's history, dating back to the arguments between Thomas Edison, who developed DC electricity transmission, and AC proponents Nikola Tesla and George Westinghouse Jr. [19]. As we develop so much offshore wind, we need to find a way to get all of that electricity from 15 miles and well beyond off the coast back to land and the cities that will use all of that power. The first issue is to decide if the electricity will be transmitted to shore either through high-voltage alternating current (HVAC) or direct current (HVDC) transmission.

HVDC cables are usually cheaper and have very limited losses, yet the costs of DC converters are significantly higher than AC transformers. This comes into play based on the distance traveled by the cables. For longer distances, most developers prefer HVDC in part because cables running underground/undersea are limited by the amount of reactive power used to energize the circuit, which limits power losses [20].

A representative of Anbaric Development Partners, which is an American electric power transmission and storage development company located in Wakefield, Massachusetts, told *Scientific American*, "I can put 1,200 MW in a direct-current cable. If I have to move it to alternating current, I would need nine of them" [21].

Now, getting the cable needed may run into further headwinds for a few reasons. First, there continue to be global supply chain delays from the COVID-19 pandemic. Second, the United States does not currently have the manufacturing capacity to meet 30 GW of offshore wind development [22], and finally, many states require a domestic and sometimes in-state supply chain, as detailed later in this chapter.

Currently, the only domestic manufacturing facility is in Charleston, South Carolina, owned and operated by 120-year-old Paris-based Nexans, the world's second largest cable manufacturer. The facility was partially subsidized by the long-term commitments to purchase the cables by Danish Ørsted Energy Company, which is the world's largest developer of offshore wind developer, and Eversource, both of whom are developing offshore wind in the United States in the northeast [23, 24, 25]. A second cable manufacturing facility is planned near Somerset, Massachusetts by Italian firm Prysmian Group, who will invest over $200 million based on a formal award of projects for cabling the Commonwealth Wind and Park Wind City offshore wind projects by Avangrid Renewables [26].

13.3.2 Find a Ship

Wesley Livsey Jones, a Republican United States senator representing Washington state from 1909 to 1932, created the Merchant Marine Act of 1920,[5] which he intended to support Seattle, Washington shipping companies to gain a better business footing after World War I. Today, this piece of legislation is commonly known as the "Jones Act" and it has the unintended consequences of significantly delaying the development and competitiveness of the US offshore wind industry.

In short, the Jones Act bans the transportation of passengers or merchandise between points in the US on ships that are not flagged and owned by US citizens. The problem is that the United States does not have any of the highly specialized, very expensive, and incredibly large vessels that can conduct all the specialized needs of offshore wind development. Labor unions fight any opportunities to revise the law and court-based waivers to get around it have been hard to get. To get around the Jones Act, two turbines recently built near Virginia Beach, Virginia had to be tended by a ship brought in from Europe and based, for legal purposes, in Halifax, Nova Scotia [21].

---

[5] www.loc.gov/item/uscode1958-009046024.

Jack-up boats[6] are designed with very large holds and heavy cranes necessary to transport and install the enormous turbines, some of which can reach 853 feet in height out to sea. The only shipbuilding project for offshore wind in the United States is by Virginia-based Dominion Energy, which is spending $500 million on a ship being built in Brownsville, Texas named *Charybdis*.[7] The ship will be 472 feet (144 meters) long and able to lift 2,200 tons. It will be ready at the end of 2023 [27]. Part of the business plan is for the ship to be utilized to develop Dominion projects off the shore of Virginia, then the vessel will be leased out to other developers across the eastern United States.

In the meantime, the Jones Act is having the unintended consequence of providing economic benefits to Nova Scotia, Canada instead of to US port cities. Nova Scotia, with a population of around 1 million, is located on the Atlantic and one of the four Atlantic provinces of Canada. Halifax, with a population of over 400,000, is Nova Scotia's largest city and its political capital [28]. Importantly, Halifax is also one of Canada's major seaports and provides the perfect workaround to the Jones Act for European companies to access the eastern offshore wind development area of the United States.

The US must rely on European vessels that are designed for the massive parts required to build an offshore wind project. Since these European ships cannot launch from US ports as they are not US-built, -owned, -crewed, or -flagged, Canadian ports, ports in Nova Scotia, and the communities where they are located will reap the benefits that US port cities will lose due to the inability to modify the Jones Act by Congress.

Fast Facts

The North American electrical infrastructure system as of 2020:

- is greater than $1 trillion in asset value
- is greater than 211,000 miles of transmission lines (roughly 8.5 times circling the earth)
- serves over 3,500 utilities and 334 million people
- exceeds 830 GW of demand.

---

[6] For a helpful video showing one of these ships in design, see www.youtube.com/watch?v=mOxNrjI3J70.

[7] After a sea monster from Greek mythology.

13.3.3 Connect to the Grid

I already introduced you to BOEM and now I am going to introduce you to another of America's many regulatory agencies – the Federal Energy Regulatory Commission (FERC).[8] FERC is an independent federal agency in the United States that regulates the transmission and wholesale sale of electricity and natural gas in interstate commerce and regulates the transportation of oil by pipeline in interstate commerce. Where FERC plays a "critical" role in offshore wind development is that they are the lynchpin for developers to connect the electricity generated offshore to the onshore electric grid.

According to a recent Lawrence Berkeley National Lab (California) report, the wait times for transmission approval to the grid in 2021 had almost doubled from a decade before to nearly four years [29]. Further, because the federal government for years failed to foresee the large growth in demand driven by renewables, they never developed a comprehensive strategy and plan for this need or identified and coordinated connection locations. FERC and the utilities have based their planning on large traditional thermoelectric power plants that take years to construct and are low in numbers versus the explosive growth of onshore and offshore renewable energy projects that are geospatially scattered and develop much more quickly.

Because of the tremendous amount of uncertainty from the applicants (developers) as to where a connection might be granted, the applicants are forced to submit multiple applications, which causes an even greater backlog. And many of those applications ultimately withdraw from the process [30].

To address the significant blowback from the broader renewable energy industry including land-based solar and wind, on June 16, 2022 FERC issued a Notice of Proposed Rulemaking focused on Improvement to Generator Interconnection Procedures and Agreements, which is intended to reform all the procedures and delays that currently exist.[9]

Testimony provided by the General Counsel for the New Jersey Board of Public Utilities, the lead energy regulatory agency for the state of New Jersey to FERC,[10] summarized the overall concerns of developers and states. The three overarching issues are:

1. How to reinforce the onshore portion of the transmission system to handle large injections over the next fifteen years
2. Whether a coordinated approach to getting power from offshore collector stations onto shore (i.e., the "beach crossing") results in better outcomes than each project constructing its own generator lead lines

[8] www.ferc.gov/what-ferc-does.   [9] www.ferc.gov/media/rm22-14-000.
[10] www.ferc.gov/sites/default/files/2020-10/Pane-3-Abe-Silverman.pdf.

3. Whether an optional ocean grid that "networks" offshore collector stations and coordinates delivery to shore is part of an optimal solution for consumers.

It will be important to the industry and transition to low-carbon renewable energy development in the US that these reforms are implemented in a timely manner.

13.4 Innovative Connection Strategies

One innovative strategy to overcome and work around the FERC gridlock is to leverage existing connection points. This strategy can be a lower-risk and lower-cost solution. And where do you find existing connection points? The answer lies in legacy thermoelectric power plants, especially coal-fired power plants that are being decommissioned because of higher operating costs and increased greenhouse gas emissions. Some exciting developments are in motion.

13.4.1 Ocean Wind in New Jersey

The 1,100 MW offshore wind project, which is led by Danish energy company Ørsted, is located between 15 and 27 miles offshore from Atlantic City, New Jersey and would connect to the north at the former Oyster Creek nuclear power plant, which received its license in 1991 as a single-unit 636 MW facility and closed in 2018 in light of substantial upgrades required [31, 32, 33]. To the south, the project will connect to the B. L. England power plant, a former 450 MW coal-generating power plant located in Upper Township, New Jersey that was decommissioned in 2019 [34]. The site is located in the Great Egg Harbor Bay, just west of the Atlantic Ocean, meaning that horizontal drilling will be required for part of the transmission connection on land under public beaches, which has brought with it community concerns and pushback [35].

13.4.2 Mayflower Wind in Massachusetts

Thirty-seven miles off the coast of Massachusetts and located south of Martha's Vineyard and Nantucket, Massachusetts will be the Mayflower 2,400 MW wind farm, which is enough electricity to power over 1 million homes and businesses. The project is backed by two global energy companies, Shell New Energies and Ocean Winds North America [36]. The first planned connection point will take place at Brayton Point Power Station, which was the largest coal power station in New England at 1,493 MW until its decommissioning in 2017

[37]. The waterfront property provides a good location for transmission connection of offshore wind projects.

13.4.3 Beacon Wind in New York

A joint venture of BP and Equinor, Beacon Wind covers 128,000 acres in federal waters approximately 60 miles east of Montauk Point and 20 miles south of Nantucket, Massachusetts. The project will be developed in phases, with the first phase bringing generation capacity of 1,230 MW of renewable offshore wind power to New York. Beacon Wind 2 will be similar in size to Beacon Wind 1 when undertaken at some time in the future – there is no specific offtake location, but it will be somewhere between New Jersey and Massachusetts. Combined, this is likely the largest project planned, providing 3.3 GW of power [38].

Beacon Wind 1 plans to connect to the Astoria Generating Station located in Queens, New York. The site is a 959 MW fuel oil and natural gas plant with five generating units and is bounded by the East River and Luyster Creek. In 2022 the facility was approved to construct 135 MW of energy storage, which should be in place by 2025 [39]. However, when the plant's owners, Houston-based NRG Energy, could not win approval for a new permit to comply with state air regulations and an effort to put a new fossil fuel generator on the site, they decided to decommission the facility and sell the land to the Beacon Wind project, thus providing a point of interconnection from the offshore transmission cables [40].

13.5 Infusion of Cash

The Inflation Reduction Act (IRA), which was signed into law in August 2022,[11] brings with it an infusion of cash that can accelerate the transition to a net-zero-carbon economy. The Energy Infrastructure Reinvestment Financing Program as detailed in the IRA will guarantee loans to projects that "retool, repower, repurpose, or replace energy infrastructure that has ceased operations, or enable operating energy infrastructure to avoid, reduce, utilize, or sequester air pollutants or anthropogenic emissions of greenhouse gases. IRA appropriates $5 billion through September 30, 2026, to carry out EIR [Energy Infrastructure Reinvestment], with a total cap on loans of up to $250 billion" [41]. This

---

[11] www.congress.gov/bill/117th-congress/house-bill/5376/text.

availability of loan guarantees can certainly aid in the development of offshore wind and the associated industries necessary for the transition.

And do these type of loan guarantees by the federal government work? In April 2010, a smaller car manufacture start-up based in San Carlos, California received a $465 million low-interest loan from the US Department of Energy to accelerate the production of EVs. That company, which we know as Tesla, used the funds to support the production of their Model S [42]. Move forward three short years and Tesla had fully repaid their loan – nine years early [43]. And as we now know, the company has the largest market cap of any automotive company in the world.

13.6 Offshore Wind and College Football

If you think that the states are competing to see who will be first to develop offshore wind for the sake of net-zero-carbon transitions, you are wrong. The bigger prize for each of these states is economic. First movers (i.e., states that begin the construction of offshore wind at scale) will likely position themselves as manufacturing hubs of the new and rapidly growing supply chains that will be necessary for the development and deployment of 30 GW of offshore wind in the United States. In fact, the uniqueness for investors is that the pace and volume of demand for manufacturing and service companies will provide quick returns on investment, something that all investors seek.

During the period of time that I was writing this book, the various American college football conferences were in a bit of chaos and realignment. To address this, the leaders of various football conferences met and announced various partnerships. In fact, on August 24, 2021 the athletic directors and university presidents from The Atlantic Coast Conference (ACC), Pac-12, and the Big 10 announced a "historic alliance" including scheduling agreements, and so on [44]. And in less than a year, on June 30, 2022 it was announced that the University of Southern California and University of California–Los Angeles had been in secret negotiations with the Big 10 and were leaving the Pac-12 to join the Big 10, despite the public-facing and non-binding agreement a year earlier [45].

These actions will actually foreshadow the future of how states will approach offshore wind development. There is a lot at stake for the states as they manipulate to be first movers and developers. Mostly, it is about jobs and the economy. Early movers can secure the investment and development of the manufacturing sectors necessary to support the offshore wind industry throughout the United States with the near-term focus on the east coast. The first movers will be states that have development contracts in place, as well as all the required federal, state, and local jurisdiction approved. Approval will comprise both the development and construction offshore and all the permitting required to connect to the grid.

These are necessary steps for companies and financial organizations to have the confidence in making the investments needed for the construction of new facilities and re-tooling of existing manufacturing facilities. The required infrastructure also needs to exist, such as port enhancements/expansions and laydown yards for the very large pieces of equipment necessary for offshore wind spanning from towers to cables. As presented in Table 13.2, a number of states along the east coast are undertaking extensive port improvements to support offshore wind while, as presented in Table 13.3, various companies are beginning to place their bets on first movers by developing new or expanded manufacturing capacity.

The first movers will most certainly have the advantage of manufacturing production that will meet not only the needs of development and deployment in their state but also the capacity and customers (developers and constructors) in other states along the Atlantic. It does not make economic sense to develop over-capacity in adjoining states.

Various state governors and state officials have been holding informal meetings,[12] some at the coordination of the White House, in part in conjunction with both the Offshore Wind Implementation Partnership and the proposed development of a National Offshore Wind Supply Chain Roadmap [46]. Yet, as was confirmed in a number of conversations with different states and state officials, many view the offshore wind supply chain in a purely competitive landscape and will do what is in the best interests of their own states. So, like the different college conference officials that agreed to historic alliances, eventually the states will follow the same path and do what is in their best interests. And consider why accelerating development and construction is important. Developing a manufacturing facility in New York requires a very different cost structure for employees and land cost in comparison, say, to the east coast of North Carolina, which can be much more competitive in the marketplace without state incentives.

---

[12] See the Offshore Wind Implementation Partnership, which includes eleven states along the east coast: https://governor.ri.gov/press-releases/governor-mckee-joins-white-house-east-coast-governors-launch-offshore-wind.

Table 13.2 *2021–2 investments in ports by states; adapted from [10]*

Projects Served	Location	Details	Sponsor	Amount (Millions)
Revolution Wind	New London, CT	Public–private investment to upgrade State Pier's infrastructure (deep-water port) and heavy-lift capabilities. Construction is expected to begin in early 2021 and be completed by August 2022. Ørsted agrees to sign a 10-year lease at that facility	Ørsted & Eversource, CT Port Authority	157
Park City Wind	Bridgeport, CT	As part of the Park City Wind winning proposal, Vineyard Wind will make Bridgeport home to Park City Wind's O&M hub for the life of the project	Vineyard Wind	Up to 26.5
Park City Wind	Bridgeport, CT	Redevelop 18.3-acre waterfront industrial property; Barnum Landing property to do critical foundation transition-piece steel fabrication and final outfitting	Vineyard Wind	Unspecified
Skipjack	Sparrows Point, MD	Trade point Atlantic will create a 3,300-acre global logistics and staging center for laydown and assembly of components for Skipjack Wind offshore wind farm. Improvements will include strengthening ground-bearing capacity	Ørsted	13.2
	New Bedford, MA	Investment to develop the first offshore wind port in the US (originally intended to support the failed Cape Wind project in 2014)	State of Massachusetts	113
	New Bedford, MA	A $50,000 grant to the New Bedford Port Authority for purposes of developing publicly owned port facilities that can support offshore wind construction, operations and maintenance, and other activities	Vineyard Wind	0.05
	New Bedford, MA	Cannon Street Power Station will be demolished and the surrounding area cleared to develop a 30-acre site for offshore wind	Cannon Street Holdings	Unspecified
	New Bedford, MA	Vineyard Wind signed a $6 million annual lease to use the New Bedford Marine Commerce Terminal for 18 months (total $9 million)	Vineyard Wind	9

Table 13.2 (cont.)

Projects Served	Location	Details	Sponsor	Amount (Millions)
Northeast projects	New Bedford, MA	Adding base of operations and terminal logistics facility including storage and laydown yards, berth facilities for tug and barge operations, and host crew transfer vessels and service operation vessels support services	Foss, Cannon Street Holdings, LLC	Unspecified
Commonwealth Wind	Salem, MA	Vineyard Wind and Crowley agreed to develop a deep-water offshore wind port for turbine assembly and staging activities	Vineyard Wind, Crowley, City of Salem	Unspecified
Ocean Wind	Atlantic City, NJ	Ørsted plans to locate its construction logistics base, foundation and transition-piece staging port, and operations and maintenance port in New Jersey	Ørsted	Unspecified
Empire Wind	Brooklyn, NY	Equinor will invest over $60 million in port upgrades throughout New York for part of its Empire Wind project. Empire Wind was proposing to invest $50 million in port upgrades state-wide, including the Port of Coeymans, Homeport Pier on Staten Island, and South Brooklyn Marine Terminal	Equinor	60
Empire Wind and Beacon Wind	Brooklyn, NY	Upgrade South Brooklyn Marine Terminal as an offshore wind hub	Equinor, BP	200–250
Sunrise Wind	New York state	Establishes a New York Ports Infrastructure Development Fund for ensuring port facilities can serve as staging areas	Ørsted, Eversource	11
	Port Jefferson, NY	New operations and maintenance hub including dockage for a 250-foot service operation vessel, a warehouse, and office facility	Ørsted, Eversource	Unspecified
Revolution Wind	Providence, RI	Port improvements for the Port of Providence, Quonset Business Park, and potentially additional ports in the state	Ørsted, Eversource	40
Park City Wind	Bridgeport, CT	Vineyard Wind has signed a lease at Barnum Landing to use as a construction and staging location Downtown Bridgeport to serve as the Connecticut headquarters for the company's offshore wind project	Vineyard Wind	Unspecified
Total Announced 2021–2022			{$ million}	**200–250 +**
Cumulative Total Announced			{$ million}	**630–630 +**

Table 13.3 *Selected supply chain announcements in the United States through May 31, 2022; adapted from [10]*

Component	Location	Investors	Announced Investment ($ Million)
Blades	Portsmouth Marine Terminal (Virginia)	Siemens Gamesa	200
Nacelles (final assembly only)	New Jersey Wind Port (New Jersey)	Vestas, Atlantic Shores	Not announced
Nacelles (final assembly only)	New Jersey Wind Port (New Jersey)	GE, Ørsted	Not announced
Towers	Port of Albany (New York)	Marmen Welcon, Equinor	$350
Monopiles	Paulsboro Marine Terminal (New Jersey)	EEW, Ørsted	$250
Monopiles	Sparrows Point (Maryland)	US Wind	$150
Array cables	Ørsted, Hellenic Cables		$140
Foundation platforms	Port of Providence (Rhode Island)	Eversource, Ørsted	$40
Secondary steel	Port of Coeymans (New York)	Eversource, Ørsted	$86
Transition pieces	Port of Albany (New York)	Marmen Welcon, Smulders	Not announced
Array and export cables	Nexans high-voltage cable facility (South Carolina)	Nexans	$200
Array and export cables	Kerite (Connecticut)	Kerite, Marmon Group, Vineyard Wind	$4
Array and export cables	Tradepoint Atlantic (Maryland)	Ørsted	$150
Array and export cables	Brayton Point (Massachusetts)	Prysmian, Avangrid	$200
Offshore substations	Ingleside (Texas)	Kiewit, Eversource, Ørsted	Not announced
Total announced investments made in 2021–2022 ($ millions)			**$1,170**

References

1. International Energy Agency (2019). World Energy Outlook 2019. www.iea.org/reports/world-energy-outlook-2019.
2. Forbes (2019). Offshore Wind Can Power the World, Say Former Skeptics. October 15. www.forbes.com/sites/davidrvetter/2019/10/25/offshore-wind-can-power-the-world-say-former-skeptics/?sh=58bf2397265f.
3. White House (2021). Fact Sheet: Biden Administration Jumpstarts Offshore Wind Energy Projects to Create Jobs. Issued on March 29. www.whitehouse.gov/briefing-room/statements-releases/2021/03/29/fact-sheet-biden-administration-jumpstarts-offshore-wind-energy-projects-to-create-jobs.
4. US Energy Information Agency (2022). Coal Will Account for 85% of U.S. Electric Generating Capacity Retirements in 2022. January 11. www.eia.gov/todayinenergy/detail.php?id=50838#:~:text=The%20majority%20of%20the%20scheduled,to%204.6%20GW%20in%202021.
5. US Department of Energy (2022). How Wind Energy Can Help Us Breathe Easier. Office of Energy Efficiency and Renewable Energy. August 16. www.energy.gov/eere/wind/articles/how-wind-energy-can-help-us-breathe-easier#:~:text=In%20general%2C%20lifecycle%20greenhouse%20gas,2%2FkWh%20for%20natural%20gas.
6. US Energy Information Agency (2022). Annual Energy Outlook 2022. March 3. www.eia.gov/outlooks/aeo.
7. Global Fleet (2022). Electric Vehicles Expected to Comprise 31% of the Global Fleet by 2050. January 21. https://tinyurl.com/54385n6f.
8. Reuters (2022). The Long Road to Electric Cars. https://graphics.reuters.com/AUTOS-ELECTRIC/USA/mopanyqxwva.
9. Dynamic Sustainability Lab (2022). Lithium Battery Manufacturing and the EV Transition. Bulletin No. 20220406. www.dynamicslab.org.
10. US Department of Energy (2022). Offshore Wind Market Report: 2022 Edition. Office of Energy Efficiency and Renewable Energy.
11. Wind Europe (2022). Europe Puts Fast Permitting of Renewables at the Heart of Its Energy Security Plan. https://windeurope.org/newsroom/press-releases/europe-puts-fast-permitting-of-renewables-at-the-heart-of-its-energy-security-plan.
12. Reuters (2022). EU to Set Out One-Year Permitting Rule for Renewables; Biden Directs Staff to Speed Up Approvals. November 2. www.reutersevents.com/renewables/wind/eu-set-out-one-year-permitting-rule-renewables-biden-directs-staff-speed-approvals.
13. European Union (2015). Denmark's Offshore Wind Farms Planning and Policy Approach – DK. https://discomap.eea.europa.eu/map/Data/Milieu/OURCOAST_097_DK/OURCOAST_097_DK_Case_OffshoreWindfarmPlanningPolicyApproach.pdf.
14. CMS (2017). Offshore Wind Law and Regulation in Denmark. https://cms.law/en/int/expert-guides/cms-expert-guide-to-offshore-wind-in-northern-europe/denmark.
15. New York State Energy Research and Development Authority (2022). Permitting and Approvals. www.nyserda.ny.gov/All-Programs U.S. DOE (2022). Offshore

Wind Market Report: 2022 Edition. Office of Energy Efficiency and Renewable Energy./Offshore-Wind/Focus-Areas/Permitting.

16. Bureau of Ocean Energy Management (2022). About Us. www.boem.gov/sites/default/files/documents/newsroom/fact-sheets/BOEM_About.pdf.

17. US Department of Energy (2022). Offshore Wind Energy Strategies. Regional and National Strategies to Accelerate and Maximize the Effectiveness, Reliability, and Sustainability of U.S. Offshore Wind Energy Deployment and Operation. January. www.energy.gov/sites/default/files/2022-01/offshore-wind-energy-strategies-report-january-2022.pdf.

18. CleanPower.org (2022). BOEM's NEPA Screening Criteria for Offshore Wind Projects Are a Big Step Toward Permitting Certainty. July 19. https://cleanpower.org/blog/boems-nepa-screening-criteria-for-offshore-wind-projects-are-a-big-step-toward-permitting-certainty.

19. M. Wincehell (2019). *The Electric War: Edison, Tesla, Westinghouse, the Race to Light the World*. New York: Henry Holt and Company.

20. Reuters (2011). HVDC vs. HVAC cables for Offshore Wind. July 22. www.reutersevents.com/renewables/wind-energy-update/hvdc-vs-hvac-cables-offshore-wind.

21. *Scientific American* (2020). U.S. Offshore Wind Needs to Clear a Key Hurdle: Connecting to the Grid. August 3. www.scientificamerican.com/article/u-s-offshore-wind-needs-to-clear-a-key-hurdle-connecting-to-the-grid.

22. M. Shields, R. Marsh, J. Stefek et al. (2022). The Demand for a Domestic Offshore Wind Energy Supply Chain. NREL. NREL/TP–5000–81602.

23. Orsted (2022). About Us. https://orsted.com/en/about-us/about-orsted.

24. Energy Global (2022). Nexans to Supply Orsted and Eversource's Offshore Wind Project. September 26. www.energyglobal.com/wind/26092022/nexans-to-supply-rsted-and-eversources-offshore-wind-project.

25. Nexans (2022). Nexans Charleston, a World Class Facility Uniquely Positioned to Serve the Rapidly Expanding U.S. Offshore Wind Market. November 9. www.nexans.com/en/newsroom/news/details/2021/11/2021-11-09-pr-nexans-charleston-world-class-facility-positioned-to-serve-rapidly-expanding-us-offshore-wind-market.html.

26. Prisimian Group (2022). Prysmian Group: New Submarine Cable Plant in the USA. February 17. Press Release. www.prysmiangroup.com/en/media/press-releases/prysmian-group-new-submarine-cable-plant-in-the-usa.

27. *New York Times* (2021). Offshore Wind Farms Show What Biden's Climate Plan Is Up Against. June 7. www.nytimes.com/2021/06/07/business/energy-environment/offshore-wind-biden-climate-change.html.

28. Canada Visa (2022). About Nova Scotia. www.canadavisa.com/about-nova-scotia.html.

29. Lawrence Berkeley National Lab (2022). Queued Up: Characteristics of Power Plants Seeking Transmission Interconnection As of the End of 2021. https://emp.lbl.gov/sites/default/files/queued_up_2021_04-13-2022.pdf.

30. Federal Energy Regulatory Commission (2020). Reliability Primer. www.ferc.gov/sites/default/files/2020-04/reliability-primer_1.pdf.

31. World Nuclear News (2018). Closure Date of Oyster Creek Brought Forward. February 2. www.world-nuclear-news.org/C-Closure-date-of-Oyster-Creek-brought-forward-0202185.html.

32. US Nuclear Regulatory Commission (2022). Oyster Creek Nuclear Generating Station. www.nrc.gov/info-finder/reactors/oc.html.

33. AP News (2022). NJ Offshore Wind to Connect at 2 Former Power Plants Onshore. April 13. https://apnews.com/article/oceans-atlantic-city-new-jersey-1e9d84449b790ffba650f927ce9d4dee.

34. NBC Philadelphia (2022). How an Offshore Wind Farm Would Come Onshore in Ocean City, NJ. March 9. www.nbcphiladelphia.com/news/national-inter national/changing-climate/how-an-offshore-wind-farm-will-come-onshore-in-ocean-city-nj/3170444.

35. Energy Central (2022). Ocean City Fights Offshore Wind Cable Planned to Run under Beach, through Town. https://energycentral.com/news/ocean-city-fights-offshore-wind-cable-planned-run-under-beach-through-town.

36. Mayflower Wind (2022). About Us. https://mayflowerwind.com/about-us.

37. Massachusetts Clean Energy Center (2022). Brayton Point Power Plant Site. www.masscec.com/resources/brayton-point-power-plant-site.

38. Beacon Wind (2022). About the Project. www.beaconwind.com/about/project.

39. QNS.com (2022). State Approves Battery Storage Project at Astoria Generating Station. June 27. https://qns.com/2022/06/state-battery-storage-astoria-generat ing-station.

40. State of New York (2022). Verified Joint Petition for Declaratory Ruling or Approval under Section 70 of the Public Service Law. September 15.

41. Energy.gov (2022). Energy Infrastructure Reinvestment. www.energy.gov/lpo/ energy-infrastructure-reinvestment.

42. Tesla (2010). Tesla Gets Loan Approval from US Department of Energy. April 20. www.tesla.com/blog/tesla-gets-loan-approval-us-department-energy.

43. Congresswoman Eshoo (2013). Tesla Motors Fully Repays $465 Million Federal Loan Nine Years Early. Forwarded from *Mercury News*. May 23. https://eshoo .house.gov/media/in-the-news/mercury-news-tesla-motors-fully-repays-465-mil lion-federal-loan-nine-years-early.

44. Pacific 12 (2021). Pac 12, ACC and Big 10 Announce Historic Alliance. https:// pac-12.com/article/2021/08/24/pac-12-acc-and-big-ten-announce-historic-alli ance–0.

45. Bleacher Report (2022). SC, UCLA Announce Move to Big Ten from Pac-12 Beginning in 2024. https://bleacherreport.com/articles/10040548-usc-ucla-announce-move-to-big-ten-from-pac-12-beginning-in–2024.

46. The White House (2022). Fact Sheet: Biden Administration Launches New Federal-State Offshore Wind Partnership to Grow American-Made Clean Energy. www.whitehouse.gov/briefing-room/statements-releases/2022/06/23/ fact-sheet-biden-administration-launches-new-federal-state-offshore-wind-part nership-to-grow-american-made-clean-energy.

PART IV

Finance and the Transition

The transition to a net-zero-carbon economy is dependent on the availability of venture funding, financial capital, loan guarantees, and insurance. In 2022, the United States unleashed an unprecedented amount of money to fund green-tech and climate investments. At the same time, there is an increasing focus on environmental and social governance. All of these factors are explored in this part.

There are a number of existing and emerging financing opportunities to support the net-zero transition. Which source(s) of funding an organization utilizes depends on the size and financial strength of the borrowing party, as well as the timeline for the loan and repayment and importantly what they need to finance; that is, research and development and prototyping, all the way to major capital equipment investments.

14.2 Research and Development (R&D)

Both emerging businesses and emerging businesses who will guide the net-zero-carbon transition will need to invest in R&D. Governments play an important role in R&D funding. They generally fund both basic research and applied research. The difference between these as defined by the US National Science Foundation (NSF) is as follows.

Applied research, with the objective of gaining the knowledge or under-standing necessary for determining the means by which a recognized need may be met, whereas basic research has the objective of gaining more complete knowledge or understanding of the fundamental aspects of phenomena and of observable facts, without specific applications toward processes or products in mind [5].

Basic research often provides new theories and insights, while applied research capitalizes on the various theories and scientific understandings to develop new or improved technologies, services, policies, and so on [5].

Development is systematic work, drawing on knowledge gained from research and practical experience and producing additional knowledge, which is directed to producing new products or processes or to improving existing products or processes [5, 6].

R&D plants include R&D facilities and fixed equipment, such as reactors, wind tunnels, and particle accelerators, as well as acquiring, construc-tion, and major repairs to structures, equipment, facilities, or land for use in R&D activities [6].

Globally, R&D expenditures achieved an all-time high of almost US$ 1.7 trillion in 2021 with ten countries account for 80 percent of spending. Certainly, the life sciences were a beneficiary due to R&D for COVID-19, yet climate-related R&D was also a driver [7]. The leading countries based on gross domestic expenditures on R&D for science, technology, and innovation in 2020 included [8]:

1. Israel at 5.43 percent
2. Republic of Korea at 4.81 percent
3. Sweden at 3.52 percent
4. United States at 3.45 percent
5. Japan at 3.26 percent.

China was at 2.45 percent, which was behind such European countries as Austria, Denmark, Finland, Germany, and Iceland but above the global average of 1.92 percent.

14.2.1 Government R&D Funding

In the United States the NSF is the most accurate repository for annual scientific R&D expenditures by both the government and industry within the country. These funds can be distributed to federal labs, research universities, and the private sector. As presented in Table 14.1, national defense is the largest

Table 14.1 *Federal budget authority for R&D and R&D plants, by budget function, ordered by financial year 2020 R&D and R&D plant total: financial years 2020–2 [10]*

Budget Function	2020 Actual	2021 Preliminary	2022 Proposed
R&D and R&D plants (millions of US$)	**169,901**	**165,560**	**179,418**
R&D and R&D plants (percent of budget)	**100.0**	**100.0**	**100.0**
National defense	48.2	48.1	43.9
Health	26.2	26.3	28.5
Space flight, research, and supporting activities	8.4	7.6	7.7
General science and basic research	8.0	8.3	8.6
Energy	2.7	2.7	3.6
Natural resources and environment	1.7	1.8	2.1
Agriculture	1.6	1.6	1.8
Transportation	1.0	1.0	1.1
Veterans benefits and services	0.8	0.9	0.8
Commerce and housing credit	0.6	0.7	0.7
Education, training, employment, and social services	0.3	0.5	0.5
Administration of justice	0.3	0.3	0.3
International affairs	0.1	0.1	0.1
Income security	0.1	0.1	0.1
Community and regional development	0.1	0.1	0.1

beneficiary. However, one must remember that military R&D has many times resulted in civilian applications – consider the internet, satellites, GPS, duct tape, microwave ovens, and so on [9].

Unique to the United States is the breadth of research-intensive universities and R&D productivity that is unsurpassed around the world. Each year approximately 651 US colleges and universities of the estimated 4,000 degree-granting American colleges and universities [11] report their R&D expend-itures annually to the NSF [12]. At the top of the list of R&D-intensive universities in terms of dollars expended are typically Johns Hopkins, the University of Michigan, the "Research Triangle" universities (Duke University, North Carolina State University, and the University of North Carolina at Chapel Hill), three of the University of California campuses (the University of California–San Francisco, the University of California–Los Angeles, and the University of California–San Diego), the University of Pennsylvania, the University of Washington, Harvard, Stanford, and Cornell, to name a few.

For 2020, the largest federal R&D funders to universities (which is consist-ent for most years) were [13]:

1. Health and Human Services: $25.4 billion
2. Department of Defense: $7.1 billion
3. NSF: $5.4 billion
4. Department of Energy: $2.0 billion
5. NASA: $1.8 billion
6. US Department of Agriculture: $1.2 billion
7. Other agencies: $3.2 billion.

Usually, the life sciences are the largest R&D thematic, with the United States Department of Health and Human Services providing large funding along with private pharmaceutical companies who depend on major medical schools to run their clinical trials for emerging drugs. However, there continues to be increased focus on and funding for the technologies that will aid in the transition to a net-zero-carbon economy. Because of the lag in the reporting and data assimilation by NSF, those trends won't be observed for a couple of years. A summary of the most recent report, which is for 2020, is presented as Table 14.2.

14.2.2 Industry R&D

In 2020 in the United State the private sector (i.e., industry) had R&D expend-itures of $538 billion, of which $36 billion (7 percent) was spent on basic research, $76 billion (14 percent) on applied research, and $426 billion

Table 14.2 *R&D expenditures at US research universities by funding source and R&D category for 2020 [13]*

Field	All R&D Expenditure	Federal Government	State and Local Government	Institution Funds	Business	Nonprofit Organizations	All Other Sources
All R&D fields	**86,296,178**	**46,143,829**	**4,596,633**	**21,946,790**	**5,184,925**	**5,745,238**	**2,678,763**
Percent of all R&D Expenditures Source of Funding		**53%**	**5%**	**25%**	**6%**	**7%**	**3%**
Science	**67,567,807**	**36,778,903**	**3,366,120**	**16,620,734**	**3,910,498**	**4,824,295**	**2,067,257**
Computer and information sciences	2,923,149	2,000,937	59,461	578,481	156,246	81,578	46,446
Geosciences, atmospheric sciences, and ocean sciences	3,281,251	2,109,065	192,307	658,966	84,585	149,331	86,997
Atmospheric science and meteorology	612,890	471,158	20,739	92,002	6,616	10,302	12,073
Geological and earth sciences	1,159,627	696,991	56,003	276,947	42,549	53,207	33,930
Ocean sciences and marine sciences	1,136,259	713,086	89,392	214,593	25,140	62,473	31,575
Sciences NEC	372,475	227,830	26,173	75,424	10,280	23,349	9,419
Life sciences	**49,640,508**	**26,254,002**	**2,699,498**	**11,954,881**	**3,388,718**	**3,725,032**	**1,618,377**
Agricultural sciences	3,626,162	1,072,057	950,453	1,160,242	145,810	153,008	144,592
Biological and biomedical sciences	15,761,876	9,339,917	558,750	3,686,204	703,545	1,108,185	365,275
	28,026,662	14,733,751	987,527	6,452,035	2,470,203	2,336,032	1,047,114
Natural resources and conservation	900,697	410,120	140,342	255,659	24,851	46,367	23,358
Life sciences NEC	1,325,111	698,157	62,426	400,741	44,309	81,440	38,038
Mathematics and statistics	**798,975**	486,259	26,640	223,162	13,335	39,436	10,143
Physical sciences	5,667,046	3,789,237	94,312	1,257,087	170,038	241,118	115,254

Table 14.2 (cont.)

Field	All R&D Expenditure	Federal Government	State and Local Government	Institution Funds	Business	Nonprofit Organizations	All Other Sources
Astronomy and astrophysics	780,080	542,725	7,009	144,050	3,872	52,890	29,534
Chemistry	1,926,772	1,166,743	38,428	523,173	81,497	78,408	38,523
Materials science	252,193	156,894	3,233	57,559	22,558	8,275	3,674
Physics	2,434,467	1,736,916	34,396	481,101	44,965	97,849	39,240
Physical sciences NEC	273,534	185,959	11,246	51,204	17,146	3,696	4,283
Psychology	1,357,081	808,565	47,653	374,133	15,469	87,853	23,408
Social sciences	2,947,338	969,278	175,297	1,163,690	49,205	451,233	138,635
Anthropology	119,329	38,847	3,855	64,794	1,954	5,480	4,399
Economics	562,192	121,461	48,994	223,229	14,023	111,551	42,934
Political science and government	425,267	78,462	13,079	202,670	7,156	86,889	37,011
Sociology, demography, and population studies	591,754	253,213	34,578	198,676	6,143	86,921	12,223
Social sciences NEC	1,248,796	477,295	74,791	474,321	19,929	160,392	42,068
Sciences NEC	952,459	361,560	70,952	410,334	32,902	48,714	27,997
Engineering	13,692,756	8,120,891	895,910	2,720,559	1,129,319	393,387	432,690
Aerospace, aeronautical, and astronautical engineering	1,295,759	957,795	33,259	130,543	129,465	4,683	40,014
Bioengineering and biomedical engineering	1,468,229	906,145	48,150	331,075	60,248	86,474	36,137
Chemical engineering	999,312	521,758	44,926	240,663	116,581	48,181	27,203
Civil engineering	1,422,418	606,519	255,959	377,850	98,399	46,087	37,604
Electrical, electronic, and communications engineering	3,048,420	2,143,397	79,138	482,858	187,270	74,512	81,245

Industrial and manufacturing engineering	588,127	384,795	35,472	113,635	36,419	12,205	5,601
Mechanical engineering	1,812,916	1,160,117	66,529	333,847	179,189	36,603	36,631
Metallurgical and materials engineering	816,610	504,528	29,785	161,984	64,388	19,043	36,882
Engineering NEC	2,240,965	935,837	302,692	548,104	257,360	65,599	131,373
Non-S&E	5,035,615	1,244,035	334,603	2,605,497	145,108	527,556	178,816
Business management and business administration	878,721	74,126	41,108	640,841	26,819	45,597	50,230
Communication and communications technologies	191,813	40,830	10,816	98,931	6,602	29,566	5,068
Education	1,603,978	667,043	131,575	520,173	53,327	201,358	30,502
Humanities	563,007	54,155	17,922	385,675	13,756	67,083	24,416
Law	267,565	26,697	12,404	158,838	7,486	44,759	17,381
Social work	307,145	140,836	29,722	93,047	5,203	35,774	2,563
Visual and performing arts	171,605	15,140	6,626	129,234	2,747	10,584	7,274
Non-S&E NEC	1,051,781	225,208	84,430	578,758	29,168	92,835	41,382

Note: Institution funds are expenditures reinvested by the university from indirect rates returned to the institution. NEC = not elsewhere classified.

(79 percent) on development. In 2020, companies in manufacturing industries performed \$308 billion (57 percent) of domestic R&D, with most of the funding coming from these companies' own funds (86 percent). Companies in nonmanufacturing industries performed \$229 billion of domestic R&D (43 percent of total domestic R&D performance), 88 percent of which was paid for by companies' own funds [14]. The global businesses with the highest reported research budgets in 2020 based on annual reports were dominated by the tech sector [15]:

1. Amazon: \$42.74 billion
2. Alphabet: \$27.57 billion
3. Huawei (China): \$22.04 billion
4. Microsoft: \$19.27 billion
5. Apple: \$18.75 billion
6. Samsung (South Korea): \$18.75 billion
7. Facebook: \$18.75 billion.

14.3 Start-Up Pathways

For those group of innovators and entrepreneurs who might have been funded for their initial R&D, they will soon learn that they require substantial more funding to build up the organizational capacity and equipment necessary to go from demonstration to protype to start-up business. And the most common formal route is to seek out venture capital and/or private equity (series A through E). I say "formal" as there of course still exist "friends and family" investments, which may be easier to obtain but have high risks for relationships if the business does not pan out.

Private equity and venture capital firms are often stereotyped as sharks, as shown on the highly successful TV show *Shark Tank*. If you have watched the show, one of the most important questions asked by the Sharks after determining if the product or service is worthy of investment is to determine how much equity is available. In other words, they want to know if others have invested and how much of a share of the company they will have. In many cases they want the controlling number of shares, though most business entrepreneurs push back, especially if they know they have a strong business. In larger opportunities the percentage of ownership offered may be very small. It is a delicate dance. And how long does it take to go from initial investment to going public? As presented in Table 14.3, there are a number of steps from securing funding to building up the company. However, the most recent data

Table 14.3 *The pathway for start-up businesses [17, 18, 19]*

	Pre-Seed	Seed	Series A	Series B	Series C	Series D	Series E
What	An entrepreneur or inventor has an idea and needs some initial funding to explore	Seed funding is used to take a start-up from idea to the first steps, such as product development or market research	In a Series A round, start-ups are expected to have a plan for developing a business model, even if they haven't proven it yet. They're also expected to use the money raised to increase revenue	Used to start scaling the product or company. Possibly have large orders or contracts that need to be fulfilled	Looking to increase their valuation before going for an IPO or an acquisition	Firms generally do not have to obtain Series D or E prior to an IPO. They may do these rounds to keep the company private during growth and raise the valuation of the company before going public. Or, they may not have met expectations and need more cash, which reduces the value (i.e., a "down round")	
Who Fund	Friends. Family. Crowdsourcing	Angel investors and/or friends and family; crowdsourcing	Venture capital firms or super angel investors	Late-stage venture capital firms	Late-stage venture capital firms, private equity firms, hedge funds, banks	Late-stage venture capital firms, private equity firms, hedge funds, banks	Late-stage venture capital firms, private equity firms, hedge funds, banks

Table 14.3 *(cont.)*

	Pre-Seed	Seed	Series A	Series B	Series C	Series D	Series E
Dollar Amounts	Varies but generally very small	$500K–$2M	$2 million to $15 million	$7 million and $10 million; companies can expect a valuation between $30 million and $60 million	An average of $26 million. Valuation of Series C companies often falls between $100 million and $120 million	Varies	
Notes		Company valuation $3M–$6M	Company valuation $10M–$15M. Less than 50% of companies are able to successfully obtain investments after Series A	Company valuation $30M–$60M	Company valuation >$100M		

show that for the years between 2000 and 2021, the average length of time between initial venture capital investment and the initial public offering (IPO) in the United States was 5.7 years; this extended to six years in 2021 likely due to the COVID-19 impacts [16].

14.3.1 Venture Capital Trends

Around the globe, venture capital funding is increasing. A recent industry research group reported that the global venture capital investment market size reached US$ 233.9 billion in 2022 and is expected to grow to US$ 708.6 billion by 2028, exhibiting a growth rate of 21.75 percent during 2023–2028 [20]. Certainly, the United States dominates the venture capital space. While not all funding is made public, pulling from disclosed deals in 2021, the United States had deals exceeding $269 billion, followed by China at $60 billion, the UK at $32 billion, India at $28 billion, Germany at $17 billion, and France at $11 billion [21]. Some of the largest venture capital firms include [22]:

1. General Atlantic (NY) $31 billion investment range $20 M to $100 M
2. Hillhouse Capital (China) $30 billion investment range $500 K to $500 M
3. Insight Venture Partners (NY) $18 billion investment range $10 M to $200 M
4. Iconiq Capital (CA) $14.5 billion investment range $5 M to $75 M
5. Tiger Global Management (NY) $10 billion investment range $1 M to $40 M
6. New Enterprise Associates (MD) $10 billion investment range $2 M to $50 M
7. Northwest Venture Partners (CA) $7.5 billion investment range $1 K to $150 M
8. Andreessen Horowitz (CA) $7 billion investment range $500 K to $40 M.

Two of the oldest and best known due to the tech revolution are:

1. Sequoia Capital (CA) $4 billion investment range $5 M to $100 M
2. Kleiner Perkins Caufield Byers (CA) $3 billion investment range $2 M to $50 M.

One of the best-known clean-tech funds was started by Microsoft founder Bill Gates. His Breakthrough Energy Ventures has plans to infuse $15 billion into clean tech. It has secured investments from Microsoft, BlackRock, General Motors, American Airlines, Boston Consulting Group, Bank of America,

ArcelorMittal, and the US Department of Energy, as well as the executive arm of the European Union, the European Commission [23].

It is important to distinguish between private equity firms and venture capital firms as both forms of finance look very similar at first glance. Private equity is capital invested in a company or other entity that is not publicly listed or traded. Private equity and venture capital buy different types of companies, invest different amounts of money, and claim different amounts of equity in the companies in which they invest. Private equity firms tend to focus on long-term investments in assets that take time to sell. The investment typically has a time horizon of ten or more years.

Private equity refers to the investment in a private company in exchange for controlling interest in the firm. A private equity firm often takes an active role in the management of the companies it invests in. When a private equity firm makes an investment, the money is typically pooled together from all the investors, then used on behalf of the fund. Investors in private equity often include high-net-worth individuals, insurance companies, pension funds, and endowments [24, 25, 26].

The companies that venture capital firms raise funding for are typically unable to seek capital from more traditional sources, like banks and public markets. This is usually because of a lack of assets, the stage of development, or the size of the company. Venture capital is technically a form of equity financing. Private firms with institutional investors purchase a stake in other companies with the goal of earning a profit. Venture capital firms often specialize in investing in young companies and startups to help them get off the ground and grow, and do not necessarily provide just financial support; the investment can be technical expertise [24–26].

One of the emerging trends in venture capital that I have both participated in and witnessed is the development of university-led venture capital funds. When you visit any research-intensive university or smaller liberal arts college, you will no doubt run into programs focused on student entrepreneurship. This links especially well to research universities who are consistently battling their peers for annual research rankings based on research expenditures. This is part of what goes into peer rankings and recognition. R&D at universities can also provide funding since faculty-led innovations researched and developed in university labs result in partial ownership by the university. Generally, student self-directed innovation is royalty free to the university, meaning the students keep the intellectual property (IP), with the university hoping the student ends up as a wealthy alumnus who gives back to their alma mater.

Hence, there is strong focus at universities to have faculty develop IP, and with that drive there is an abundance of early investment to take the research out of the lab and generate a business. So instead of having just family supporting pre-seed and seed with third venture capital firms, universities themselves have been developing venture capital networks dominated by alumni and friends of the university.

I was fortunate to be at Duke University when the person who occupied the office next to me was Dr. Eric Toone,[2] who previously led Advanced Research Projects Agency–Energy (ARPA–E). I was at the time a faculty member, executive director of Duke Corporate Relations, and the number two administrator in Duke's Research Office, which had reached over $1 billion in research expenditures. In 2015, Eric, who remains one of the brightest individuals I have ever met and also one of the nicest, developed the Duke Angel Network, which is now called Duke Capital Partners. The fund provides capital and expertise to help Duke startups and also trains Duke students. The fund has deployed more than $50 million in capital [27].

The North Carolina universities are a great example of leadership in this space and are among the global leaders for innovation, along with Boston-based and Bay-area-based research universities. North Carolina State University, the University of North Carolina at Chapel Hill, and East Carolina University[3] have all developed highly successful innovation and entrepreneurship programs and venture funding schemes.

While venture capital funding is still heavily dominated by the life sciences and high-tech, there is the beginning of a rapid expansion and demand for clean tech and climate-smart feedstocks and products, and venture capital funds are quickly entering the market. For instance, in 2021, venture capital deals for advanced batteries (electric vehicles, storage) increase a reported 850 percent year on year. One such example is the US-based SES, who in April 2021 raised $139 million led by the venture capital of General Motors and others [28].

14.4 Clean-Tech Manufacturing Financing

14.4.1 Government Loan Guarantees

For the last year in addition to this book I worked on researching the effectiveness of the US government's Biorefinery, Renewable Chemical, and Biobased Product Manufacturing Assistance Program, also known as the 9003 Loan Guarantee

---

[2] Eric is now a principal at Breakthrough Energy Ventures.
[3] For transparency, while serving as vice chancellor at East Carolina University I created an Innovation Office, which has expanded and built on the highly ranked Miller School of Entrepreneurship. I continue to this date to individually contribute to the venture funds.

Program [29].[4] The research for the report offered a wonderful set of insights into the challenges the emerging American industry with novel technologies faces in the development and deployment of new clean-tech manufacturing capacity.

If you are a company with existing and proven technologies, such as photo-voltaic cell manufacturing or ethanol production, there is a standard set of approaches that you can take such as self-financing or seeking private funding from lenders or a combination of both. It is far easier to secure financing for these type of established technologies as they present a much lower risk to the lender as compared to unproven or novel low-carbon technologies. This is where the US government steps in. They provide loan guarantees so that the lending institution such as a bank is not caught with very large, failed loans on their books, which can impact the larger financial sector.

Congress has authorized and established two important programs for financing the clean-tech sector. The first is the US Department of Energy's Loan Programs Office (LPO).[5] The Title 17 Innovative Clean Energy Projects loan program and Advanced Technology Vehicles Manufacturing loan program are the cornerstones of the LPO. The LPO has a portfolio comprising more than $30 billion of loans, loan guarantees, and conditional commitments covering more than thirty projects, which have resulted in more than $50 billion in total project investment. The US Department of Agriculture's 9003 Program has not been as successful in funding projects in part because biobased solutions are not as sexy to investors and are dependent on high oil prices. However, the program plays a critical role and represents an opportunity [29, 30].

Both programs require a very arduous and detailed technical review to ensure that the technologies are capable of performing and importantly capable of scaling. This rationale is obvious as the agencies are providing loan guarantees with taxpayer money. However, if not managed effectively, these reviews can result in drawn-out government bureaucracies that adversely impact the goal of companies to be first to market. Further, traditional lenders do not like to have to wait one to two years for the government to provide the loan guarantee [29].

14.4.2 Green Bonds and Green Banks

Green bonds function the same way as any other bonds in that they are a fixed-income issuance, but their proceeds are allocated solely to financing new or existing projects focused on climate and/or environmental

[4] For a copy of the report, see the reports section at www.dynamicslab.org.
[5] https://stage.energy.gov/lpo/loan-programs-office.

sustainability. Green bonds can be issued by private companies, financial institutions, and governments. A private company such as a power utility may issue a green bond to finance a large-scale renewable energy development. Financial institutions can issue green bonds as part of their environmental and social governance and net-zero-carbon commitments, similar to the way in which local and regional governments can issue green bonds [31].

A more recent development has been the development of green banks, especially at the state level. A green bank leverages public capital to attract private investment by private capital partners to enter clean-tech markets at scale without green bank assistance. According to the DC Green Bank, the national mobilization ratio (overall investment/green bank investment) of American green banks was 3.7 to 1 as of the end of the calendar year 2020, resulting in $3.70 of overall investment in the American clean-energy economy for every $1.00 green bank investment [32].

In the United States, the first green bank launched in 2010 [33] and the largest green bank is the state of New York's NY Green Bank. The bank is a state-sponsored, specialized financial entity working with the private sector to increase investments into New York's clean-energy markets. Its formation was seen as a critical component of the state's climate and clean-energy agenda formalized under the Climate Leadership and Community Protection Act (Climate Act), which seeks economy-wide carbon neutrality by mandating an 85 percent reduction in greenhouse gas emissions by 2050 and 100 percent clean electric grid by 2040. The bank has made cumulative overall investments of $1.6 billion as of June 2021 [34]. Across the country there are twenty-one green banks and there will soon be a major addition.

The Inflation Reduction Act of 2022 establishes a $27 billion National Green Bank program to provide grants to national and local green banks. The fund's money is divided into three groupings [35]:

1. $7 billion that is earmarked for projects intended to help low-income and disadvantaged communities deploy or benefit from zero-emission technology or other greenhouse gas emission reduction activities.
2. The second pot is also earmarked to support low-income and disadvantaged communities by funding direct or indirect investments in renewable energy projects that would otherwise lack access to financing.
3. Almost $12 billion can be used broadly to support eligible direct and indirect investments in renewable energy projects nationwide.

14.4.3 Tax Incentives

An indirect approach that the government takes is to provide tax incentives for clean tech. One example is the federal government's tax-incentive approach to drive the development of carbon capture and sequestration (CCS). Section 45Q of the tax code was enacted as part of the energy improvement and extension act in 2008. The US Treasury Department and Internal Revenue Service (IRS) issued final regulations regarding the Section 45Q tax credit for qualified "carbon oxide" sequestration using carbon-capture equipment placed in service on or after the date of the enactment of the Bipartisan Budget Act of 2018 [36, 37].

45Q is a performance-based tax credit incentivizing CCS or carbon capture utilization. Much like with the production tax credit for wind, under 45Q, qualifying power generation and industrial facilities can "generate" a tax liability offset per captured ton of carbon dioxide. The amount of the credit per ton varies depending on whether the facility sequesters the carbon in permanent geological storage or captures the carbon for "utilization" in enhanced oil recovery (EOR) or other processes, but generally the credit value ranges from \$10 to \$50 per metric ton, depending on when the carbon-capture equipment is placed in service and what is done with the carbon oxide after it is captured. The credit is worth more if the carbon oxide is permanently buried as opposed to used in an enhanced oil or natural-gas recovery project or other process [37, 38].

To qualify for the tax credit, the facilities must begin construction before January 1, 2026 and facilities must emit no less than [39]:

- 500,000 tons of CO_2 in a taxable year for electricity generating facilities that permanently store the emissions underground or via EOR
- 100,000 tons of CO_2 in a taxable year for other industrial and direct air-capture facilities that permanently store the emissions underground or via EOR
- 25,000 tons of CO_2 in a taxable year for all type of facilities that use the emissions for other utilization processes.

Why is the tax credit important? Because unlike other countries, the United States does not have a national carbon tax or national government carbon trading scheme.

14.5 Government-Backed Carbon Tax and Carbon Trading

A carbon tax establishes a price on carbon in dollars per ton of emissions, while a cap is the limit of the amount of certain greenhouse gases that can be emitted. Companies can trade the so-called emission allowances, which they can buy or sell with one another as needed. The cap is reduced over time so that total emissions could fall. In the United States there is no national government level carbon tax or cap-and-trade program. A country can also limit the total quantity of greenhouse gas emissions by year and implement a cap-and-trade program, which limits the total quantity of emissions per year. This limit is enforced using tradable emissions permits that any emissions source must own to cover its emissions. The market for buying and selling these allowances creates the carbon price in a cap-and-trade program. In the European Union (EU), such a program exists as the EU emissions trading system (EU ETS). The EU ETS works on the cap-and-trade principle. In fact, as of 2022 there were twenty-seven countries with some form of a carbon tax, including China – yet the US does not have a carbon tax [39, 40, 41].

However, two states in the US do have important cap-and-trade programs. The world's fifth largest economy, California, has had a cap-and-trade system since 2013 and Massachusetts has had a program for the power and energy sectors since 2018. The current price of California carbon emissions is $28.26 per ton, which many believe is still too low [41, 42, 43, 44].

Currently, carbon credits trade at €34.25 per ton of CO_2. However, analysts have estimated that an EU carbon permit could cost €89 per ton of CO_2 by 2030. That is the amount needed for the EU to reach its 55 percent emissions-cutting goal by that time.

References

1. B. Gates (2021). Bill Gates: Funding Clean Technology Is the Way to Avoid Climate Disaster. *Financial Times*. October 31. www.ft.com/content/ea71f4f8-e5d8-4324-a42c-8fa09ccb1cc5.
2. World Economic Forum (2021). How to Finance Industry's Net-Zero Transition. January 22. The Davos Agenda. www.weforum.org/agenda/2021/01/how-to-finance-the-industry-net-zero-transition.
3. BlackRock (2022). How to Finance the Net-Zero Transition in Emerging Markets. Blackrock Investment Institute. www.blackrock.com/corporate/insights/black rock-investment-institute/financing-the-net-zero-transition.
4. Casaplorer (2022). US Federal Reserve Interest Rate. Latest Updates and History since 1982. https://casaplorer.com/fed-interest-rate.
5. National Science Foundation (2022). Glossary of Terms. Federal Funds Survey. www.nsf.gov/statistics/fedfunds/glossary/def.htm.
6. National Science Foundation (2018). Definitions of Research and Development: An Annotated Compilation of Official Sources. www.nsf.gov/statistics/randdef/rd-definitions.pdf.
7. UNESCO (2022). How Much Does Your Country Invest in R&D? UNESCO Institute of Statistics. http://uis.unesco.org/apps/visualisations/research-and-

development-spending/#:~:text=Global%20spending%20on%20R%26D%20has%20reached%20a%20record,well%20as%20the%20number%20of%20researchers%20by%202030.

8. UNESCO (2022). GERD as a Percent of GDP. http://data.uis.unesco.org/Index.aspx?DataSetCode=SCN_DS&lang=en.

9. UKEssays (2018). Military Innovations in Civilian Use. www.ukessays.com/essays/military/military-innovations-in-civilian-use.php?vref=1.

10. National Science Foundation (2022). Federal R&D Funding, by Budget Function: Fiscal Years 2020–22. April. https://ncses.nsf.gov/pubs/nsf22316.

11. US News & World Report (2021). A Guide to the Changing Number of U.S. Universities. www.usnews.com/education/best-colleges/articles/how-many-universities-are-in-the-us-and-why-that-number-is-changing.

12. National Science Foundation (2021). Higher Education Research and Development: Fiscal Year 2020. NSF 22–311 Tables. https://ncses.nsf.gov/pubs/nsf22311.

13. National Science Foundation (2022). Federally Financed Higher Education R&D Expenditures, by Federal Agency and R&D field: FY 2020. https://ncses.nsf.gov/surveys/higher-education-research-development/2020.

14. National Science Foundation (2022). Businesses Spent Over a Half Trillion Dollars for R&D Performance in the United States During 2020, a 9.1% Increase Over 2019. NSF 22–343 October 4. https://ncses.nsf.gov/pubs/nsf22343.

15. Nasdaq (2021). Which Companies Spend the Most in Research and Development? June 21. www.nasdaq.com/articles/which-companies-spend-the-most-in-research-and-development-rd-2021-06-21.

16. Statista (2022). Median Time from Initial Equity Financing to IPO Exit in the U.S. 2000–2021. www.statista.com/statistics/320793/median-time-venture-capital-exit-usa.

17. E. McGowan (2022). Series A, B, C, D, and E Funding: How It Works. Start-ups.com. www.startups.com/library/expert-advice/series-funding-a-b-c-d-e.

18. R. Law (2017). From Pre-Seed to Series C: Startup Funding Rounds Explained. August 29. https://medium.com/the-saas-growth-blog/from-pre-seed-to-series-c-startup-funding-rounds-explained-f6647156e28b.

19. Silicon Valley Bank (2022). Stages of Venture Capital. www.svb.com/startup-insights/vc-relations/stages-of-venture-capital.

20. Imarc (2022). Venture Capital Investment Market: Global Industry Trends, Share, Size, Growth, Opportunity and Forecast 2023–2028. www.imarcgroup.com/venture-capital-investment-market.

21. Washington Note (2022). Which Countries Have the Most Venture Capital Investments? https://thewashingtonnote.com/venture-capital-investment-by-country.

22. FundComb (2022). The Largest Venture Capital Funds. https://fundcomb.com/lists/largest/venture-capital.

23. CNBC (2022). Bill Gates Climate Fund Plans to Mobilize $15 Billion into Clean Tech. January 10. www.cnbc.com/2022/01/10/bill-gates-bec-climate-fund-plans-to-invest-15-billion-in-clean-tech.html.

24. Investopedia (2022). Private Equity vs. Venture Capital: What's the Difference? January 27. www.investopedia.com/ask/answers/020415/what-difference-

between-private-equity-and-venture-capital.asp#:~:text=Private%20equity%
20is%20capital%20invested,potential%20for%20long%2Dterm%20growth.

25. Financial Edge (2022). Private Equity vs Venture Capital. November 1. www.fe
.training/free-resources/private-equity/private-equity-vs-venture-capital.

26. Harvard Law (2022). Private Equity, Venture Capital, and Hedge Funds. https://
guides.library.harvard.edu/law/private_equity.

27. Duke (2022). Duke Angel Network Is Now Duke Capital Partners. November 9.
https://otc.duke.edu/news/duke-angel-network-is-now-duke-capital-partners.

28. Batteries News (2022). Venture Capital Deals Value in Advanced Batteries
Skyrocket 850% Yoy in 2021, Finds Globaldata. April 27. https://batteriesnews
.com/venture-capital-advanced-batteries.

29. J. S. Golden, R. Handfield, N. Falkenburg, A. J. Otis, and A. Greenberg (2022).
The Biorefinery, Renewable Chemical, and Biobased Product Manufacturing
Assistance (9003) Program: An External Review Conducted for the U.S.D.A.
Technical Report #2022–11–1: Issued by the Dynamic Sustainability Lab at
Syracuse University. www.dynamicslab.org.

30. Department of Energy (2022). LPO Portfolio. https://stage.energy.gov/lpo/
portfolio.

31. Deloitte (2022). Green Bonds Issuance and Support Offering. www2.deloitte
.com/lt/en/pages/legal/articles/Green-Bonds-Issuance-and-Support-Offering.html.

32. DC Greenbank (2021). Green Banks in the United States: 2021 U.S. Green Bank
Industry Report. https://dcgreenbank.com/press/green-banks-in-the-united-
states-2021-u-s-green-bank-industry-report.

33. US Environmental Protection Agency (n.d.). Clean Energy Finance: Green
Banking Strategies for Local Governments. Updated November 15, 2022. www
.epa.gov/statelocalenergy/clean-energy-finance-green-banking-strategies-local-
governments.

34. New York State Energy Research and Development Authority (2022). NY Green
Bank: Agent for Greater Private Sector Investment in Sustainable Infrastructure.
https://greenbank.ny.gov/About/About.

35. Morgan Lewis (2022). Inflation Reduction Act Creates $27B Green Bank Fund
for Clean Energy Projects, but False Claims Exist. August 16. www.morganlewis
.com/pubs/2022/08/inflation-reduction-act-creates-27b-green-bank-fund-for-
clean-energy-projects-but-false-claims-risks-exist.

36. Congress (2008). H.R. 6049-Energy Improvement and Extension Act of 2008.
www.congress.gov/bill/110th-congress/house-bill/6049.

37. JPT (2021). IRS Issues Final Rules on CCS Tax-Credits Regulations. https://jpt
.spe.org/irs-issues-final-rules-on-ccs-tax-credits-regulations.

38. Energy Ventures Analysis (2020). Understanding 45Q: The Carbon Capture Tax
Credit. October 8. www.evainc.com/energy-blog/45q-the-carbon-capture-tax-
credit.

39. Carbon Herald (2022). What Is the 45Q Tax Credit? November 19. https://
carbonherald.com/what-is-45q-tax-credit.

40. Columbia (2022). What You Need to Know about a Federal Carbon Tax in
the United States. Columbia Center on Global Energy Policy. www.energy
policy.columbia.edu/what-you-need-know-about-federal-carbon-tax-united-
states.

41. Earth.org (2022). Carbon Tax in the USA. January 26. https://earth.org/carbon-tax-in-the-usa.

42. California Air Resources Board (2022). Cap-and-Trade Program. https://ww2.arb.ca.gov/our-work/programs/cap-and-trade-program.

43. International Carbon Action Partnership (2017). Massachusetts Introduces Additional Cap-and-Trade System. August 23. https://icapcarbonaction.com/en/news/massachusetts-introduces-additional-cap-and-trade-system.

44. Bloomberg (2021). California Carbon Sets Record Price in Cap-and-Trade Auction. November 24. www.bloomberg.com/news/articles/2021-11-24/california-carbon-sets-record-price-in-cap-and-trade-auction?leadSource=uverify%20wall#xj4y7vzkg.

15

Finance and Environmental and Social Governance

Canada Pension will sell firms that don't take ESG seriously.
Canada Pension Plan Investment Board chief executive officer John Graham on the intentions of one of the world's largest institutional investors – greater than $400 billion – November 16, 2022 [1]

NC treasurer seeks BlackRock CEO's ouster because of firm's environmental investments.
News and Observer, December 9, 2022 [2]

15.1 Environmental and Social Governance (ESG) Overview

These days so many of us use the term ESG without first understanding its background. So, a bit of history. ESG was first coined in 2004 in a report entitled "Who Cares Wins," which was initiated by the United Nations (UN) secretary general and UN Global Compact in collaboration with the Swiss government. The initiative was endorsed by twenty-three financial institutions collectively representing more than US$6 trillion in assets. ESG as a term builds on the Socially Responsible Investment (SRI) movement that has been around much longer.

But unlike SRI, which is based on ethical and moral criteria and uses mostly negative screens, such as not investing in alcohol, tobacco, or firearms, ESG investing is based on the assumption that ESG factors have financial relevance and will produce stronger returns for the investors. It also builds on Elkington's triple-bottom-line foundations of evaluating businesses performance in a broader perspective to create stronger business value through a focus on ESG lenses [42]. However, the uniqueness, as will be discussed in this section, is that ESG has been adapted as a means to leverage shareholder pressures to

direct corporations to develop a new set of organizational strategies to primarily meet the challenges of climate change in the environment and in the
marketplace [3, 4].

How big is ESG? Well, it is a bit difficult for anyone to state with 100 percent
confidence, in large part because there really is no universally accepted and
regulatory binding definition. However, in one well-publicized study by the
Global Sustainable Investment Alliance [5], ESG assets reached $35.3 trillion
in 2020, which represents 36 percent of all assets under management, and in
2021 Bloomberg Intelligence estimated that this number would rise to $50
trillion by 2025 [6].

The Dow Jones recently (2022) undertook research on the market and the
role of ESG investments. Their findings were:

> According to Dow Jones's survey of 200 financial leaders, ESG investments are
> projected to more than double in the next three years, accounting for 15% of all
> investments by 2025. Survey respondents cited the opportunity to drive positive
> change as the primary driver for this growth, followed by fiduciary responsibilities
> and tightening regulation.
>
> However, more than half (56%) of financial professionals say traditional ways of
> valuing companies are inadequate for assessing sustainable investments, believing
> that the quality of ESG data available today is not yet sufficient to make investment
> decisions (52%). [7]

And who is driving ESG investments in the United States? Well, a 2021 study
conducted by RBC Wealth Management of its US client base showed that it is
women who are leading the ESG investment focus. The firm's female clients
were "more than twice as likely as men to say it is extremely important that the
companies they invest in integrate ESG factors into their policies and decisions." The survey also found that 74 percent of women were interested in
increasing their share of ESG investments in their current portfolios and were
significantly more likely than men to have an interest in learning more about
ESG investing [8].

Similarly, a UBS Wealth Management 2022 report indicated women
are twice as likely as men to say that it's extremely important that the
companies they invest in incorporate ESG factors into their policies and
procedures, and that women in the US under age sixty favor ESG
investing. The UBS survey has laid out that more women (71 percent)
take into account sustainable considerations when investing compared to
men (58 percent) [9].

Similarly, a 2022 study by Harvard researchers indicates that "investors are
willing, on average, to pay 20 basis points more per annum for an investment in
a fund with an ESG mandate as compared to an otherwise identical mutual fund

without an ESG mandate, suggesting that investors as a group expect commensurately higher pre-fee, gross returns, either financial or non-financial, from an ESG mandate" [10].

Related, if you are wondering who are better investors, men or women, the Warwick Business School found that women who invest tend to outperform men by 1.8 percent per annum. This is largely because women trade less often, therefore incurring fewer trading costs, which subtract from market performance [11]. Some might add that women are smarter than men and that is the reason. Being the father of only daughters and brother to only sisters, I would concur.

15.1.1 ESG Products

For the general public, when we consider investing in ESG funds, there are a number of investment products that are promoted as ESG funds, such as mutual funds, exchange-traded funds (ETFs), and index funds [12] (see also Table 15.1). A bit of an overview:

- **ESG mutual funds** are professionally managed funds that contain stocks and bonds with predetermined ESG criteria. They offer investors the benefits of diversification, liquidity, and professional management. Just like companies being traded on a stock exchange, mutual funds are required by law to disclose their performance and associated fund activities publicly. Examples of ESG mutual funds include Parnassus Core Equity Fund, Vanguard FTSE Social Index Fund, and TIAA-CREF Core Impact Bond. There are hundreds of similar funds available.[1]
- **ESG ETFs** are similar to mutual funds in the sense that they contain a variety of ESG-centric stocks, bonds, and other financial instruments. However, unlike a mutual fund (which is bought and sold from the issuer), ETFs are traded freely on stock exchanges. In general, ETFs tend to have lower fees, including management expense ratios, than mutual funds. And because of the lower fees, the downturn in the market, and the Federal Reserve's efforts to tackle inflation, many more sophisticated investors have pulled away from bonds and into ETFs. In fact, the *Wall Street Journal* reported [13] that 2022 has seen the largest net annual swing toward ETFs with over $454 billion pulled from bond mutual funds on net, while $157 billion has entered bond exchange-traded funds through the end of October 2022. Examples of ESG

---

[1] The listed funds here and throughout the book are not endorsed or promoted by the author. Readers need to seek professional financial investment advice before investing.

Table 15.1 *Basic design elements of ESG funds [5, 12]*

GLOBAL SUSTAINABLE INVESTMENT ALLIANCE – Core approaches to sustainable investment	
ESG integration	The systematic and explicit, inclusion by investment managers of environmental, social and governance factors into financial analysis
Corporate engagement and shareholder action	Employing shareholder power to influence corporate behavior, including through direct corporate engagement (i.e., communicating with senior management and/or boards of companies), filing or co-filing shareholder proposals, and prosy voting that is guided by comprehensive ESG guidelines
Norms-based screening	Screening of investments against minimum standards of business or issuer practice based on international norms, such as those issued by the UN, International Labour Organization, Organisation for Economic Co-operation and Development, and non-governmental organizations (e.g., Transparency International)
Negative/exclusionary screening	The exclusion from a fund or portfolio of certain sectors, companies, countries, or other issuers based on activities considered not investable. Exclusion criteria (based on norms and values) can refer, for example, to product categories (e.g., weapons, tobacco), company practices (e.g., animal testing, violation of human rights, corruption), or controversies
Best-in-class/positive screening	Investment in sectors, companies, or projects selected for positive ESG performance relative to industry peers and that achieve a rating above a defined threshold
Sustainability themed/thematic investing	Investing in themes or assets specifically contributing to sustainable solutions – environmental and social (e.g., sustainable agriculture, green buildings, lower-carbon-tilted portfolio, gender equity, diversity)
Impact investing	Investing to achieve positive, social, and environmental impacts – requires measuring and reporting against these impacts, demonstrating the intentionality of investor and underlying asset/investee, and demonstrating the investor contribution
Community investing	Where capital is specifically directed to traditionally underserved individuals or communities, as well as financing that is provided to businesses with a clear social or environmental purpose. Some community investing is impact investing, but community investing is broader and considers other forms of investing and targeted lending activities

GENERALIZED ESG FUND CONSTRUCTION EXAMPLES

Negative screening	Negative screening is sometimes referred to as exclusion. This technique involves identifying undesirable characteristics (that don't meet certain sustainability criteria or expectations) and then running a stock screener (like Refinitiv or Capital IQ) to exclude investments that don't qualify
	Screens that eliminate an entire SIC or NAICS code (like businesses in the oil and gas industry)
	Screens that exclude external ESG scores that are below X (as rated by external rating agencies like Moody's or Sustainalytics, etc.)
Positive screening	Positive screening, sometimes called inclusion, is the opposite of negative screening. Analysts and fund managers at asset management firms can instead run screens to search out top performers (often scored by the same external rating agencies), measured against important ESG criteria
	The screening tool may be searching out top scores overall; alternatively, they can be seeking out top performers in the "S" (social) pillar or in some subset of it (like DE&I or corporate culture metrics). Capital markets platforms are designed to allow analysts to drill down in considerable detail when screening for securities
Thematic investing	Thematic investing is where an ESG fund manager identifies longer-term macroeconomic trends that they feel have tailwinds and that should collectively contribute to better ESG performance
	BlackRock is widely credited with making the concept of thematic ESG investing more mainstream. Thematic ESG funds may still use screening tools, but many also employ proprietary models and criteria to achieve their investment objectives

ETFs include XTrackers S&P ESG Dividend Aristocrats ETF, Invesco ESG NASDAQ 100 ETF, and IQ MacKay ESG Core Plus Bond ETF.

- **ESG index funds** are a type of ESG mutual fund. While ESG mutual funds are actively managed by a portfolio manager, an ESG index fund passively tracks the ESG-centric companies that trade on an index, such as the S&P 500. Examples of ESG index funds include Vanguard's FTSE Social Index Fund (VFTAX) and Fidelity US Sustainability Index Fund (FITLX).

15.1.2 Establishing a US Definition

Potter Stewart was an associate justice on the US Supreme Court. He is famous for having described hard-core pornography and obscenity in 1964 in the *Jacobellis* v. *Ohio* case as "I know it when I see it" [14]. Unfortunately, in some bizarre ways that is analogous to the current ESG world, where one is left to think they know if a fund is an ESG fund. However, there is an opportunity to change that.

On May 25, 2022, the US Securities and Exchange Commission (SEC) proposed new rules to under both the Investment Advisers Act of 1940 (Advisers Act) and the Investment Company Act of 1940 (Investment Company Act) to enhance the regulatory framework for disclosures concerning investment funds and investment advisers' ESG-related investing strategies [15].

This action comes after three related and significant actions by the SEC:

1. The SEC proposal announced on March 21, 2022 requiring public companies to disclose extensive climate-related information in their SEC filings [16].
2. The recent formation of the SEC's Climate and ESG Task Force in the Division of Enforcement [17].
3. May 2022 when SEC charged BNY Melon Investment Advisor, Inc. for material misstatements and omissions about a sub-adviser's ESG quality reviews – BNY Melon Investments agreed to a $1.5 million penalty [18].

If adopted, the Proposed Rules would require SEC-registered advisers to include ESG factors and strategies for investors in fund prospectuses, annual summaries, and brochures. More specifically, they would [15]:

- require specific disclosures on ESG strategies in fund prospectuses, annual reports, and adviser brochures including progress toward stated impact, key performance indicators, the time horizon the adviser uses, the relationship between ESG impacts and financial returns, and any material conflicts of interest
- introduce a standard table for ESG funds to disclose information, allowing investors to compare ESG funds quickly
- require certain environmentally focused funds to disclose greenhouse gas (GHG) emissions of their portfolio investments; funds that disclose they do not consider GHG emissions as part of their ESG strategy would not be expected to report this metric
- require registered investment funds to be categorized into an ESG fund-type depending on the extent that the funds advertise or utilize ESG factors in investment decision-making
- require fund annual summaries to disclose additional ESG-related information, including progress on achieving stated impacts, disclosure of aggregated GHG emissions, and enhanced narrative disclosure of how proxy voting or engagement with issuers is a means of implementing an ESG strategy.

The SEC proposal also develops three categories of ESG funds [15, 19, 20]:

1. Integration funds
2. ESG-focused funds
3. Impact funds.

Integration funds: these integrate both ESG factors and non-ESG factors in their investment decisions such that ESG factors are not considered dispositive. Integration funds would be required to disclose how ESG factors guide their investment process. The disclosure would be brief to avoid overstating the role of ESG factors. Integration funds that consider GHG emissions would be required to disclose how the fund considers GHG emissions, including the methodology and data sources consulted by the fund.

   ESG-focused funds: these significantly center on ESG factors and would be required to submit detailed disclosures, including in the form of an ESG strategy overview table. The proposal would also obligate certain ESG-focused funds to provide about their ESG strategies, including any inclusionary or exclusionary screens, and information about the impacts they are pursuing. ESG-focused funds that utilize proxy voting or engagement with issuers to implement their ESG strategy would also be required to disclose how they voted proxies relating to portfolio securities on particular ESG-related voting matters and information regarding their ESG engagement meetings. ESG-focused funds that have environmentally focused investment strategies would be required to disclose additional information on the GHG emissions associated with their investments, including the carbon footprint and the weighted average carbon intensity of their portfolio.

   Impact funds: these are a subset of ESG-focused funds pursuing a specific ESG impact (e.g., financing the construction of affordable housing or improving availability of clean water). Impact funds would be required to disclose how they measure progress (in qualitative and quantitative terms) and summarize achievements toward their stated ESG goal.

15.1.3 The European Union Taxonomy

The European Union in 2020 established a taxonomy [21] of a list of environmentally sustainable economic activities with the goal of informing companies, investors, and policymakers with appropriate definitions of which economic activities can be considered environmentally sustainable. The regulation established the criteria for determining whether an economic activity qualifies as environmentally sustainable for the purposes of establishing the degree to which an investment is environmentally sustainable. The regulation applies to:

- measures adopted by member states or by the Union that set out requirements for financial market participants or issuers in respect of financial products or corporate bonds that are made available as environmentally sustainable
- financial market participants that make available financial products.

15.2 ESG Market Performance

To understand the market performance of ESG funds, you need to have a comparative, and for this I have used S&P's 500, which is a stock market index that measures the performance of 500 leading public companies in the US. It includes companies across eleven sectors to offer a picture of the health of the US stock market and the broader economy. This includes companies such as Apple and Microsoft as well as Bank of America and Goldman Sachs, Walmart, Boeing, and Nike. It is not an exact list of the top 500 US companies by market cap because there are other criteria that the index includes. Another market performance comparative could be the Dow Jones Industrial Average (DJIA) [22, 23].

Throughout 2019 the S&P 500 and the S&P 500 ESG index had similar performances; both indexes were weighted to similar industries as the S&P 500 followed the leading 500 companies in the United States. By the fourth quarter of 2020, the S&P 500 ESG index began to steadily outperform the S&P 500 by four points on average. By April 4, 2022, the S&P ESG index had a score of 187.42 index points as compared to the S&P 500 at 176.45 [24].

This compares to a study by Morgan Stanley that analyzed more than 3,000 US mutual funds and ETFs in 2020. Their findings indicated that sustainable equity funds outperformed their traditional peer funds by a median total return of 4.3 percentage points in 2020 [25].

15.2.1 Countering Version

While those prior studies tell one story, there are countering versions of performance. The first is already outdated but has been broadly put forward by some who seek to countervail the ESG movement. A study by two researchers from the London School of Economics and the University of Columbia [26] examined self-claimed ESG mutual funds (as identified by Morningstar) in the United States from 2010 to 2018. During this pre-COVID-19 period, they found those funds had worse track records for compliance with labor and environmental laws as compared to non-ESG funds managed by the same financial institutions in the same years. Relative to other funds offered by the same asset managers in the same years, ESG funds hold stocks that are more likely to voluntarily disclose carbon emissions performance but also stocks with higher carbon emissions per unit of revenue.

They also state that the ESG funds "appear" to underperform financially relative to other funds within the same asset manager and year, and to charge higher fees. In other words, without the regulatory structures and oversight, these offerings can be confusing at best to an individual investor and greenwashing at worse.

And most recently, as of the end of 2022, the ten largest ESG funds by assets have all posted double-digit losses, with eight of them falling even more than the S&P 500's 14.8 percent decline [27]. As a whole, the market took a hit in 2022 and ESG funds were also hit if compared to the market as the fossil fuel industry. In fact, as reported by the *New York Times*, for the S&P's first half of 2022, nineteen of the top twenty spots belonged to companies connected, in one way or another, with fossil fuel. The best performer with a 142 percent gain was Occidental Petroleum [28]. Yet the price of a barrel of oil by the end of 2022 went from a high of $122 per barrel on June 13, 2022 to $77 by December 12, 2022, so the final comparisons of fund performances for the end of 2022 and for 2023 are yet to be understood [29].

15.3 The Politicization of Climate and ESG

Certainly, the issue of climate change has been both partisan and contentious at best, pitting conservatives versus liberals as well as pitting fossil fuel industry states against more progressive clean-tech states. For example, back in 2011 the then governor of Texas Rick Perry was on the presidential campaign trail when he famously said, "there are a substantial number of scientists who have manipulated data so that they will have dollars rolling into their projects" and "the issue of global warming has been politicized," and argued that America should not spend billions of dollars addressing "a scientific theory that has not been proven, and from my perspective is more and more being put into question" [30]. And to be fair, years later when serving as US secretary of energy, then Secretary Perry contradicted his boss Donald Trump when he told the press, "We're going to address the climate. It makes sense for us to have policies that reduce emissions, that reduce the pollutants that are in the air, to reduce the particles that cause massive health problems around the world," he said. "Common sense tells you, bring the cleaner burning fuels, bring the things that bring the emissions down. That's just common sense" [31].

The point of this is not to call out one individual on a change of opinion, but to highlight that politics has played a key role in the climate debate and unfortunately put it into terms of blue versus red rather than let's work together and support Americans and the American economy.

And the partisanship can and does continue, as states can also preempt local jurisdictions as a new trend in respect to climate change. Laws by state, traditionally conservative state legislatures, are developed to nullify existing municipal or county ordinances deemed progressive [32]. A case in point occurred in the state of Arizona when Regina Romero (D) became mayor of Tucson in 2019 and sought to address climate change through building codes. The Arizona state legislature passed House Bill 2686 on February 24, 2020, which is a law that mandates that natural gas utilities are "not subject to further regulation by a municipality" [33, 34].

However, there are times where preemption can be overridden. One such example is what happened in the state of Colorado where on April 3, 2019 the Colorado state assembly passed SB 19–181, which placed the regulation of oil and gas exploration back with local communities as equals to the state, over-riding the Colorado Supreme Court precedent that made state law the highest law. This in effect makes the state law the floor and local law the ceiling [35].

15.3.1 State Treasurers Enter the Fray

As one could expect, the momentum of ESG has garnered the attention of elected conservative state treasurers. At the root of the issue is that there are a number of states dominated by and dependent on the fossil fuels industry, as well as politicians who feel that it is good politics to take on what is perceived as a liberal ESG agenda. In the recent 2022 national elections, some Republican campaigns for state financial officers focused on ESG, arguing that investing in ESG is harming capital markets and domestic energy production. Kansas offers such an example as Stephen Johnson (R) beat out the democratic incumbent for state treasurer with anti-ESG as part of his platform [36].

Florida and Texas politicians are among the leaders of the anti-ESG political movement. In August 2022, the Florida State Board of Administration trustees, led by Governor Ron DeSantis, voted to ban ESG considerations from the asset allocator's investment decisions. "I want to have the values not of Davos imposed on us, but of places like Destin and Dunedin, where I grew up," the Republican governor added. He has also proposed that the GOP-controlled state legislature pass a law forbidding ESG investing [37].

In August 2022, nineteen state attorneys-general penned a letter to the chief executive officer of BlackRock, Larry Fink. The letter stated in the opening that

"BlackRock's past public commitments indicate that it has used citizens' assets to pressure companies to comply with international agreements such as the Paris Agreement that force the phase-out of fossil fuels, increase energy prices, drive inflation, and weaken the national security of the United States" [38].

Additionally, the letter stated, "BlackRock's public commitments treat the 'energy transition' as a fait accompli. As noted above, you have committed to manage all assets under management to achieve net zero emissions by 2050 or sooner. BlackRock's belief that the world will require net zero by 2050 could be a pretext to force companies to adopt your preferred climate policies" [38]. This was signed by the state attorneys-general for:

1. Arizona
2. Alabama
3. Arkansas
4. Georgia
5. Idaho
6. Indiana
7. Kansas
8. Kentucky
9. Louisiana
10. Missouri
11. Mississippi
12. Montana
13. Nebraska
14. Ohio
15. Oklahoma
16. South Carolina
17. Texas
18. Utah
19. West Virginia.

Beyond the letter, there are a number of proposed and enacted pieces of legislation like Florida seeking to curb ESG and contracting with investment firms that use ESG in their financial considerations. In September 2021, Texas implemented a ban on municipalities[2] doing business with financial firms that they accuse of boycotting the gun and fossil fuel industries [39]. In part, this was self-preservation of their reliance on these industries, as well as political. The implications of these actions are that five of the largest underwriters exited

---

[2] Texas Senate Bills 13 and 19, which took effect on September 1, 2021.

the market: JPMorgan Chase, Goldman Sachs, Citigroup, Bank of America, and Fidelity.

A related study by the Wharton School of Business and a researcher who is also a member of the Board of Governors of the Federal Reserve System documented the financial impact of the Texas actions. Their findings estimated that Texas cities will pay an additional $303 million to $532 million in interest on $32 billion in bonds based on analyzed data from the first eight months of the law [40].

So, what does this all mean? Well, from my perspective, not much. The politics may continue to be heated, just as they were in the earlier days of the global climate debate. When you compare the top pensions and their assets, California and New York overwhelm those of Texas, Florida, and North Carolina, who are all aggressively pushing back on ESG. The assets of just California and New York pensions[3] in 2022 were three times larger, with over $1.6 trillion, as compared to the three other states that came in at $554 billion [41]. And that investment strength influences the role of ESG in funds and the companies that funds invest in.

And, while certain conservative governors and state politicians can continue to raise ESG as a political platform agenda, global industry, not just domestic industry, is ignoring the politics and meeting shareholder and consumer demands of firms to address climate and related imperatives, and these voices are only getting stronger with the elevation of the next generation of consumers.

My work with numbers of major multinational corporations in various sectors, including energy, shows that they understand that the net-zero-carbon transition is underway and there is no looking back. They also understand that the political landscape can change every two years and that the political hot-buttons can change even sooner. Most importantly, these leaders and the future corporate leaders know that to be financially sustainable and competitive in a global economy, they will need to produce goods and services with lower environmental impacts.

References

1.   Bloomberg (2022). Canada Pension Will Sell Firms That Don't Take ESG Seriously. November 16. www.bloomberg.com/news/articles/2022-11-16/canada-pension-will-sell-firms-that-don-t-take-esg-seriously#xj4y7vzkg.

---

[3] A number of teacher and retirement pension plans.

2. News and Observer (2022). NC Treasurer Seeks BlackRock CEO's Ouster Because of Firm's Environmental Investments. December 9. www.newsobser ver.com/news/politics-government/article269816167.html.

3. International Finance Corporation (n.d.). Who Cares Wins, 2004–08: Issue Brief. World Bank Group. Washington, DC. https://documents1.worldbank.org/curated/en/444801491483640669/pdf/113850-BRI-IFC-Breif-whocares-PUBLIC.pdf.

4. Forbes (2018). The Remarkable Rise Of ESG. July 11. www.forbes.com/sites/georgkell/2018/07/11/the-remarkable-rise-of-esg/?sh=36b81fd01695.

5. Global Sustainable Investment (2021). Global Sustainable Investment Review 2020. http://www.gsi-alliance.org/wp-content/uploads/2021/08/GSIR-20201.pdf.

6. Bloomberg Intelligence (2021). ESG Assets Rising to $50 Trillion Will Reshape $140.5 Trillion of Global AUM by 2025, Finds Bloomberg Intelligence. www.bloomberg.com/company/press/esg-assets-rising-to-50-trillion-will-reshape-140-5-trillion-of-global-aum-by-2025-finds-bloomberg-intelligence.

7. Dow Jones (2022). Beyond Buzzwords: An Outside-In Approach to ESG and Long-Term Investing Trends. https://visit.dowjones.com/esg/content/beyond-buzzwords.

8. RBC (2021). Women Are Leading the Charge for Environmental, Social and Governance (ESG) Investing in the U.S. amid Growing Demand for Responsible Investing Solutions. www.rbcwealthmanagement.com/en-us/newsroom/2021-04-06/women-are-leading-the-charge-for-environmental-social-and-gov ernance-esg-investing-in-the-us-amid-growing-demand-for-responsible-invest ing-solutions.

9. UBS (2022). What Makes Women's Wealth Journey Different? www.ubs.com/global/en/wealth-management/our-approach/marketnews/article.1560217.html.

10. M. Baker, M. Egan, and S. Sarkar (2022). How Do Investors Value ESG? Working paper for the National Bureau of Economic Research. December. www.nber.org/papers/w30708.

11. Warwick Business School (2018). Are Women Better Investors Than Men? www.wbs.ac.uk/news/are-women-better-investors-than-men.

12. Corporate Finance Institute (2022). Understanding ESG Funds. https://corporate financeinstitute.com/resources/esg/esg-fund.

13. *Wall Street Journal* (2022). Bond Investors Swap Mutual Funds for ETFs at Record Pace. December 10. www.wsj.com/articles/bond-investors-swap-mutual-funds-for-etfs-at-record-pace-11670651567?mod=rss_markets_main.

14. *Wall Street Journal* (2007). The Origins of Justice Stewart's "I Know It When I See It." September 27. www.wsj.com/articles/BL-LB-4558.

15. Securities and Exchange Commission (2022). Enhanced Disclosures by Certain Investment Advisers and Investment Companies about Environmental, Social, and Governance Investment Practice. www.sec.gov/rules/proposed/2022/ia-6034.pdf.

16. Securities and Exchange Commission (2022). SEC Proposes Rules to Enhance and Standardize Climate-Related Disclosures for Investors. www.sec.gov/news/press-release/2022–46.

17. Securities and Exchange Commission (2021). Enforcement Task Force Focused on Climate and ESG Issues. www.sec.gov/spotlight/enforcement-task-force-focused-climate-esg-issues.

18. Securities and Exchange Commission (2022). SEC Charges BNY Mellon Investment Adviser for Misstatements and Omissions Concerning ESG Considerations. www.sec.gov/news/press-release/2022–86.

19. White and Case (2022). SEC Proposes Amendments to Rules to Regulate ESG Disclosures for Investment Advisers & Investment Companies. www.whitecase .com/insight-alert/sec-proposes-amendments-rules-regulate-esg-disclosures-investment-advisers-investment#:~:text=On%20May%2025%2C%202022%2C %20the%20US%20Securities%20and,disclose%20extensive%20climate-related %20information%20in%20their%20SEC%20filings.2.

20. Norton Rose Fulbright (2022). US SEC Proposes New ESG Disclosure Rules for Funds and Advisers. www.nortonrosefulbright.com/en/knowledge/publications/ 915ef285/us-sec-proposes-new-esg-disclosure-rules-for-funds-and-advisers#:~: text=To%20that%20end%2C%20the%20SEC%20has%20defined%20two,% 282%29%20ESG-Focused%20Funds%20and%20%283%29%20ESG% 20Impact%20Funds.

21. European Union (2020). Regulation (EU) 2020/852 of the European Parliament and of the Council of 18 June 2020 on the Establishment of a Framework to Facilitate Sustainable Investment, and Amending Regulation (EU) 2019/2088.

22. Investopedia (2022). S&P 500 Index: What It's for and Why It's Important in Investing. www.investopedia.com/terms/s/sp500.asp.

23. S&P Dow Jones Indices (2022). Investment Theme U.S Core. www.spglobal .com/spdji/en/landing/investment-themes/us-core.

24. Statista (2022). Comparison of the Effect of the S&P 500 ESG and S&P 500 Indices between March 2019 and November 2022. www.statista.com/statistics/ 1269643/s-p-500-esg-normal-index-comparison/#:~:text=The%20major%20dif ferences%20between%20the,than%20the%20S%26P%20500%20index.

25. Morgan Stanley (2021). Sustainable Funds Outperform Their Peers in 2020 during Coronavirus. www.morganstanley.com/ideas/esg-funds-outperform-peers-coronavirus.

26. A. Raghunandan and S. Rajgopal (2022). Do ESG Funds Make Stakeholder-Friendly Investments? *Review of Accounting Studies*. http://dx.doi.org/10.2139/ ssrn.3826357.

27. Bloomberg (2022). Big ESG Funds Are Doing Worse Than the S&P 500. December 7. www.bloomberg.com/news/articles/2022-12-07/big-esg-funds-are-doing-worse-than-the-s-p-500-green-insight.

28. *New York Times* (2022). Fossil-Fuel Shares Lead the Stock Market. How Awkward. June 3. www.nytimes.com/2022/06/03/business/stock-market-energy-climate-change.html.

29. Statista (2022). Weekly Oil Prices in Brent, OPEC Basket, and WTI Futures 2020–2022. www.statista.com/statistics/326017/weekly-crude-oil-prices.

30. CBS News (2011). Rick Perry Suggests Global Warming Is a Hoax. August 17. www.cbsnews.com/news/rick-perry-suggests-global-warming-is-a-hoax.

31. CNBC (2019). Energy Secretary Rick Perry Contradicts Trump, Says Humans Do Play a Role in Causing Climate Change. July 31. www.cnbc.com/2019/07/31/

energy-secretary-rick-perry-humans-play-a-role-in-climate-change.html#:~:
text=Energy%20Secretary%20Rick%20Perry%2C%20veering,Man%2C%20it's
%20been%20changing%20forever.

32. *Harvard Law Review* (2022). Zoning Laws As an Intersectional Climate Policy. April 11. 135 Harv. L. Rev 1592.
33. *Phoenix New Times* (2020). Cities Hate It, but Ducey Signs Bill Banning Local Bans on Natural Gas Anyway. www.phoenixnewtimes.com/news/ducey-signs-bill-banning-local-bans-on-natural-gas-into-law–11445713.
34. Arizona Legislature (2020). HB 2686. www.azleg.gov/legtext/54leg/2R/bills/HB2686P.pdf.
35. Cobar (2019). Springtime for Home Rule over Oil and Gas. www.cobar.org/Portals/COBAR/TCL/2019/July/CL_July2019_Feat_Gov.pdf.
36. Rollcall (2022). Republicans Ride ESG Backlash to State Financial Offices. November 17. https://rollcall.com/2022/11/17/republicans-ride-esg-backlash-to-state-financial-offices.
37. Chief Investment Officer (2022). DeSantis and Allies Bar Florida SBA from ESG Investing. August 23. www.ai-cio.com/news/desantis-and-allies-bar-florida-sba-from-esg-investing.
38. Letter from 19 Attorneys General to Larry Fink, CEO of Blackrock. August 4, 2022. www.texasattorneygeneral.gov/sites/default/files/images/executive-management/BlackRock%20Letter.pdf.
39. National Public Radio (2022). Texas Ban on Firms That Don't Invest in Firearms and Fossil Fuels Is Costing Taxpayers. www.npr.org/2022/09/01/1120457153/texas-ban-on-firms-who-dont-invest-in-firearms-and-fossil-fuels-are-cost-taxpaye.
40. D. Garrett and I. Ivanov (2022). Gas, Guns, and Governments: Financial Costs of Anti-ESG Policies. July 11. http://dx.doi.org/10.2139/ssrn.4123366.
41. Pensions and Investments (2022). The P&I 1,000 Largest U.S. Retirement Funds: 2022. www.pionline.com/pi-1000-largest-retirement-plans/2022-full-list.
42. J. Elkington (1994). Towards the Sustainable Corporation: Win-Win-Win Business Strategies for Sustainable Development. *California Management Review*, 36: 90–100.

16

Insuring the Transition

We really don't underwrite or like to see companies that are using carbon offsets.

Zachary Bogue, co-founder of Silicon Valley Venture Capital Firm
DCVC CNBC, October 7, 2022 [1]

In the short term, Delta intends to achieve carbon neutrality by directly reducing emissions through fleet and operational efficiencies and addressing remaining emissions through carbon offset project investments that maintain, protect and expand forests.

Delta Airlines News Hub, April 22, 2021 [2]

16.1 The Carbon Conundrum

The quotes I offered up to introduce this chapter are indicative of the conflicting views of the voluntary carbon offsets market. Companies and governments are committing to achieve a net-zero-carbon transition, and in order to achieve the "net," they are by default in need of carbon offsets during the transition. Yet, at the same time, there is strong pushback by a variety of actors spanning environmental activists and politicians to conservative members of the financial sectors all the way to late-night TV hosts. On August 22, 2022, John Oliver, host of the HBO show *Last Week Tonight*, went off on a twenty-three-minute tirade highlighting all the worst of the voluntary carbon market – and he did a very good job. In the segment, Oliver presented what many would consider "bullshit" or "greenwashing" offset strategies. While over the top, there was truth in his segment.

However, a more cerebral approach is to examine both the values and the risks of voluntary carbon market and corporate carbon reduction strategies, as presented in Figure 16.1. And importantly, what are the operational gaps that exist that, if not addressed, will result in the failure of the carbon market?

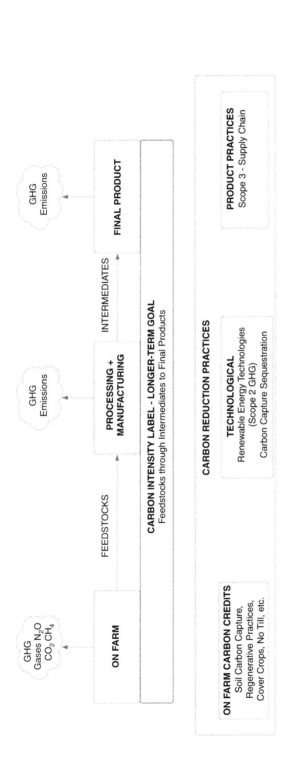

Figure 16.1 Carbon reduction strategies and operational needs.

16.2 Insurance 101

First, we need a bit of overview of the insurance industry itself. Way back in 1688 Edward Lloyd's coffee house in Tower Street, London was providing important information about shipping and the marine insurance market to those engaged in the shipping industry. This was the precursor of Lloyd's of London, which is now the world's largest insurance marketplace and global distribution network [3, 4].

Today, the global insurance industry, which is expected to reach $6.4 trillion by 2025 [5], has very selfish reasons for entering the voluntary carbon offsets and carbon mitigation marketplace. The first reason is that insurance payouts resulting from climate change are rapidly increasing and having major impacts on the industry. As climate change brings stronger storms, flooding, forest fires, and other impacts, the industry is facing uncertain future payouts. As an example, 2017 was the worst year financially of the US insurance sector with losses of over $132 billion, due to weather disasters, with 60 percent of global insurance payouts in the year caused by Hurricanes Harvey, Irma, and Maria [6]. Then in 2018, the most destructive wildfires in California history further contributed to the industry and nearly 1.9 million acres were burned. In all, the California Insurance Department tallied more than 56,000 claims and $12.4 billion in insured losses due to the wildfires [7].

As a result, the industry is now more focused on reversing these losses and exploring how to leverage the emerging market so that the overall sector can move from an increasingly trending "payout" industry from the increasing impacts from climate change to become a "policy payment" industry helping to mitigate climate change.

The industry makes money, namely through: (1) underwriting profit; (2) investments; and (3) reduced overall claims expense.

1. An underwriting profit occurs when an insurance company insures policy-holders who have few or no losses. As climate change intensifies, this becomes problematic.
2. Investment income, like underwriting profits, is also largely beyond the control of the insurance companies. Insurers are scrutinized with respect to their investment portfolios. State laws and the National Association of Insurance Commissioners regulate total percentages of stock market and other riskier investments in which an insurance company may invest. However, the insurance sector can play an important role through possible investments in companies that are committing and properly transitioning to net-zero-carbon emissions. They can also play a critical role in the possible

investment in carbon mitigation strategies – both nature-based and technologies.

3. Of the three factors, managing claims expense is the one factor that is more or less within the full control of the insurance company. Insurance companies develop models and strategies based on "prior" occurrences that provide the insights needed to minimize losses. The difficulty with climate change as an insurable product is that there are too many uncertainties about the impacts and intensity of the impacts related to increased climate change.

Related to claims expense is the fact that insurance companies have a general reputation of being aggressive to deny or reduce a claim – hence, the large legal industry that has grown that we all witness for car accident attorneys.

Managing all of this are generally five broad departments: (1) claims, (2) finance, (3) legal, (4) marketing, and (5) underwriting. Marketing and underwriting are the departments that work to bring in business, while the claims and finance units are the more risk-averse departments. The legal department is often the referee between these competing interests. Underwriters seek to develop insurance products that can be sold to their customers for a profit, which requires a strong reliance on historic claims data and predictive models.

16.3 Corporate Carbon Reduction Strategies

In addition to the insurance sector needing to find ways to reduce payouts resulting from the impacts of climate change, they must also find insurance solutions to drive natural and technological solutions to mitigate climate change.

16.3.1 Nature-Based Solutions

Nature-based solutions provide a pathway for carbon that is in the atmosphere to be captured and stored various methods. The most prominent due to the low cost is for carbon to be sequestered in soils, forests, wetlands, and oceans. In addition to price, these solutions help to protect important ecosystems, which themselves are necessary to support the biodiversity needed to sequester the carbon. And as discussed in Chapter 4, organizations can enter the carbon market and purchase carbon offsets.

The risk, of course, for the corporations purchasing the voluntary carbon offsets is two-fold. The first risk is that the offsets they are purchasing are not legitimate or that harmful activities take place such as deforestation, for which they not only lose the ability to capture and sequester the carbon but the carbon itself is also released during operational activities, such as deforestation and tilling of soils or from catastrophic events such as forest fires, droughts, or flooding [8–11].

16.3.2 Technological Solutions

There are a number of historically proven technologies that have lower insurance risks. These include the deployment of renewable energy sources in lieu of legacy fossil fuels such as generating or purchasing electricity from wind or solar versus coal and natural gas and obtaining renewable energy credits. Technology, especially unproven technology, generally has greater risks and greater costs.

However, it can also provide more direct benefits. Take, for instance, a manufacturing company. Rather than having to "offset" their carbon emissions through a voluntary carbon credit market that likely is using nature-based solutions far from their facility, the company could deploy in-situ or on-site technologies. An example of a technological solution is carbon capture and storage (CCS). This is where the carbon dioxide (CO_2) emissions from an industrial process such as generating energy, steel, or cement are captured then compressed and transported through a pipeline or some other form and injected and stored deep underground in geological formations [8, 12]. A fuller review is provided in Table 16.1 [8, 13–17].

Table 16.1 *Selected nature- and technology-based carbon dioxide removal techniques [8, 13–17, 39]*

Nature-Based	Definition	Land Usage ha/tCO$_2$/Yr	Current Scalability Barriers
Reforestation (RF) + afforestation (AF)	Reforestation includes planting trees or allowing trees to regrow on land that had recently been covered with forest. Afforestation involves planting trees on land that has not recently been covered with forest	0.03–0.7	Land requirements and competition with crops. Benefits can take decades to realize

Table 16.1 *(cont.)*

Nature-Based	Definition	Land Usage ha/tCO$_2$/Yr	Current Scalability Barriers
Improved forest mgt. (IMF)	Forest management activities that result in increased carbon stocks within forests and/or reduce greenhouse gas emissions from forestry activities when compared to business as usual forestry practices		
Soil carbon sequestration (SCS)	Soil carbon sequestration, also known as "regenerative agriculture," includes various ways of managing land, especially farmland so that soils absorb and hold more carbon, such as (1) reducing soil disturbance by switching to low-till or no-till practices or planting perennial crops; (2) changing planting schedules or rotations, such as by planting cover crops or double crops instead of leaving fields fallow; (3) managed grazing of livestock; and (4) applying compost or crop residues to fields	No additional land beyond what is used for agriculture	Lack of incentives to drive growth by farmers when subsidy systems are tied to high yield of monocultural commodity crops. Difficulties in measuring soil carbon
Blue carbon (BC)	Carbon captured by the world's ocean and coastal ecosystems through such resources as sea grasses, mangroves, and salt marshes along the coast	0.2 for mangroves, other systems will vary	Conflicts in use of coastal zones. Lack of incentives. Impacts from water pollution. Negative public perceptions of mangroves and wetlands

Table 16.1 *(cont.)*

Technology-Based	Definition	Energy Usage GJ/tCO$_2$	Current Barriers
Direct air capture and storage (DACS)	In Prototype Phase Climateworks (Switzerland) opened an operational facility Ocra in Iceland. The plant will capture 4,000 tons of CO$_2$ a year (~250 US residents) and is primarily removing carbon and storing it underground by mineralizing it with basalt rock. Selling captured carbon dioxide for use in soda drinks or in greenhouses	6.7–12.3	Very high costs, slow development of geological storage infrastructure, risks of leakage, lack of regulations and standards
Enhanced weathering	Strategy based on amending soils with crushed calcium- and magnesium-rich silicate rocks to accelerate CO$_2$ sequestration and/or ocean alkalinity is increased through depositing rock particles into the ocean	12.5	Lack of understanding of the impacts and effectiveness. Very slow sequestration rates. Costs and energy of transporting minerals
Bio energy with carbon capture and storage (BECCS)	Involves any energy pathway where CO$_2$ is captured from a biogenic source and permanently stored BECCS is the only carbon dioxide removal technique that can also provide energy. The Illinois Industrial CCS Project has been capturing 1 Mt CO$_2$ per year for permanent storage in a deep geological formation since 2018 from corn to ethanol fermentation	Energy production 0.8–10.9	Costs of industrial capture and storage. Availability of biomass and competition for farm land, lack of consistent regulations and standards, leakage in system

Table 16.1 *(cont.)*

Technology-Based	Definition	Energy Usage GJ/tCO$_2$	Current Barriers
Biochar	Biochar recovers and stores a large fraction of carbon in the ground Biochar also reduces the need for fertilizer and raises agricultural productivity in marginal soils, significantly reduces runoff. Biochar can be made through agriculture and/or human wastes through reactors	0.0–0.01	Costs of pyrolysis (heating of organic materials), lack of understanding to date of full greenhouse gas benefits

16.4 Corporate Carbon Management Strategies

Any corporate strategy to commit to a net-zero-carbon transition, or not to transition, starts with the executive leadership and namely the board. And that too is where the responsibility from those decisions faces the greatest scrutiny. Therefore, it should be the executive leadership that takes the leadership to have the organization fully evaluate the opportunities, risks, and unintended consequences that can potentially impact both the organization and the individuals that comprise the board.

So let us consider how companies can be impacted by climate change and carbon. The examples can be fairly straightforward, such as resource sourcing and the supply chain. While straightforward, they can still be incredibly frustrating and complex. Companies need to be able to delve deep into their multitier and global supply chains as part of due diligence to minimize the risks of supply chain interruption. And increasingly, interruptions are occurring as a result of carbon and climate change. Physical climate risks are either acute or chronic. Acute risks include droughts, floods, extreme precipitation, and wildfires, which can interrupt energy systems and navigational and transportation pathways, and of course can destroy natural resources. Similarly, chronic risks include rising temperatures, the expansion of tropical pests and diseases into temperate zones, which can impact the workforce, and an accelerating loss of biodiversity. These threats pose both idiosyncratic and systemic risks to shareholders and investors [18, 19].

And, increasingly, shareholders feel emboldened to seek compensatory damages for management decisions or lack of oversight that result in reduced stock prices and shareholder value through a process of either "securities fraud" or another pathway known as a "shareholder derivative claim." Plaintiffs in derivative suits may allege various breaches of fiduciary duty by the corporation's board of directors, including negligence and mismanagement that leads a shareholder to step in and bring suit on behalf of the corporation to compel it to correct the alleged wrongs being perpetrated by the officers and/or directors [20, 21].

Therefore, it is incumbent upon the organization and leadership within the organization to protect themselves and the company through appropriate insurance instruments to counter the risks, such as:

1. Pre-purchase risk: many carbon-reducing activities are new scientific techniques and systems. These businesses are funding their buildout and operations by selling future carbon credits to be delivered in five to ten years. If the company goes bankrupt or otherwise never delivers, that risk could be insurable.
2. Fraud risk: fully fraudulent greenwashers who are selling duplicate carbon credits. Buyers could purchase this insurance to pay indemnity in this case.
3. Scientific protocol risk: each carbon removal method (direct carbon air capture, ocean alkalinity, algae, forest biomes, carbon char/oil, etc.) has a scientific protocol about how to do it. These protocols are all backed by science, but some of it is recent or not widely peer tested.
4. Execution/measurement risk: even when following the protocols exactly, business make mistakes that can affect the amount of carbon removed or the amount of energy it took to make it happen. An insurance product could fill in the missing gap.
5. Durability risk: once the carbon has been removed from the atmosphere, it needs to stay out for 100–1,000 years to be considered "removed." Most protocols and removal methods declare their expectation of durability. Periodic monitoring to ensure that carbon has not leaked back into the atmosphere can check on this status. Insurance could fill in any gaps.
6. Directors and officers liability insurance: protecting the personal assets of corporate directors and officers, and their spouses, in the event they are personally sued by employees, vendors, competitors, investors, customers, or other parties, for actual or alleged wrongful acts in managing a company (i.e., not being prepared for/mismanaging impacts from climate or management of the company to develop strategies to adapt to climate change [thinking of the fossil fuel industry]).

7. Error and omissions or environmental liability insurance: this covers engineers, geologists, contractors, and so on, in the development of a carbon sequestration offset or other scientists for developing or validating carbon offsets.

16.5 Third-Party Carbon Certifiers

It is important to understand that carbon credits are not a tangible, visible asset but are in fact digital assets that are intended to represent a "verified" emission reduction or removal and that the voluntary carbon market exists in different contexts in different national regulatory frameworks [22]. Article 6 of the Paris Agreement now provides a framework for governments to authorize the use of carbon emission reductions and/or removals obtained within their borders, which provides for the right to control the use of carbon credits [23]. And while some countries require activities to be registered, such as the National Registry of Reduction of Greenhouse Gas Emissions (RENARE) in Colombia, there are no current examples of governments requiring carbon credits under the Clean Development Mechanism to approve projects serving the voluntary carbon market [22]. Given this lack of government oversight, there is an uneven field of non-government organizations (NGOs) and for-profit entities seeking to occupy the space to of carbon credit verification.

A few organizations are emerging as market leaders. Washington, DC-based Verra, which was founded in 2007, is a nonprofit 501c (3) NGO that markets itself as setting the "world's leading standards for climate action" and operates the Verified Carbon Standard (VCS) program, which is the "world's most widely used greenhouse gas crediting program" [24]. Developers of projects seek to be both registered by Verra and to receive Verified Carbon Units (VCUs), which equate to the reduction or removal of one ton of carbon dioxide equivalent (CO_2-eq). The VCUs can also be labeled with certifications externally that have been approved by VCS [25]. Similar to Carbon Disclosure Project (CDP) carbon accounting submissions, which must follow a structured set of guidance and guidelines as presented in earlier chapters, so too developers must follow a set of transparent VCS standards and program rules.

Following submittals, an independent validation and verification process is undertaken by qualified independent third-party auditors (i.e., validation/verification bodies [VVBs]) that compare the submittal to the established rules for the submitted carbon removal/reduction methodology [25]. To date, Verra claims over 1 billion greenhouse gas emissions removed from over 1,865 projects in 56 countries [26]. Verra is the largest of the certifying bodies – in 2021, Verra issued 295 million VCUs, representing 83 percent of the total issued certified credit tons in that year [27].

In addition to Verra, the Gold Standard, which was established in 2003 by the World Wide Fund for Nature and other international NGOs, has the goal of "ensur[ing] projects that reduced carbon emissions featured the highest levels of environmental integrity and also contributed to sustainable development" [28]. The not-for-profit organization headquartered in Geneva, Switzerland claims to have 2,600 projects in 98 countries and over 209 million CO_2-eq reduced [28]. One of the distinctions of the Gold Standard is their focus on "co-benefits" of projects, specifically how they benefit social and community needs. And while Verra focuses mostly on nature-based carbon mitigation strategies, the Gold Standard's portfolio of nature-based projects is much smaller at only 4 percent in 2021 [27]. Examples of their projects include a 20 MW biomass power project in Chhattisgarh, India, improved cookstoves in Guinea, and improved cookstoves in schools in Uganda [29].

16.6 Emergence of Improved Science and Quality

One of the issues that diminishes confidence in the voluntary carbon market is the current level of science to monitor and track the sequestration as well as the quality of the data that can be used to undertake risk and forecasting modeling. There are a number of emerging efforts that if successful can transform the voluntary carbon market.

16.6.1 Sylvera

A 2020 entrant into the carbon market certification sector is a company based in London, UK called Sylvera. Rather than simply relying on standards, Sylvera seeks to leverage science to quantify the validity of proposed and existing nature-based carbon offsets. The company uses a scoring scheme, with AAA being the highest rating, going down to AA, A, BBB, BB, B, C, and D. The rating system is based on three pillars: carbon, additionality, and performance.

The organization quantifies the carbon reduction performance as compared to the developers' claims. They accomplish this via remote satellite imagery coupled with machine learning. One hundred is the baseline for scoring; if the measurements equal claims, then the score is 100. If the project is performing greater than the claims, then the score is above 100, and likewise poor per-formance equates to scores lower than 100 [30, 31].

The performance score focuses on the ability of the project to be successful in the future; that is, in about 100 years. The performance risks include natural such as forest fires, severe weather, and so on, as well as anthropogenic such as geopolitical stability, land and insurance risks, access to sustained capital, and prior and informed consent of Indigenous people. This score is ranked 1–5, with 5 being the highest score [30, 31].

Finally, the additionality score is based on two important factors. The first is if the carbon reduction would have occurred irrespective of the financial project. The second portion examines the appropriateness of the number of carbon credits issued for the project and whether claims are science-based and not overstated. Similar to performance, the score range is 1–5 [30, 31].

While not part of the rating criteria, Sylvera also provides a score for co-benefits such as to biodiversity and/or to a community. A project with a high score and high additionality would in theory provide a premium price on the marketplace [30, 31].

Sylvera will use the inputs from carbon registries, such as Verra and the Gold Standard and supplement them with optical, light detection, and ranging lidar and synthetic aperture radar satellite, as well as forest databases, NASA fire databases, and a number of other data-rich repositories [30, 31].

16.6.2 Sensors

Currently, most risk analysis and verification is based on remote sensing; that is, satellites and models. In some respects, this is appropriate for forestry projects. But farm-based carbon mitigation and sequestration solutions require greater inputs from real-time data, especially when quantifying greenhouse gas emissions from nitrous oxide (N_2O), which is emitted into the atmosphere when micro-organisms act on nitrogen introduced to the soil via animal urine and dung, synthetic fertilizers, and legumes. N_2O is a powerful greenhouse gas with 298 times the warming potential of carbon dioxide (CO_2) over 100 years and is also the leading contributor to stratospheric ozone depletion [32]. Helping to lead the development of cost-effective sensing technologies to combat climate change is the US Department of Energy's Advanced Research Projects Agency–Energy (ARPA–E). One such company that I am currently supporting with sustainable business and finance research that is funded by ARPA–E is out of Princeton University in partnership with Intelligent Material Solutions and Paige Wireless called NitroNet. This is an autonomous sensing system designed to monitor N_2O emissions that uses laser-beams and inexpensive reflectors and sensitive detectors. The system holds the promise to affordably monitor fields without disrupting normal operation at high temporal and spatial resolutions over an entire growing season [33]. These types of technologies will play an important role to increase transparency and accuracy while reducing dependence on third-party verification.

16.6.3 Blockchain

First and most importantly, blockchain is not cryptocurrency. While there has been much negative and justified condemnation of cryptocurrency in the press lately, especially after the November 2022 collapses of both FTX and BlockFi [34], blockchain is a database that stores encrypted blocks of data and then links them together to form a chronological single-source-of-truth for the data. These digital assets are then made available for distribution in lieu of being of copied or transferred, creating an immutable record of an asset. One of the clear additional advantages of blockchain is that it is decentralized, allowing full real-time access and a transparent ledger of changes to the public, which itself generates trust [35].

There are four major types of blockchain networks [35]:

1. Public blockchain: non-restrictive, decentralized and permission-less distributed ledger technology. Anyone can join the network and verify transactions to be added to the platform. Any user can become an authorized node (i.e., be a part of the blockchain network). They can access past and current recorded data, as well as do mining or verify transactions. Users often do not know each other, and strict security protocols have to followed. This type of blockchain is commonly used for Bitcoin and Litecoin.
2. Private blockchain: operates as a closed network and is controlled by a single entity. It uses peer-to-peer connections and decentralization, but on a smaller scale than public blockchain. Only a small number of users with specific authentication and permission can participate in that network. Users of this type of blockchain usually know and have already established a relationship of trust with each other. It is also known as a permissioned ledger or enterprise blockchain. This type of blockchain is often used in agricultural supply chains.
3. Hybrid blockchain: a combination of a private and public blockchain. Users can control who gains access to which data stored in the network. It works in a closed ecosystem without the need to make everything public. In hybrid blockchain, rules can be changed as needed. Transactions are usually verified within that network, but the verification process can also be released into the public network.

4. Consortium blockchain: decentralized with more than one organization in charge of the network. This means that a consortium formed by a group of members controls this blockchain. More than one organization can act as a node and do mining. These types of distributed ledger technologies are usually used by government organizations and banks. A consortium block-chain can also be used in agricultural supply chains.

One example of blockchain at work comes from a relatively new company – Regen Network, which launched its Regen Ledger. This is a public, proof-of-stake blockchain developed with the Cosmos Software Development Kit to verify claims, agreements, and data related to ecological state, which allows multiple registries to communicate and transact with each other, producing a public ecological accounting system. Their goals are to index claims and assertions pertaining to ecological health and to securely track Ecosystem Service Credits tied to measurable changes in ecological health [36, 37]. Ultimately, the ledger is used as a mechanism to financially reward farmers undertaking climate-smart agriculture practices.

Given the focus by both the scientific community and the financial commu-nity, we soon may see the opportunity to capture accurate greenhouse gas emissions calculated from actual measurements, not estimates, across the full value chain spanning from farm to processing to manufacturing and eventually to customer acquisition. This will provide us the opportunity to acquire a better understanding of real-time climate and sustainability impacts and to be able to automatically calculate total emissions, as well as carbon intensity, of particular operations emissions on a daily basis.

With blockchain and the underpinning science of monitoring, the data that are captured by the industrial internet of things and connected devices can provide real-time measurements and other information to confirm pre-agreed contractual terms have been satisfied based on actual numbers, not esti-mates [38].

References

1. CNBC (2022). Why this Investor Doesn't Back Companies That Use Carbon Offsets. October 7. www.cnbc.com/2022/10/07/silicon-valley-vc-we-dont-back-companies-that-use-carbon-offsets-.html.
2. Delta Airlines (2021). Delta Spotlights Ambitious Carbon Neutrality Plan on Path to Zero-Impact Aviation this Earth Month. April 22. https://news.delta.com/delta-spotlights-ambitious-carbon-neutrality-plan-path-zero-impact-aviation-earth-month.

3. Lloyd's Register (n.d.). Edward Lloyd and His Coffee House. www.lr.org/en/who-we-are/brief-history/edward-lloyd-coffee-house/#:~:text=The%20first%20recorded%20news%20of,of%20the%20maritime%20business%20district.

4. Lloyds (2022). Why Coverholders Bring Their Business to Lloyd's. www.lloyds.com/about-lloyds/value-proposition-coverholder.

5. Statista (2022). Estimated Size of the Global Insurance Market 2020, with Forecasts Up until 2025. January 11. www.statista.com/statistics/1192960/forecast-global-insurance-market.

6. Reuters (2018). 2017 Second-Costliest Year on Record for Natural-Disaster Insured Losses: Aon. January 24. www.reuters.com/article/us-global-insurance-aon/2017-second-costliest-year-on-record-for-natural-disaster-insured-losses-aon-idUSKBN1FD22Y.

7. *Los Angeles Times* (2019). Insured Losses from California Wildfires Top $11 Billion As Claims Keep Rolling In. January 28. www.latimes.com/business/la-fi-california-wildfires-insurance-20190128-story.html.

8. Swiss Re Institute (2021). The Insurance Rationale for Carbon Removal Solutions. July. www.swissre.com/institute/research/topics-and-risk-dialogues/climate-and-natural-catastrophe-risk/expertise-publication-carbon-removal-technologies.html.

9. B. W. Griscom, J. Adams, P. W. Ellis et al. (2017). Natural Climate Solutions. *Proceedings of the National Academy of Sciences*, 114(44): 11645–11650.

10. J. E. Fargione, S. Bassett, T. Boucher et al. (2018). Natural Climate Solutions for the United States. *Science Advances*, 4(11): eaat1869.

11. R. Bellamy and S. Osaka (2020). Unnatural Climate Solutions? *Nature Climate Change*, 10: 98–99.

12. National Grid (2022). What Is Carbon Capture and Storage? www.nationalgrid.com/stories/energy-explained/what-is-ccs-how-does-it-work#:~:text=CCS%20involves%20the%20capture%20of,deep%20underground%20in%20geological%20formations.

13. American University (2020). What Is Forestation? www.american.edu/sis/centers/carbon-removal/fact-sheet-forestation.cfm#:~:text=Reforestation%20includes%20planting%20trees%20or,recently%20been%20covered%20with%20forest.

14. Un-REDD Program (2022). Improved Forest Management (IFM). www.un-redd.org/glossary/improved-forest-management-ifm.

15. National Oceanic and Atmospheric Administration (2022). Understanding Blue Carbon. September 29. www.climate.gov/news-features/understanding-climate/understanding-blue-carbon.

16. Bloomberg (2021). World's Largest Carbon-Sucking Plant Starts Making Tiny Dent in Emissions. www.bloomberg.com/news/features/2021-09-08/inside-the-world-s-largest-direct-carbon-capture-plant?leadSource=uverify%20wall.

17. D. J. Beerling, E. P. Kantzas, M. R. Lomas et al. (2020). Potential for Large-Scale CO_2 Removal via Enhanced Rock Weathering with Croplands. *Nature*, 583: 242–248.

18. Impax (2021). Physical Climate Risks: Designing a Resilient Response to the Inevitable Impact of Climate Change. https://impaxam.com/wp-content/uploads/2020/09/20200924_physical_climate_risk.pdf.

19. Bank for International Settlements (2021). Basel Committee on Banking Supervision: Climate-Related Risk Drivers and Their Transmission Channels. ISBN 978-92-9259-472–5.

20. M. Levine (2021). Money Stuff: Boards Have to Pay Attention. Bloomberg. September 13. www.bloomberg.com/news/newsletters/2021-09-13/money-stuff-boards-have-to-pay-attention.

21. M. Gelter (2022). Preliminary Procedures in Shareholder Derivative Litigation: A Beneficial Legal Transplant? Harvard Law School Forum: Corporate Governance. https://corpgov.law.harvard.edu/2022/03/14/preliminary-proced ures-in-shareholder-derivative-litigation-a-beneficial-legal-transplant.

22. Ernst and Young (2022). Carbon Credit Rights under the Paris Agreement: How Article 6 and the Implementation of NDCS May Shape Government Approaches to the Carbon Market, and What This Means for Rights Related to Carbon Credits. November. www.ey.com/en_pl/law/carbon-credit-rights-under-the-paris-agreement.

23. United Nations (2015). Article 6 of the Paris Agreement. https://unfccc.int/files/ meetings/paris_nov_2015/application/pdf/paris_agreement_english_.pdf.

24. Verra (2022). Overview. https://verra.org/about/overview.

25. Verra (2022). VCS Program Details. https://verra.org/programs/verified-carbon-standard/vcs-program-details.

26. Verra (2022). Validation and Verification. https://verra.org/programs/verified-car bon-standard/#validation-and-verification.

27. Arbonics (2022). ABC: Who Are Verra and Gold Standard? Why They Matter. September 13. www.arbonics.com/knowledge-hub/abc-verra-and-gold-standard.

28. Gold Standard (2022). About Us. www.goldstandard.org/about-us/vision-and-mission.

29. Gold Standard (2022). Marketplace. https://marketplace.goldstandard.org/collec tions/projects.

30. Personal conversations with various members of Sylvera during the months of September through December 2022.

31. Sylvera (2022). Sylvera Carbon Credit Ratings. Frameworks and Processes White Paper.

32. N. C. Lawrence, C. G. Tenesaca, A. VanLoocke, and S. J. Hall (2021). Nitrous Oxide Emissions from Agricultural Soils Challenge Climate Sustainability in the US Corn Belt. *Proceedings of the National Academy of Sciences*, 118(46).

33. Intelligent Material (2022). Sensors for Sustainable Agriculture. www.intelligen tmaterial.com/sustainable-agriculture.

34. CNBC (2022). Crypto Firm BlockFi Files for Bankruptcy As FTX Fallout Spreads. November 28. www.cnbc.com/2022/11/28/blockfi-files-for-bank ruptcy-as-ftx-fallout-spreads.html.

35. CBI (2022). Blockchain Technology for Agricultural Ingredients. Published by the Centre for the Promotion of Imports from Developing Countries – Netherlands Ministry of Foreign Affairs. www.cbi.eu/market-information/nat ural-ingredients-health-products/blockchain-technology-agricultural.

36. Regen Network (2022). www.regen.network/developers.

37. G. Booman, A. Craelius, B. Deriemaeker et al. (2021). Regen Network
     Whitepaper. February 15. https://regen-network.gitlab.io/whitepaper/
     WhitePaper.pdf.
38. A. Bruce (2021). The Near-Term Future of Blockchain: Tracking Carbon Offsets.
     Forbes. August 16. www.forbes.com/sites/forbestechcouncil/2021/08/16/the-
     near-term-future-of-blockchain-tracking-carbon-offsets/?sh=3726e53a5790.
39. International Energy Agency (2022). Bioenergy with Carbon Capture and
     Storage. www.iea.org/reports/bioenergy-with-carbon-capture-and-storage.

17

Biden and Congress Open the Checkbook

But simply put . . . [it] will be the most important investment – not hyperbole – the most important investment that we've ever made in our energy security, and developing cost savings and job-creating clean energy solutions for the future. It's a big deal.
President Biden on the Inflation Reduction Act, July 28, 2022 [1]

China Threatens Action Against "Discriminatory" US EV Tax Breaks
Bloomberg, September 22, 2022 [2]

17.1 Federal Infusion of Funding

While private equity plays an important role to achieve a clean-tech and net-zero-carbon transition, money will not flow unless there is confidence that those investments will offer a return. Further, as has been presented, there is a strong national security set of interests, both national defense and economic, that the United States should be the leader in the manufacturing and distribution of technologies and services that will drive the clean-tech economy for the foreseeable future.

And while much general attention is focused on the manufacturing of electric vehicles, semiconductor chips, and offshore wind, there is so much more that must be developed or renewed within the domestic economy for the transition to be successful from civil infrastructure to the electrical grid all the way to workforce development and reducing unnecessary regulatory burdens.

The federal government is the only entity with the wealth and span that can address this. So while many of us want a smaller government, we ultimately depend on the government to keep the nation secure and competitive and make prudent investments to ensure that this happens.

253

17.2 Bipartisan Infrastructure Bill

The first large-scale federal funding mechanism for the transition in recent years arrived on November 15, 2021 when President Biden signed into law the $1.2 trillion "Bipartisan Infrastructure Law for State, Local, Tribal and Territorial Governments and Other Partners"[1] [3, 4]. If you think this book might be a lot of reading, the guidebook produced by the White House the following year (2022) is over 455 pages long [4]. Yes, it is a rather large bill.

While the bill is heavily focused on civil engineering infrastructure such as bridges, tunnels, transportation, highways, congestion relief, and so on, there are very specific elements that focus on climate and the net-zero-carbon transition. These include large-scale funding of lower emission transportation options such as inter-city rail ($36 billion), Amtrak passenger rail ($21.7 billion) and other public transit ($82.5 billion), such as bus transportation, and urbanized ferry programs, as well as the specific deployments below [3, 4].

1. $6.4 billion over four years for a Carbon Reduction Program to provide grants to states to reduce transportation emissions or the development of carbon reduction strategies.
2. $50 million to states to develop a pilot program to demonstrate a national motor vehicle per-mile user fee to maintain the long-term solvency of the highway trust fund. Perhaps this can be used to develop a strategy to mitigate the impacts of the transition to electric vehicles?
3. $21.3 billion for delivering clean power.
4. $21.5 billion for clean energy demonstrations, which is related to the US Department of Energy establishing a new Office of Clean Energy Demonstrations to oversee the funding.
5. $6.5 billion for energy efficiency and retrofits for homes, buildings, and communities.
6. $8.6 billion for funding clean energy manufacturing and workforce development.

Within the larger grouping of climate, energy, and the environment listed above, there are also investments in battery manufacturing and recycling, critical mineral innovation, large-scale carbon capture, rare-earth demonstration facilities, energy and minerals research facilities, wind energy technology programs, critical material supply chain research facilities, state and local cybersecurity, and so on.

---

[1] Public Law 117–58. See www.govinfo.gov/content/pkg/PLAW-117publ58/pdf/PLAW-117publ58.pdf.

17.3 Inflation Reduction Act

As the Bipartisan Infrastructure Act ultimately came into law, in 2021 the Biden Administration was trying to push forward a $1.7 trillion Build Back Better (BBB) Act. However, Democratic senator Joe Manchin from West Virginia ultimately blocked and killed the legislation [5]. Ultimately, the social provisions of the BBB were removed and the budget was reduced to $740 billion to garner Manchin's favor. The BBB was then signed into law on August 16, 2022 as the Inflation Reduction Act of 2022[2] (IRA) [6, 7].

The IRA directs around $400 billion for climate efforts, including [8]:

1. $250.6 billion for the energy sector
2. $47.7 billion for the manufacturing sector
3. $46.4 billion for the environmental sector
4. $23.4 billion for the transportation and electric vehicle (EV) sectors
5. $20.9 billion for the agriculture sector
6. $4.7 billion for the water sector.

17.3.1 Green-Tech Loans

The Department of Energy's Loan Programs Office received $11.7 billion to support the issuance of new bonds, increase the existing loan program authority by $100 billion, and appropriate $5 billion for a new loan program called the Energy Infrastructure Reinvestment Program for up to $250 billion in loans [9].

17.3.2 Consumer Clean-Tech Incentives

A sum of $43 billion is provided for consumer incentives, which, if successful, will support market pull mechanisms that can result in manufacturing growth in the United States. Consider the incentives for EVs listed below. Not only will these help create market pull and manufacturing demand from American EV manufacturers but they will also require the domestic expansion of the vast supply network, such as batteries, chips, electronics, components, and so on.

If you're a consumer and want to add renewables to your home between now and 2032, well, with the IRA you can get back 30 percent on what you pay for new solar, wind, or geothermal systems that produce electricity or heating – as well as the labor to install them and the fees for permitting, inspection, and development. This also covers the purchase of standalone batteries with more than 3 kilowatt-hours of storage. There is no cap on the total spent. So, spend

---

[2] Public Law 117–169.

$5,000 or $50,000 and still get a 30 percent tax credit. If you don't owe that much in federal taxes, the remainder of the credit rolls over into the next tax year.

Want to buy that new EV? Well, you probably should wait until 2024 when the new incentives take effect and run until 2032. You can get $7,500 Clean Vehicle Credit for new EVs or a 30 percent tax credit (capped at $4,000) for used EVs. Starting in 2024, you can transfer these credits to a dealer, which allows for a point-of-sale discount rather than waiting until tax season. And if you need to install an EV charger at home, the IRA renews a recently expired tax credit that covers 30 percent of the cost.

On-shoring and building up American green-tech manufacturing means that all eligible vehicles have to satisfy a requirement for final assembly in North America. Further changes around critical mineral and battery sourcing requirements begin phasing in as soon as 2023.

Used vehicles incentives start in 2023 and run until the end of 2032. They also do away with manufacturer caps. The incentives come with some qualifications you need to be aware of; namely, for a new car credit, single taxpayers making $150,000 or less, heads of household making $225,000 or less, and households filing jointly making $300,000 or less qualify.

For the used car credit, single taxpayers must make $75,000 or less; heads of household must make $112,500 or less, and households filing jointly must make $150,000 or less. There are vehicle price caps to qualify too. Smaller cars and sedans can cost up to $55,000; SUVs, trucks, and vans up to $80,000. For used cars, the price cap to qualify is $25,000.

17.3.3 Small Business Benefits

While large businesses focused on green-tech and the net-zero-carbon transition will benefit in many ways through expanded research and development (R&D) funding, capital, and loan guarantees, small businesses can also benefit. The IRA provides small businesses a tax credit that covers 30 percent of the cost of switching to low-cost solar power, as well as eligibility to receive a tax credit up to $5 per square foot to support energy efficiency improvements that deliver lower utility bills. And, as small businesses switch to zero-emission vehicles for their companies, they can receive tax credits covering 30 percent of purchase costs for clean commercial vehicles, like electric and fuel cell models.

Small businesses can also realize R&D benefits. The IRA increases the refundable R&D tax credit for small businesses from $250,000 to $500,000. Starting in 2023, small businesses can use the credit to further reduce payroll taxes and several other business expenses by up to $500,000 annually.

17.3.4 Large Investments for Corporations

The IRA impacts federal income tax benefits for renewable energy, including the existing Section 45 production tax credit (PTC) and Section 48 investment tax credit (ITC), and adds Section 45Y, the Clean Energy Production Tax Credit, and Section 48E, the Clean Electricity Investment Credit, to the Internal Revenue Code [10].

Production Tax Credits

The IRA reinstates the PTC for solar energy facilities, which were last eligible for the PTC if placed in service before 2006. Additionally, qualified facilities include wind, closed- and open-loop biomass, geothermal, landfill gas, trash, qualified hydropower, and marine and hydrokinetic facilities, but note the base credit amount is reduced by one-half for open-loop biomass facilities, small irrigation power facilities, landfill gas facilities, and trash facilities. There are a number of determinants for qualification that need to be examined by the applicant.

Investment Tax Credits

This includes facilities such as solar, fiber-optic solar, qualified fuel cell, qualified microturbine, combined heat and power system, qualified small wind, and waste energy recovery properties. The Act also permits taxpayers to claim the ITC with respect to several additional technologies, including standalone energy storage, qualified biogas property, fuel cells using electromechanical processes, dynamic glass, and microgrid controllers. The election to claim the ITC in lieu of the PTC for otherwise eligible PTC facilities is retained.

Clean Energy Production Tax Credits and the Clean Electricity Investment Credits

These newly created credits are intended to be technology neutral and apply to any qualified facility or energy storage used for the generation of electricity, which is placed in service on or after January 1, 2025 and has an anticipated greenhouse gas emissions rate of not more than zero. Qualified facilities also include any additions of capacity that are placed in service on or after January 1, 2025.

Additionally, the IRA provides $500 million to use the Defense Production Act to speed manufacturing of things like heat pumps, as well as processing critical minerals and $2 billion in grants to help automaker facilities transition to clean vehicle production, and up to $20 billion in loans to construct new manufacturing facilities for clean vehicles.

Tax credits in the IRA were restricted in four very impactful ways [11]:

1. **Certainty in the marketplace**: The tax credits will be extended at their full value for at least ten years, which gives investors, manufacturers, utilities, and developers the long-term sense of security they need for their investments. Coupled with the expansion of the Department of Energy's Loan Program Office program, this should add robustness to the clean-tech expansion.

2. **Expands to allow new zero-emissions technologies**: Energy storage technologies are now also eligible for ITC. A new PTC for existing nuclear power should keep most US nuclear plants online, empowering new renewables to displace fossil fuels instead of zero-carbon electricity.

3. **Seeks to increase US labor practices**: Project developers can only earn one-fifth of the credits' original value unless they meet worker training and competitive wage conditions. They gain additional credit value by sourcing components from domestic manufacturers and siting facilities in fossil-dependent communities. Clean energy tax credits more than offset the minimal cost of these high-road labor policies.

4. **Tax credits are now transferable:** This reduces reliance on the very large financial institutions to monetize tax credits and now allows clean-tech developers to sell credits directly to anyone with tax liability, circumventing waste and making each federal dollar go much further. It also offers cash grants to tax-exempt entities like municipal utilities and rural electric cooperatives, further simplifying the process.

17.4 Offshore Wind and the IRA

In addition to financial benefits, the IRA will also reverse President Trump's ten-year moratorium for offshore wind leasing for Florida, North Carolina, South Carolina, and Georgia, as well as have the Bureau of Ocean Energy Management begin planning for the development of offshore wind in US territories such as Guam and Puerto Rico [12].

17.5 Pushback by Friends and Foes

Many books have been written in regard to trade and policy between the United States and China, and really nowhere is the tension more evident than in regard to clean-tech manufacturing as both countries seek to be the dominant player in the world; or, at the very least for the United States, to reduce reliance on China for resources and goods. The passage of the IRA has added fuel to the fire with not just China articulating anger but also allied countries within the European Union (EU). CNBC reported [13] that German finance minister Christian Linder stated, "We are concerned about the consequences due to the Inflation Reduction Act." He added, "Our common approach should be that value partners should stay preferred trade partners."

Similarly, EU news outlet France 24 reported [14] that "EU leaders are looking for ways to counter aspects of the US Inflation Reduction Act (IRA) that they fear will unfairly discriminate against European firms. With the IRA giving generous subsidies and priority access to American businesses, the EU is now considering a subsidy program of its own." The article included a statement by Belgian Prime Minister Alexander De Croo that "We are in Europe, really, at the point where we risk to be de-industrialized." Without such an EU-wide plan, "we'd just be competing against one another, while the United States would be running away with everything."

No doubt the EU will press on with creating their own green-tech subsidy plan while at the same time seeking to negotiate a mutually beneficial trade agreement with the United States to try to keep a balanced and favored nation trade partnership. The same will not occur with China given the current geopolitical landscape.

References

1. The White House (2022). Remarks by President Biden on the Inflation Reduction Act of 2022. July 28. www.whitehouse.gov/briefing-room/speeches-remarks/2022/07/28/remarks-by-president-biden-on-the-inflation-reduction-act-of-2022.
2. Bloomberg (2022). China Threatens Action against "Discriminatory" US EV Tax Breaks. September 22. www.bloomberg.com/news/articles/2022-09-22/china-threatens-action-against-discriminatory-us-ev-tax-breaks#xj4y7vzkg.
3. Fox News (2021). Biden to Sign Bipartisan Infrastructure Bill on Monday. www.foxbusiness.com/politics/biden-to-sign-bipartisan-infrastructure-bill-on-monday.
4. White House (2022). Building a Better America: A Guidebook to the Bipartisan Infrastructure Law for State, Local, Tribal and Territorial Governments and Other Partners. www.whitehouse.gov/wp-content/uploads/2022/05/BUILDING-A-BETTER-AMERICA-V2.pdf.
5. Fox News (2021). Manchin Kills Build Back Better and Gives Nation – and Republicans – a Big Win. December 19. www.foxnews.com/opinion/manchin-kills-build-back-better-nation-republicans-win-david-marcus.
6. Gov. (2022). Public Law 117–169. 117th Congress. www.govinfo.gov/content/pkg/PLAW-117publ169/pdf/PLAW-117publ169.pdf.

7. CNN (2022). Biden Signs Inflation Reduction Act into Law. August 16. www.cnn.com/2022/08/16/politics/biden-inflation-reduction-act-signing/index.html.

8. McKinsey and Company (2022). The Inflation Reduction Act: Here's What's in It. https://avidsolutionsinc.com/wp-content/uploads/2023/06/the-inflation-reduction-act-heres-whats-in-it_final.pdf.

9. Department of Energy (2022). Inflation Reduction Act of 2022 Loan Programs Office. www.energy.gov/lpo/inflation-reduction-act–2022.

10. *National Law Review* (2022). The Inflation Reduction Act: Key Provisions Regarding the ITC and PTC. December 17. Volume XII, Number 351.

11. Forbes (2022). Inflation Reduction Act Benefits: Clean Energy Tax Credits Could Double Deployment. August 28. www.forbes.com/sites/energyinnovation/2022/08/23/inflation-reduction-act-benefits-clean-energy-tax-credits-could-double-deployment/?sh=710834f67272.

12. National Conference of State Legislatures (2022). Inflation Reduction Act of 2022 Provisions by the National Conference of State Legislatures. Issued at the Council of States Conference, August 2022. https://documents.ncsl.org/wwwncsl/State-Federal/NCSL-Summary-Inflation-Reduction-Act.pdf.

13. CNBC (2022). EU Says It Has Serious Concerns about Biden's Inflation Reduction Act. www.cnbc.com/2022/11/07/us-inflation-reduction-act-eu-raises-concerns-risks-wto-dispute.html.

14. France 24 (2022). Why EU Leaders Are Upset over Biden's Inflation Reduction Act. December 16. www.france24.com/en/europe/20221216-why-eu-leaders-are-upset-over-biden-s-inflation-reduction-act.

PART V

Wrap Up and What Is Next

Don't allow your desire for quick change to be the cause of longer-term failures.

Jay Golden, talk to US national security leaders, 2023

18

Crystal Ball

Imagination is more important than knowledge. For knowledge is limited to all we now know and understand, while imagination embraces the entire world, and all there ever will be to know and understand.

Albert Einstein [1]

There is no greater thing you can do with your life and your work than follow your passions – in a way that serves the world and you.

Sir Richard Branson, billionaire, entrepreneur, and founder and chief executive officer of Virgin Group [2]

18.1 Looking into a Crystal Ball

Given all that I have written about, I thought it would be fun to put down on paper some of the winners and losers resulting from the transition to a net-zero-carbon economy. Which of these will be able to leverage dynamic sustainability? The list is not exhaustive but is broad enough to give a bit of perspective. I urge you not to use what is listed below as investment advice. For that, seek a professional adviser. But it will be interesting to return to this list in a few years to see how wrong or right I was.

18.2 Possible Winners

I am going to bypass further detailing the obvious winners such as green-tech entrepreneurs and astute green-tech investors. The environment, US manufacturing, labor, and defense, as well as electric vehicle (EV) sectors and traditional renewables sectors such as photovoltaics and wind will also win. Most of this has been carried throughout this book.

I think it is simpler to state that the set of winners are those organizations, chief executives, and boards that are the most effective in identifying the risks, unintended consequences, and opportunities of the net-zero-carbon and sustainable technologies transition. In other words, those organizations, public or private, that can manage dynamic sustainability will win.

18.2.1 Nuclear Fusion Breakthroughs

Congratulations to the scientists at Lawrence Livermore National Laboratory (LLNL) in California, who on December 13, 2022 announced that they were actually able to achieve a "net energy" fusion reaction on December 5. The team placed 192 high-energy lasers and converged them onto a target of combined deuterium and tritium. The lasers heated the compound to over 3 million degrees Celsius and put about 2.05 megajoules (Mj) into the reaction, which resulted in a 3.15 Mj output – a gain of 1.5 [3, 4]. To put this in perspective, this energy burst was so intense that, for a split second, it produced 10,000 times more power than the combined output of every power station on earth [5].

Is fusion safe? The idea dates back to the 1960s and LLNL where John Nuckolls and scientists hypothesized that lasers could be used to induce fusion in a laboratory setting. Nuclear "fission" is the splitting of atoms and is what is used when we think of nuclear weapons where uranium and plutonium are most commonly used. Fusion entails the safer process of combining atoms.

Fission is used to produce the nuclear fuel for nuclear power generation. The heat from fission heats water in reactors and uses the steam to produce low-carbon thermoelectric power. There are significant issues with the potential accidents and with the wastes. For instance, low-level nuclear wastes (i.e., transuranic wastes) have half-lives of up to 1,000 years (half the radioactivity will decay in 1,000 years), while plutonium-239 has a half-life of 24,000 years [6, 7]. Fusion, on the other hand, does not create any long-lived nuclear wastes. And unlike a nuclear reactor using fission, a fusion facility is not based on a chain reaction so you would not have accidents similar to existing fission facilities [8].

Many hurdles still exist. Because laser fusion is a pulsed technology, it requires an incredible amount of energy to achieve what amounts to a very short energy burst that lasts less than a billionth of a second. If we want to use fusion to supplant traditional power generation facilities, scientists have to be able to achieve rapid repetition of the energy burst to achieve the fusion. That is a major hurdle. So is the electricity requirement for the lasers, which currently are highly inefficient [5]. Still, over $5 billion in private investment has been placed into companies trying to break through as fusion start-ups [4], so the long-term future is very bright for fusion.

18.2.2 Green Cement

Cement is the main ingredient that goes into the production of concrete, which is used for our highways, sidewalks, bridges, airport runways, buildings, and so on. Over 5 billion tons of cement are produced and 30 billion tons of concrete are used each year and the demand continues to increase. While cement and concrete are instrumental to support our society, cement itself contributes almost 8 percent of global greenhouse gas emissions [9, 10]. It is the production of cement that is the carbon-intensive process where energy is used to heat a mixture of limestone and clay to more than 1,400 °C in a kiln, and limestone (calcium carbonate) is heated with clays, resulting in roughly 600 kilograms of carbon dioxide being released for every ton of cement produced [11].

The impact is not just from the energy used in the production process; it also results from the chemical reaction from the calcium carbonate being heated with clay called calcination. The byproducts are calcium silicates, which are cooled and used to produce cement and carbon dioxide is released into the atmosphere. One mitigation option, as detailed below, is for the sector to undertake carbon capture and sequestration technologies. However, a potential coupling technology would be to re-inject the sequestered carbon back into the process (reverse calcination), which could result in a CO_2 reduction of up to 30 percent eventually as the technologies mature [12].

Two additional potential emerging green cement technologies are also on the horizon. The first comes out of Longmont, Colorado where a company called Prometheus Materials, started by some University of Colorado–Boulder engineering professors, began research on engineered living materials and producing bio-cement grown from micro-algae. With the assistance of a $2 million grant from the Department of Defense, the process approach is to undertake biomineralizing cyanobacteria that are grown using sunlight, seawater, and CO_2 instead of the more traditional and energy-intensive processes.

The bio-cement is a hydrogel-based living building material (LBM) containing bacteria capable of microbially induced calcium-carbonate precipitation. LBMs are made by microorganisms. Cement blocks are currently produced by mixing this bio-cement with aggregate to create a low-carbon building material with mechanical, physical, and thermal properties comparable to Portland cement-based concrete, with up to 90 percent less embodied carbon. The firm has already closed on an $8 million series A round of financing [13, 14]. Finally, the US government in 2022 developed a National Institute of Standards and Technology in the Department of Commerce (NIST-DOC) carbon cements and concretes consortium with the goal to "evaluate, develop, and standardize methods to characterize and quantify the carbon and carbonates in new low carbon cements and concretes," which is an important step to accelerate and standardize the green cement industry [15].

The bio-cement could be mass-produced as an alternative to Portland cement, which is a huge source of carbon emissions as it relies on clinker made from crushed and burned limestone. The process separates the calcium, which is a key ingredient in cement, from the carbon, which is released into the atmosphere.

18.2.3 Gyrotron Technologies: Achieving Large-Scale Geothermal Energy

Around the United States and around the world, there will be more and more decommissioned coal power plants. Yet each of these facilities has the value of being connected to a grid in addition to the large property footprints. For those facilities located on the coasts, they can serve offshore wind development. However, for the rest of these retired facilities, we need to reimagine how they can be repurposed.

The recent development with fusion relates to this big bet technology: gyrotron drilling for deep earth geothermal energy. Originally developed by Russia in the 1960s, gyrotrons generate electromagnetic waves in the millimeter-wave part of the spectrum, with wavelengths shorter than microwaves but longer than visible or infrared light. Researchers in the 1970s working on designs for fusion reactors discovered these millimeter waves were an excellent way to substantially heat up plasma and subsequently there have been continued improvements to the technology. Today, gyrotrons are capable of generating continuous energy beams over a megawatt [16, 17, 18, 19].

The development of this technology is perhaps the key required to untap large-scale and cost-effective geothermal energy around the world. The earth's core depths from 2,886 kilometers to the center at 6,371 kilometers (1,794 to 3,960 miles) are predominantly iron, and temperatures in the iron center of the core are estimated to be 3,500 to 5,500 kelvins (5,800 to 9,400°F) at the base of the earth's mantle [20]. Because of this potential of an untapped energy source, scientists have continually attempted to find ways to access deep geothermal pockets. The deepest effort to date was at the Kola Superdeep Borehole in

Russia near the Norwegian border with a goal to puncture the crust right down to the mantle.

One of its bore holes reached a vertical depth of 12,289 m (40,318 ft) in 1989 before the team decided it was unfeasible to go any deeper using conventional technologies [21]. The issues have to do with the drill bit. However, if you could use directed energy beams to heat, melt, and vaporize the rock, then you could overcome these issues. This is a process called spallation [22].

In 2018, MIT's Plasma Science and Fusion Center spun out a business that combines traditional rotary drilling with gyrotron-powered millimeter-wave technology, while pumping in argon as a purge gas to clean and cool the bore while firing rock particles back up to the surface and out of the way. They plan to drill holes up to 20 km (12.4 miles) deep, significantly deeper than the Kola Superdeep Borehole. Of note is that the Kola team took nearly twenty years to reach their limit, but the MIT spinout called Quaise expects its gyrotron-enhanced process to take just 100 days using a 1 MW gyrotron [23].

If they are successful, they could develop large-scale geothermal facilities basically anywhere on the planet – starting with repurposing legacy coal power plants. And Quaise is not alone. There are a number of other start-ups looking to exploit large-scale renewable geothermal energy using different technologies such as dual-circulation wet-hammer systems. Will these technologies work at scale? That is yet to be seen but it is worth tracking.

18.2.4 US Carbon-Intensity Labels

Because US companies have committed to a net-zero-carbon transition and associated reductions, they will be highly dependent on their supply chain to contribute to these reductions (i.e., scope 3 greenhouse gas emissions). It will be too expensive in both time and costs to individually evaluate varied technical approaches to obtain an inventory of emissions. Rather, industry is smart enough to place the onus on the federal government. Without the leadership of government, there will be a confusing and scattered tapestry of state, industry, and non-governmental organization approaches and labels. In my crystal ball I see the US Department of Agriculture being given primacy as a non-regulatory agency to develop a carbon-intensity label for feedstocks and products.

18.2.5 Carbon Capture and Sequestration

With tax and financial incentives in place and growing, and the expansive funds now available for clean-tech manufacturing in the United States, the demand for low-carbon and carbon-negative manufacturing is high and expanding. And while renewable electricity will continue to be developed, there is still a great need for technologies to sequester carbon. It will take the concurrence of policymakers to address eminent domains, geologists to find appropriate regions to safely store carbon underground, and the insurance industry to protect these investments. I believe this will all come together in the next few years both domestically and around the world. The insurance industry will be critical to ensure a level of technical and scientific approaches to sequestration and scientists to monitor its application long term. But the market for low- and negative-carbon products will drive the industry.

18.2.6 Vertical Agriculture

It is simply a win–win when considering vertical agriculture. It does not make sense to use carbon-intensive air freight to move certain seasonal crops around the United States, let alone import them from countries around the world. A recent study in *Nature* found that global food-miles correspond to about 3.0 $GtCO_2e$ (3.5–7.5 times higher than previously estimated), indicating that transport accounts for about 19 percent of total food-system emissions and global freight transport associated with vegetable and fruit consumption contributes 36 percent of food-miles emissions – almost twice the amount of greenhouse gases released during their production [24].

Coupled with the continued growth in renewable electricity deployment in the United States, this will drive the development of large-scale vertical agriculture facilities, primarily in urban regions and near major retail distribution centers. Additionally, these crops will not just be low carbon but also low water and pesticide/herbicide free. But don't worry, land-based farmers, as the total agriculture demand will not be impacted by vertical farming. The interesting conversation will be between vertical agriculture companies and those who brand themselves US Department of Agriculture organic.

18.2.7 Mass Timber Construction

Mass timber construction is moving from niche to mainstay in a big way and it is happening in Bentonville, Arkansas. The world's largest company, Walmart, is constructing a new campus with their office buildings of over 2.4 million square feet on a 350-acre campus being constructed from pre-engineered mass timber. This is the largest mass timber campus development currently under construction in the United States and should be completed by 2024 [25, 26].

Traditional building construction materials such as cement, glass, and steel are reported to account for 10 percent of global greenhouse gas emissions [27]. Mass timber construction was studied by researchers at Oregon State University and Skidmore, Owings and Merrill. Their research report details that wood is approximately 50 percent carbon by weight with the additional benefit that wood sequesters carbon from the atmosphere. Structural wood also uses far less energy than cement and steel for building construction. Their findings showed that a modeled forty-two-story timber building in Chicago had a 60–70 percent lower embodied carbon footprint than an existing forty-two-story high-rise apartment building in Chicago [28].

Why is this going to make a difference in the market? In 2019, New York City passed local law 97. The law requires most buildings over 25,000 square feet to meet new energy efficiency and greenhouse gas emissions limits by 2024, with stricter limits coming into effect in 2030. The goal is to reduce the emissions produced by the city's largest buildings by 40 percent by 2030 and 80 percent by 2050. Buildings account for approximately two-thirds of greenhouse gas emissions in New York City and this trend is similar in other dense urban regions around the country and world [29].

Finally, for those who are concerned with fires in buildings, mass timber structures can resist fire as well as or better than steel. That's because wood exposed to fire naturally produces a layer of char, which is highly insulating and can protect the bulk of the wood for more than 2 hours. Steel, in contrast, can fail suddenly when heat softens it and causes it to buckle [30]. So there is great momentum for the transition to mass timber buildings as part of the transition to a net-zero-carbon economy.

18.3 Possible Losers

For all the winners, there also have to be some losers as a result of market shifts. Those listed below are not what I would consider to be immediate losers but rather longer-term ones. The one exception is green diplomacy, which I could have just as easily listed as status quo rather than a possible loser.

18.3.1 Green Diplomacy

What would be the results if you could get the world's two largest greenhouse gas emitters to work together to advance a net-zero-carbon economy? While the United States continues to make efforts to reduce greenhouse gas emissions, moving from 5.8 $GtCO_2$ in 2000 to 4.4 $GtCO_2$ in 2020,[1] China increased from 3.5 $GtCO_2$ in 2000 to emitting a world-leading 11.4 $GtCO_2$ in 2020 [31]. Yet both play an incredibly important role in the transition, as has been laid out in this book. However, the current political climate in both countries does not foretell any meaningful progress. In fact, trade wars, competition in market entries for technologies, and continued efforts to reduce America's reliance on imports of critical minerals and other supply chain mainstays from China will continue. Both countries will continue to seek diplomatic relations and financing tactics with resource-rich countries around the globe in order to secure the resources necessary to grow domestic manufacturing and meet key national security imperatives. At best, we can hope this can be accomplished without conflict.

18.3.2 The University of Texas

You may be asking yourself why I am putting in universities and how they connect to the net-zero-carbon economy. Both Texas A&M and especially the University of Texas are likely to feel the pinch of the dynamics, which will see a significantly diminished reliance on oil and gas. While many institutions around the country will need to re-envision colleges and departments in their universities that focus on fossil fuel research activities (think of petroleum engineering degree programs), the Texas universities have much bigger problems potentially awaiting them.

The University of Texas dates back to 1883 and the state of Texas has a history of appropriating state lands, starting in 1839, to fund higher education. As the University of Texas began to operate, the state appropriated an additional million acres of unpopulated land in West Texas for their endowment, known today as the Permanent University Fund (PUF). The land had very little economic value with the income from grazing leases. In fact, at the turn of the twentieth century, the income was only $40,000.

However, all of this changed in 1923 with the development of the Santa Rita oil well in Regan County. In 1931 the legislature authorized a split in the net income from PUF investments, with the University of Texas to receive two-thirds of the money and Texas A&M to receive one-third. By the late 1950s, the market value of the PUF exceeded $283,642,000 and provided investment income of more than $8,513,000 annually for distribution to the two university

---

[1] Note that per-capita emissions in the United States still remain higher than China at 14 tons per capita versus 8.2 on average in China.

systems. In 1990 the PUF stood at $3,541,314,800 and generated $266,119,000 for the available fund [32, 33].

Push forward to 2022, and the revenues are now generated from over 2.2 million acres of land, with the University of Texas system having grown to thirteen institutions across the state and the Texas A&M system reaching eleven institutions. Because of the large financial rebound of the fossil fuel industry in 2021, the University of Texas endowment surged past Yale, reaching $42.9 billion compared to Yale's $42.3 billion as reported in December 2022. The fund at the University of Texas still trails behind Harvard University's $53.2 billion endowment, the largest higher education endowment in the world [34]. However, of note is that the University of Texas system endowment serves around 240,000 students, while Yale, like Harvard, Duke, and Stanford, serves much fewer students (approximately 11,000).

Hence, the value of the endowment of the University of Texas system averages $176,000 per student, while Yale's value per student is closer to $2.9 million [34, 35]. Of course, these funds don't focus just on the student but the interest on the funds, which is generally capped at 4 percent per year to not impact the overall health of the funds, and can be used in a number of ways. This includes capital expenditures, professorships, research, and athletics, all in addition to scholarships and so on.

While the PUF has been an economic engine for Texas higher education, and certainly will continue to produce results in the near term, the longer-term outlook is not nearly as bright. With the reduction of global dependence on fossil fuels there exist cascading implications if state revenues and budgets match a decline of the once prominent donors to the universities currently flush with oil and gas cash.

18.3.3 Tesla

No manufacturing company in the last decade has come close to the meteoric rise in brand name recognition and market value as Tesla. Yet, a number of factors are at play that will possibly impact these gains.

First, Tesla had the benefit of being a first mover, and the organization and its leadership in the name of Elon Musk needs to be recognized for this foresight and vision. This has allowed the firm to produce the highest number of EVs and importantly to build up a niche of "green-" and "tech"-savvy affluent customers willing to pay for their product. This was embodied in their 2015 marketing plan, which identified their target customer as "business executives and entrepreneurs who are city dwellers, tech-savvy and green-friendly … wealthy, early adopters in the upper-middle class segment" [36, 37].

Those with affluence and who are buying in the green-tech space are likely concerned with the perception of Elon Musk's purchase and managerial public relations mishaps with Twitter. Further, there has been very public pushback and concern with his lack of oversight at Tesla since the Twitter purchase. Even the third largest shareholder[2] of Tesla has called for a new chief executive officer as recently as December 2022 [38, 39]. And all of this is bleeding over to the media, with recent headlines such as:

1. CNBC: "Oppenheimer downgrades Tesla, says Elon Musk's handling of Twitter could hurt electric vehicle maker" [40].
2. Reuters: "Musk Twitter play sparks concerns about distraction, Tesla stock sales" [41].
3. Forbes: "Elon Musk's Twitter antics are tarnishing Tesla – just as its EV rivals are catching up" [42].
4. *The Washington Post*: "Tesla's value dropped Tuesday by more than double the cost of Twitter" [43].

Of all the above-listed and other headlines, the one that has the most resonance with me is that of Forbes as it calls out the obvious. Rivals, the well-known automotive manufacturers with greater market penetration, greater manufacturing capacity, and a much more expansive global sales and service offering, are in fact catching up and will soon bypass the sales of Tesla. And the markets reflect this perspective with Tesla share prices reaching a high of $371 per share on October 29, 2021 and closing at $157 on December 16, 2022.

Clearly, Tesla will remain a viable EV manufacturer. Yet, their placement at the top of the sector is clearly in jeopardy, as is their dominance in the market.

18.3.4 Local Gas Stations and Convenience Stores

Take a drive around any US city and the major streets are dotted with gas stations and convenience stores. And while they will not completely disappear in the near and mid-term, the longer-term prospects are not good. While some may find ways to reconfigure to support EV charging, national networks and national retailers such as McDonalds, Starbucks, and many others are rapidly developing plans to incorporate EV charging stations at store properties. Let's hope that the feds and states figure out a way to manage the hundreds of thousands of underground storage tanks left behind.

---

[2] Indonesian billionaire KoGuan Leo, who has approximately 22.7 million shares as of September 2022.

18.3.5 Fast Fashion

Fast fashion is the term we use to describe the rapid increase in apparel retailers selling cheap and low-quality clothing that has a very short life and eventually is thrown away in the near term. In fact, each year US consumers throw out more than 34 billion pounds of used textiles or roughly 100 pounds per person each year, with over 66 percent sent to landfills in the US where they decompose and generate greenhouse gases such as methane.

Globally, between 2000 and 2015, clothing production doubled, while over the same period utilization – the number of times an item of clothing is worn before it is thrown away – decreased by 36 percent. As a result, the global fashion industry is reported to have produced around 2.1 billion tons of greenhouse gas emissions in 2018, which was a staggering 4–8 percent of the global greenhouse gas emissions total. And worse for the sector's impacts is that global apparel production is projected to rise by 63 percent by 2030, from 62 million tons today to 102 million tons – equivalent to more than 500 billion additional T-shirts. If this happens, the industry's greenhouse gas emissions will rise to around 2.7 billion tons a year by 2030 [44, 45, 46, 47]. As consumer awareness and corporate net-zero-carbon commitments gain greater transparency, the business approach of fast fashion will be under great pressure to change. Interestingly, a group of researchers in my lab have been focusing on the global apparel retail sector and their commitments and transparency. Some of the name-brand stores you find in malls and standalone stores have very questionable business practices when it comes to transparency. These few firms are stating broad sustainability and climate goals without providing any substantive metrics to track, let alone using third-party auditors. By the time this book comes out, you will be able to view their findings on the Dynamics Lab website.[3]

References

1. Goodreads (n.d.). Albert Einstein Quotes. www.goodreads.com/quotes/556030-imagination-is-more-important-than-knowledge-for-knowledge-is-limited.
2. Forbes (2013). 11 Quotes from Sir Richard Branson on Business, Leadership, and Passion. www.forbes.com/sites/erikaandersen/2013/03/16/11-quotes-from-sir-richard-branson-on-business-leadership-and-passion/?sh=4b574b9969e7.
3. Lawrence Livermore National Laboratory (2022). National Ignition Facility Achieves Fusion Ignition. Press Release. www.llnl.gov/news/national-ignition-facility-achieves-fusion-ignition.

[3] www.dynamicslab.org.

4. CNBC (2022). Nuclear Fusion Breakthrough: Scientists Generate More Power Than Used to Create Reaction. www.cnbc.com/2022/12/13/nuclear-fusion-passes-major-milestone-net-energy.html.

5. J. Pasley (2022). Nuclear Fusion: How Scientists Can Turn Latest Breakthrough into a New Clean Power Source. Phys.org. December 15. https://phys.org/news/2022-12-nuclear-fusion-scientists-latest-breakthrough.html.

6. Office of Nuclear Energy (2021). Fission and Fusion: What Is the Difference? www.energy.gov/ne/articles/fission-and-fusion-what-difference.

7. US Nuclear Regulatory Commission (2019). Backgrounder on Radioactive Wastes. U.S. Nuclear Regulatory Commission. www.nrc.gov/reading-rm/doc-collections/fact-sheets/radwaste.html.

8. International Atomic Energy Agency (n.d.). Fusion – Frequently Asked Questions. www.iaea.org/topics/energy/fusion/faqs#:~:text=Fusion%20on%20the%20other%20hand,its%20half%20life%20is%20short.

9. *Nature* (2021). Concrete Needs to Lose Its Colossal Carbon Footprint. Editorial. www.nature.com/articles/d41586-021-02612-5.

10. *The Economist* (2021). Set in Green Concrete. November 6, pp. 69–72.

11. Imperial College London (2021). Best Ways to Cut Carbon Emissions from the Cement Industry Explored. www.imperial.ac.uk/news/221654/best-ways-carbon-emissions-from-cement.

12. T. Czigler, S. Reiter, P. Schulze, and K. Somers (2020). Laying the Foundation for Zero-Carbon Cement. McKinsey. May 14. www.mckinsey.com/industries/chemicals/our-insights/laying-the-foundation-for-zero-carbon-cement.

13. Dezeen (2022). Prometheus Materials Uses Algae-Based Cement to Make Masonry Blocks. www.dezeen.com/2022/06/07/prometheus-biocomposite-cement-blocks.

14. Engineering News (2022). Prometheus "Bio-cement" Touted As Portland Cement Sub. www.enr.com/articles/54236-prometheus-bio-cement-touted-as-portland-cement-sub.

15. National Institute of Standards and Technology (2022). Low Carbon Cements and Concretes Consortium. www.nist.gov/programs-projects/low-carbon-cements-and-concretes-consortium.

16. New Atlas (2022). Fusion Tech Is Set to Unlock Near-Limitless Ultra-Deep Geothermal Energy. https://newatlas.com/energy/quaise-deep-geothermal-milli meter-wave-drill.

17. MIT News (2022). Tapping into the Million-Year Energy Source below Our Feet: MIT Spinout Quaise Energy Is Working to Create Geothermal Wells Made from the Deepest Holes in the World. https://news.mit.edu/2022/quaise-energy-geother mal-0628.

18. K. Oglesby, P. Woskov, H. Einstein, and B. Livesay (2014). Deep Geothermal Drilling Using Millimeter Wave Technology (Final Technical Research Report) (No. DE-EE0005504Final). Impact Technologies LLC, Tulsa, OK.

19. Geoengineering Global (n.d.). Geothermal Energy with Millimeter Wave or Direct Energy Drilling. https://geoengineering.global/geothermal-energy.

20. *Scientific American* (1997). Why Is the Earth's Core So Hot? And How Do Scientists Measure Its Temperature? October 6.

21. BBC (2019). The Deepest Hole We Have Ever Dug. www.bbc.com/future/article/20190503-the-deepest-hole-we-have-ever-dug.
22. R. Williams (1986). The Thermal Spallation Drilling Process. *Geothermics*, 15(1): 17–22. https://doi.org/10.1016/0375-6505(86)90026-X.
23. Quaise (2022). Unlocking the True Power of Clean Geothermal Energy. www.quaise.energy.
24. M. Li, N. Jia, M. Lenzen et al. (2022). Global Food-Miles Account for Nearly 20% of Total Food-Systems Emissions. *Nature Food*, 3: 445–453.
25. Walmart (2022). Mass Timber Construction. https://corporate.walmart.com/newhomeoffice/mass-timber.
26. CBS News (2019). Walmart Moving into New HQ That Looks Like a Tech Campus. www.cbsnews.com/news/walmart-new-headquarters-inspired-by-tech-campus.
27. United Nations Environment Programme (2021). 2021 Global Status Report for Buildings and Construction: Towards a Zero-Emissions, Efficient and Resilient Buildings and Construction Sector. https://globalabc.org/sites/default/files/2021-10/GABC_Buildings-GSR-2021_BOOK.pdf.
28. Skidmore, Owings, and Merrill (2013). Timber Tower Research Project: Final Report. www.som.com/wp-content/uploads/2021/08/timber-tower-final-report-and-sketches-1633640951.pdf.
29. New York City (2022). Local Law 97. www.nyc.gov/site/sustainablebuildings/ll97/local-law-97.page#:~:text=Buildings%20account%20for%20approximately%20two-thirds%20of%20greenhouse%20gas,ambitious%20plans%20for%20reducing%20emissions%20in%20the%20nation.
30. MIT (2018). Mass Timber: Thinking Big about Sustainable Construction – MIT Class Designs a Prototype Building to Demonstrate That Even Huge Buildings Can Be Built Primarily with Wood. https://news.mit.edu/2018/mass-timber-sustainable-construction–0807.
31. International Energy Agency (2022). Global Energy Review: CO_2 Emissions in 2021. March. www.iea.org/reports/global-energy-review-co2-emissions-in–2021-2.
32. V. E. Smyrl (n.d.). "Permanent University Fund," *Handbook of Texas Online*. www.tshaonline.org/handbook/entries/permanent-university-fund.
33. B. R. Haigh (1955). Land, Oil and Education (El Paso: Texas Western Press, 1986). Vernon's Annotated Constitution of the State of Texas. Kansas City, MO: Vernon Law Book Company.
34. Yale News (2022). Yale's Endowment Falls from Silver Medal Position As University of Texas Surges Ahead. December 18. https://yaledailynews.com/blog/2022/09/01/yales-endowment-falls-from-silver-medal-position-as-university-of-texas-surges-ahead.
35. The University of Texas System (2022). About the University of Texas System. https://utsystem.edu/about.
36. Investopedia (2021). What Drives Consumer Demand for Tesla? www.investopedia.com/articles/personal-finance/021715/what-drives-consumer-demand-tesla.asp#citation–2.
37. LinkedIn Slideshare (n.d.). Tesla Marketing Plan. www.slideshare.net/dpayne05/tesla-marketing-plan.

38. Markets Insider (2022). "Elon Abandoned Tesla": The EV Maker's 3rd-Largest Individual Shareholder Calls for a New CEO As the Twitter Circus Tests Investor Patience. December 15. https://markets.businessinsider.com/news/stocks/tesla-investor-koguan-leo-new-ceo-elon-musk-twitter-focus–2022–12.
39. Fox Business (2022). Third-Largest Tesla Stock Owner Says Elon Musk Should Step Down As CEO. December 17. www.foxbusiness.com/markets/third-largest-tesla-stock-owner-says-elon-musk-step-down-ceo.
40. CNBC (2022). Oppenheimer Downgrades Tesla, Says Elon Musk's Handling of Twitter Could Hurt Electric Vehicle Maker. December 19. www.cnbc.com/2022/12/19/oppenheimer-downgrades-tesla-says-elon-musks-handling-of-twitter-could-hurt-electric-vehicle-maker.html.
41. Reuters (2022). Musk Twitter Play Sparks Concerns about Distraction, Tesla Stock Sales. April 14. www.reuters.com/technology/musks-twitter-play-sparks-concerns-about-distraction-stock-sales-tesla-2022-04-15.
42. Forbes (2022). Elon Musk's Twitter Antics Are Tarnishing Tesla – Just As Its EV Rivals Are Catching Up. December 2. www.forbes.com/sites/alanohnsman/2022/12/02/elon-musks-twitter-antics-are-tarnishing-teslajust-as-its-ev-rivals-are-catching-up/?sh=40fb5a522018.
43. *The Washington Post* (2022). Tesla's Value Dropped Tuesday by More Than Double the Cost of Twitter. April 26. www.washingtonpost.com/technology/2022/04/26/elon-musk-tesla-twitter-stock.
44. Ellen MacArthur Foundation (2021). Circular Business Models: Rethinking Business Models for a Thriving Fashion Industry. A study produced by the Ellen MacArthur Foundation with analytical support from Boston Consulting Group. https://emf.thirdlight.com/file/24/Om5sTEKOmmfEeVOm7xNOmq6S2k/Circular%20business%20models.pdf.
45. Global Fashion Agenda and Boston Consulting Group (2017). Pulse of the Fashion Industry. www.globalfashionagenda.com/publications-and-policy/pulse-of-the-industry.
46. United Nations (2019). UN Alliance For Sustainable Fashion Addresses Damage of "Fast Fashion." www.unep.org/news-and-stories/press-release/un-alliance-sustainable-fashion-addresses-damage-fast-fashion.
47. Boston University (2022). The Aftermath of Fast Fashion: How Discarded Clothes Impact Public Health and the Environment. September 22. www.bu.edu/sph/news/articles/2022/the-aftermath-of-fast-fashion-how-discarded-clothes-impact-public-health-and-the-environment.

19

Epilogue

The best leaders understand the world is dynamic and harness the opportunities for good.

Jay Golden, keynote address to business leaders at the American Council of Engineering Companies, New York, September 10, 2023

The experience of writing this book has been both a wonderfully fulfilling and exciting journey. It has also served as a catalyst for self-awareness as I reflect on the dynamics at play across our globe. I have had the privilege to meet and interview various leaders around the globe and to read from so many brilliant thought leaders and researchers. In addition to spanning traditional peer-reviewed research articles and local publications around the world, I must now be one of the leading readers of the *Financial Times*, *Wall Street Journal*, *New York Times*, Bloomberg, and, of course, *The Economist*, as well as many other global publications.

I had to deviate a bit from the traditional utilization of peer-reviewed academic publication primarily because the net-zero-carbon economy transition is happening so quickly, with updates almost every day. For this I relied more on real-time news, which only made the task of writing this book more complex as I tried to keep the information current. I believe this has without a doubt made me a better mentor to my students and a more effective consultant and adviser to leaders in industry and governments around the world.

Whether you agree or disagree with the policies of the Biden Administration, one must acknowledge that his administration has done a more effective job than many thought he could achieve. While in my opinion there is still much work that needs to be done, his administration has done a good job of grasping the complexities of the transition and focusing on jobs and the economy.

At the top of my list of work that still needs to be done is my greatest concern – the rural–urban divide. The US government is stuck in old thinking by delegating the focus of its rural citizens, businesses, and communities to that of the United States Department of Agriculture. Agriculture plays a vital role for rural America but there is much more than just agriculture. Too much of the current investments and policies have benefited urban areas and the coasts. At a minimum, the president should appoint a person or office to focus exclusively on the rural–urban divide and break through traditional government agency barriers.

But it is even more important to be the voice of the administration and bring bipartisan efforts to the US's rural communities. These Americans deserve nothing less. Without this effort, we not only risk the successes the green economy can bring but also risk providing continued divisiveness of what we cherish – the "United" States of America.

For me, the road next traveled is to take the interviews of leaders around the world that I have amassed as background for this book and pull them into a new book and podcast on dynamic leadership. I hope you have found this book to be interesting and, more importantly, informative. Wishing you all a bright and healthy future.

Index

Printed in the USA
CPSIA information can be obtained
at www.ICGtesting.com
LVHW051021211223
766986LV00002B/88